Case Study Research

Praise for the book

'Comprehensive, passionate, right out at the growing edge of the psychotherapy research and even slightly beyond it, this book maps out where case study research has come from, what it looks like today, and what its future will look like.'
Robert Elliott, Professor of Counselling, University of Strathclyde

'This is an excellent book that has been needed by the counselling and psychotherapy profession for some considerable time. It has been worth the wait. John McLeod writes in a clearly accessible style easy to read and absorb and his comprehensive book both captures existing methods and identifies potential methods ripe for development.'
Sue Wheeler, Professor of Counselling, University of Leicester

'This is an excellent book, and a very much needed addition to the case study methodology literature. It is very comprehensive and covers all aspects of case study methodology. The text addresses the issue intelligently, but is also an introduction for those engaging in case study research.'
Mark Widdowson, Director of Training, CPTI Edinburgh

'This book does an outstanding job in pulling together the crucially important literature on case studies in psychotherapy practice and research into a coherent, engaging and scholarly whole.'
Daniel Fishman, Editor-in-Chief, Pragmatic Case Studies in Psychotherapy, Graduate School of Applied and Professional Psychology, Rutgers University

Case Study Research

IN COUNSELLING
AND PSYCHOTHERAPY

John McLeod

British Association for
Counselling & Psychotherapy

Los Angeles | London | New Delhi
Singapore | Washington DC

SAGE Publications Ltd
1 Oliver's Yard
55 City Road
London EC1Y 1SP

SAGE Publications Inc.
2455 Teller Road
Thousand Oaks, California 91320

SAGE Publications India Pvt Ltd
B 1/I 1 Mohan Cooperative Industrial Area
Mathura Road
New Delhi 110 044

SAGE Publications Asia-Pacific Pte Ltd
33 Pekin Street #02-01
Far East Square
Singapore 048763

Library of Congress Control Number: 2010922460

British Library Cataloguing in Publication data

A catalogue record for this book is available from
the British Library

ISBN 978-1-84920-804-8
ISBN 978-1-84920-805-5 (pbk)

Typeset by C&M Digitals (P) Ltd, Chennai, India
Printed by MPG Books Group, Bodmin, Cornwall
Printed on paper from sustainable resources

For Julia

Contents

Foreword

Many of the major ideas and theories associated with psychotherapy have been created and empirically demonstrated through case study research. Immediate examples that come to mind in psychoanalysis are Sigmund Freud's cases of 'Dora' and 'Little Hans'; in behavior therapy, J.B. Watson's case of 'Little Albert' and B.F. Skinner's insistence that behavioral principles of learning be studied one organism at a time; in cognitive therapy, Aaron Beck and colleagues' book, *Cognitive Therapy in Clinical Practice: An Illustrative Casebook*; in client-centered therapy, Virginia Axline's case of 'Dibbs'; and in existential therapy, Irvin Yalom's book of cases, *Love's Executioner & Other Tales of Psychotherapy*.

However, in spite of the case study's impressive contributions to psychotherapy theory and practice, starting in the 1920s and gaining strength and going forward until recently was the view that case studies were by their nature unscientifically journalistic and subjectively biased, and they became marginalized in psychotherapy research. The major source of this negative view of case studies was the domination in psychology – psychotherapy's main research discipline – of a positivistically inspired research paradigm. This paradigm privileges the deductive search for general, context-independent knowledge by the quantitative, experimental comparison of groups, dealing with statistically simplified individuals.

In contrast, practitioners know that therapy knowledge always starts with the contextually specific, qualitatively rich case that is naturalistically situated, that deals with real persons (not statistical composites), and that generalizes via induction from the specific. Case-based knowledge is thus the polar opposite of knowledge based on group experiments – that is, qualitative vs quantitative, naturalistic vs experimental, context-dependent vs context-independent, inductive vs deductive, and individual-based vs group-based, respectively. These dramatic differences in the epistemology of traditional researchers and practitioners have created tensions between these two groups, with each frequently dismissing the other for being off-base in advancing our understanding and the effectiveness of psychotherapy.

In recent years, with the rise in psychology of a postmodern alternative to positivistic epistemology, there has been a re-emergence of interest in the case study as a credible and useful vehicle for therapy research, complementing experimental group studies. However, this re-emergence has been quite fragmented geographically, conceptually, and methodologically, and it has been hidden from the view of many academic researchers and practicing therapists. John McLeod's book, *Case Study Research in Counselling and Psychotherapy*, does a brilliant job of pulling these fragments together into a persuasive and coherent whole. Using accessible and engaging language, concepts, and examples, McLeod provides clarity and insight as he guides the reader through challenging clinical and epistemological terrains, along the way showing how the researcher–clinician divide can be bridged. McLeod accomplishes these goals in three ways.

First, in Chapters 1–3, McLeod describes in detail the historical development of case study research towards methods that create systematic, observation-based, rigorous, critically interpreted information – that is, 'scientific' knowledge in the usual sense of the word. This type of information links the experiences of the practitioner to the general scientific knowledge base of the field, at the same time providing credibility for case-based knowledge in the eyes of traditional psychotherapy researchers.

Second, McLeod lays out and discusses specific methods and considerations in conducting systematic and rigorous case studies, including ethical issues around ensuring the privacy of the clients being studied (Chapter 4) and how to collect and analyze case study data about the process and outcome of therapy (Chapters 5 and 11). McLeod pays particular attention to procedures for clinicians – not just academic researchers – to conduct systematic case studies that can contribute to the discipline's knowledge base.

Finally, McLeod catalogues and describes the ways in which the case study field has differentiated into five distinct, complementary models of systematic and rigorous case study research. Each model has a distinct purpose, method of data design and collection, and strategy for data summary and interpretation. And each model has unique value in expanding the field's knowledge base, both practical and theoretical. The models include an emphasis upon the use of case studies as exemplars of best clinical practice (Chapter 6); as settings for single-case experiments (Chapter 7); as vehicles for intensively evaluating efficacy via multiple types of data as analyzed by multiple judges (Chapter 8); as a means for theory-building (Chapter 9); and as a way to explore the narrative meaning of the therapy experience for both client and clinician (Chapter 10).

In short, McLeod's accomplishment is extraordinary. He has cogently and persuasively pulled the separated strands of the multifaceted field of case study research in counselling and therapy into an intricate, integrated tapestry that lays out a detailed and effective stellar roadmap for future goals in the field and pathways for getting there.

Daniel B. Fishman, PhD, Graduate School of Applied and Professional Psychology, Rutgers University

Foreword

As a non-researcher I found this book both fascinating and educational. As long as I have been involved with BACP, the debate between quantitative and qualitative research has been raging, with the balance tipping ever more in favour of large randomised trials – or so it seemed. It has been a depressing and demoralising time for counsellors and psychotherapists whose work has been dismissed in some quarters in favour of approaches that are supported by 'robust' evidence in the form of RCTs. This book is important and timely because it helps us to understand how qualitative research in general, and case study research in particular, can and should develop in order to strengthen their position and begin to really influence practice and policy. Case studies, McLeod reminds us, are widely accepted within medicine as having scientific as well as educational value. Large randomised trials can miss vital evidence, illustrated by instances where drugs are introduced following such large-scale studies, only to be withdrawn from the market on the basis of evidence coming from single case reports.

McLeod tracks the history of single case study research, from Freud to Yalom, demonstrating the weaknesses of some approaches and the consequences of this for the profession. Case studies based on the views, memories and notes of a sole practitioner, however interesting and eloquently written, should be treated with caution. Humble counsellor or master practitioner, we are all subject to bias, blind spots and selective memories. It is not just our evidence-based culture that now demands that research be more methodologically rigorous. McLeod argues that what happens in a therapy case is so complex and multi-faceted that it is beyond the capacity of an individual therapist who is also involved in the case to really do justice to what has happened in therapy.

If case study research is to have a future and be regarded as a source of reliable evidence, then a radically different approach needs to be found. McLeod describes the main innovations in case study research which need to be adopted. These include among other things, working with a team of researchers who facilitate dialogue and debate around theoretical interpretations of case material; being critical and scholarly rather than using a case study to sell an approach to therapy; and always inviting the client's perspective both on the therapy and on the analysis of the case data.

Whilst you never feel that McLeod is trying to sell you something, his own passion for case study research is present on every page of this book. Case study research is published much less frequently than other types of research and is seldom cited by authors when reviewing the therapy literature. This should change and it seems to me that this book is an important step in effecting that change.

Laurie Clarke, BACP Chief Executive

Preface

In counselling and psychotherapy, a 'case' reflects the entirety of the involvement of the client, couple or family, with the therapist and therapy agency where they have gone for help. It is inevitable that counselling and psychotherapy practitioners should be interested in 'cases'. To be a practitioner is to inhabit a world that is dominated by cases: case allocation meetings, case reviews, writing case reports. Learning to be a counsellor or psychotherapist involves the study of exemplar cases written by leading figures in the field. Key points in the transition from trainee to qualified status are marked by the presentation of case studies that demonstrate the development of professional competence. However, counselling and psychotherapy case studies are also of interest to people who are not practitioners. Members of the public, some of them potential clients, are keen to know about what happens in therapy, and how the course of therapy unfolds. For example, *Love's Executioner*, the collection of case studies published by the existential therapist Irvin Yalom (1989), has been an international best-seller for many years. Managers and policy-makers who are responsible for the organization and funding of therapy services are also interested in cases, as evidence for the effectiveness of different types of therapeutic intervention.

The aim of this book is to provide the conceptual understanding and practical tools required to conduct systematic, high-quality therapy case studies. The book will also be valuable to people who are not intending to do actual studies, but to use them to inform their practice. The focus of the book is on case studies that can be disseminated, by being published in books and journals, and which can therefore make a contribution to the global network of evidence and ideas that constitutes the counselling and psychotherapy research literature. At the present time, the majority of counselling and psychotherapy trainees write and present case reports as part of their courses. Many of these cases are of high quality, but few are ever published. Similarly, many experienced practitioners have fascinating stories to tell about their work with clients, that are never published. This book explains how trainees and practitioners can use their clinical experience to generate publishable case studies, by drawing on some straightforward principles of data collection and analysis.

Within this book, the terms 'counselling' and 'psychotherapy' are used interchangeably. Although it is possible to argue that counselling and psychotherapy each represent distinct traditions of practice, it is also clear that they draw on a shared set of methods and concepts. The book is solely concerned with case studies of work with clients, rather than case studies of counselling and psychotherapy service delivery organizations.

Counselling and psychotherapy case studies are mainly carried out and written up by therapists reporting on their own cases. Many of the examples of case studies discussed in this book are of this type. However, reference is also made to case studies that have been carried out by external researchers, or by clients. Each of these vantage points has its own distinctive strengths and weaknesses – a thriving and robust case study research literature requires all three approaches.

When thinking about case study research in counselling and psychotherapy, it is important to keep in mind that this kind of inquiry needs to be understood in relation to a multiple set of purposes:

1 to make a contribution to shared professional and scientific knowledge, by presenting carefully documented and rigorously analysed case-based evidence;
2 to enable users of therapy (clients, purchasers) and practitioners to gain an understanding of what actually happens in different forms of therapy for different client problems;
3 to provide a structure for personal and professional development in therapists, in the form of opportunities to reflect on practice.

The message of this book is that it is essential to give equal weighting to all three of these purposes. If case study reports are not systematically carried out, then they will be disregarded by the profession, as not capable of yielding reliable and valid evidence. If a case study does not tell a story, which conveys meaning and understanding that is accessible to reasonably informed readers, then it will not be read, and as a result will fail to have any influence on the field. Finally, if practitioners view case study research as boring and a chore, and as something that is done only by people in universities, then few case studies will be attempted, and even fewer will be published.

The material in this book is organized into three broad sections. Chapters 1–5 review essential background knowledge: the role of systematic case study research, the nature of methodological issues, challenges and solutions in this field of inquiry; the basis for ethical good practice. Chapters 6–10 then present a series of different approaches to doing good-quality, publishable case studies. The intention in these chapters is to provide readers with the information they need in order to make a choice of which type of case study is most appropriate in respect of their interests and circumstances, and to design and conduct a case study project. Chapter 11 offers some ideas around ways that practitioners and students/trainees can work in groups to carry out case study research.

Throughout the book, the discussion focuses on a number of exemplar studies, which have been selected to represent what is possible in case study research. Anyone interested in conducting case study research in counselling and psychotherapy is strongly advised to track down these studies, and have a close look at them. Within each chapter, there are also boxes that highlight key issues, suggested topics for further personal reflection and discussion, and lists of suggested further reading. The emphasis throughout the book is on concrete examples of counselling and psychotherapy case study research that have been published and have had an impact on the field. Influential social scientists such as Gerring (2006), Stake (2005) and Yin (2009) have produced detailed analyses of the complex methodological issues and choices associated with case research. The approach taken in the present book makes every effort not to get bogged down in these complexities, but instead seeks to focus on the practical realities of different genres of therapy case study research, and their contribution to knowledge.

This book has been written at a point in the history of counselling and psychotherapy at which there is enormous external pressure on the profession to produce evidence of its effectiveness. This drive toward evidence-based practice and quality standards has been powerfully influenced by what has happened within medicine, where strict systems have had to be established to regulate the marketing and use of an endless stream of new drug treatments produced by the pharmacology industry. The criterion of effectiveness, the 'gold standard', that has been imported from medicine and the drug industry, has been the randomized controlled (or clinical) trial (RCT). Valuable though RCTs might be, it is necessary to recognize that they represent a 'top-down' approach to the production of knowledge. Such an approach is probably inevitable within contemporary industrialized and bureaucratized societies. At the same time, however, it always necessary to retain a balance, by holding on to the possibility of 'bottom-up' knowledge, based on the effort and ingenuity of small groups of people. In the realm of counselling and psychotherapy, systematic case studies are one of the ways in which ordinary practitioners and clients can personally 'own' the knowledge that they create and consume, and provide a contextualized counterpoint to the abstract conclusions of large-scale mega-research.

Acknowledgements

I would like to thank the following colleagues, for the generosity and patience in sharing with me their knowledge and experience in relation to the field of counselling and psychotherapy case study research: Sophia Balamoutsou, Art Bohart, Tim Bond, Ole Dreier, Robert Elliott, Kim Etherington, Dan Fishman, Soti Grafanaki, Thomas Mackrill, Ron Miller, Alison Shoemark, Kate Smith, Bill Stiles, Jeanne Watson and Sue Wheeler.

The role of case studies in the development of theory and practice in counselling and psychotherapy

Counselling and psychotherapy emerged as discrete areas of professional activity in the late 19th and early 20th centuries (Cushman 1995; McLeod 2009). At the time when counselling and psychotherapy were becoming established, research in psychology was almost entirely focused on the laboratory study of processes of memory, attention and learning, and had not reached the stage of examining real-world applied problems. There were few methods available for evaluating the effectiveness of therapy, or exploring the processes that were associated with good or poor outcome therapy. The only option available to Sigmund Freud and other pioneers of psychotherapy who sought to analyse their practice, was to follow the example of the medical profession, and write up their work in the form of detailed clinical case studies. Since that period, case studies have remained a central strand of the knowledge base for counselling and psychotherapy. Case reports have had a significant impact on the field of counselling and psychotherapy in a variety of ways, and an appreciation of the different styles and purposes of case study report is necessary in order to be able to make sense of current debates around this methodological approach. The chapter offers an overview of the various forms of case study knowledge in counselling and psychotherapy that have been developed over the past century.

The use of case study methods in developing a knowledge base for counselling and psychotherapy

Case study methods have been used in counselling and psychotherapy to generate many different kinds of knowledge. Case study reports have contributed to research, theory-building, training, organizational and political change, marketing and public awareness. It is not possible to be a counsellor or psychotherapist, or to be a lay person who is interested in therapy, and not to have been influenced by case study evidence in some way.

Documenting, evaluating and disseminating new approaches to therapy

When an innovative approach to therapy is first developed, it is necessary to be able to provide evidence of how it operates, and how effective it is, in order to persuade colleagues of its potential. At this stage in the development of an approach, it is likely that there are few practitioners actually using the new methods. It is therefore hard to carry out an extensive study, involving many cases. In recent times, it would also be difficult to secure ethical approval to conduct a large-scale study of an unproven method. In these circumstances, the only way to generate convincing evidence of the possible value of a new approach is to publish case study reports. The history of counselling and psychotherapy encompasses many examples of case reports that were highly influential during the formative phase of new treatment approaches. The early development of psychoanalysis, by Sigmund Freud and his colleagues, depended on presentation and discussion of case studies at conferences and seminars, and their eventual publication (Freud 1901, 1909, 1910). The establishment of behaviour therapy as a credible approach was built on a series of case studies by Joseph Wolpe (1958). Likewise the sex therapy of Masters and Johnson (1970) and the use of eye movement desensitization and reprocessing (EMDR) (McCann 1992; Shapiro 1989) also depended on the publication of plausible and persuasive case reports. Typically, the publication of case reports leads to further research, with larger samples, and to the provision of training programmes for practitioners who are convinced by the case evidence and want to learn how to use the new methods.

Contributing to public understanding of counselling and psychotherapy

Counselling and psychotherapy are forms of help that require active commitment on the part of users, who need to attend regular sessions, explore painful areas of personal experience, and put therapeutic learning into practice in everyday life situations. They are also forms of help whose legitimacy cannot be taken for granted within society – there are many critics who deny the basic validity and worth of therapy (Furedi 2004). It has always been essential therefore, to find ways to let members of the general public know about how therapy works. There have been several memorable case studies that have had a significant impact on how the general public makes sense of therapy. In the 1960s, the spirit of client-centred therapy was captured effectively in the best-selling case study *Dibs*, written by Virginia Axline (1971), who had been a colleague and student of Carl Rogers. In the 1990s, many people became convinced about the value of therapy by reading the case studies in *Love's Executioner*, by Irvin Yalom (1989). More recently, the drama and impact of psychotherapy have been disseminated to a wider public through the series of case study books edited by Jeffrey Kottler and Jon Carlson (2002, 2003, 2006, 2008, 2009) and the TV series *In Treatment*.

The development of theory

Theories of therapy necessarily involve complex sets of propositions that seek to reflect the way different factors interact and unfold over time. One of the most effective ways in which to develop and test theoretical ideas is through analysis of individual cases; it is at the level of the case that the operation of different factors can best be observed. By contrast, research that attempts to analyse what is happening at the level of a single session, or an event within a session, is in danger of either failing to take into account important contextual factors, or of not being able to access sufficient instances of the phenomenon being examined. There are many examples within the counselling and psychotherapy literature of the use of case studies as a means of advancing theoretical understanding. The historical development of psychoanalysis and psychodynamic psychotherapy has been built around discussion of the theoretical implications of detailed case presentations. Within the client-centred/person-centred tradition, Carl Rogers published transcripts of some of his cases, which have served as the basis for further investigation into the process of client-centred/person-centred therapy (Farber et al. 1996). One of the major areas of theoretical debate within the past 30 years has been around the relative contribution to therapy outcome of non-specific or 'common factors' (e.g., instillation of hope), as against specific therapeutic techniques (e.g., the use of systematic desensitization). Hill (1989) carried out an analysis of eight cases of brief psychotherapy, focusing on this theoretical question. A recent trend within the use of case analysis as a means of developing theory, has been the practice of comparing good outcome and poor outcome cases, as a strategy for identifying theoretical factors that are associated with effective practice. This approach was used by Watson, Goldman and Greenberg (2007) in the development of a model of the effectiveness of emotion focused therapy (EFT). The work of Bill Stiles and his colleagues, into the assimilation model of therapeutic change, provides a further example of how a new theoretical perspective can be articulated through case analyses (Stiles 2002).

Drawing attention to critical issues and areas of practice

A notable area of application of case study methodology in counselling and psychotherapy has been its use in highlighting issues that have been previously neglected within the professional and research literature. When a practitioner becomes aware of a topic that he or she feels deserves to be taken more seriously by colleagues, one option is to write and publish a 'personal opinion' article. However, a more convincing alternative strategy is to write and publish a detailed case example. There are several areas within the therapy field where case studies have been used both to convince sceptical colleagues to give more serious consideration to a particular issue, and to function as a rallying point for like-minded colleagues. *Sex in the Therapy Hour: A Case of Professional Incest* is a detailed case study of an episode of sexual exploitation of a client (Bates and Brodsky 1989), which had a significant impact on changing the climate of opinion around the serious nature of client–therapist sexual contact. *Shouldn't I Be Feeling Better by Now? Client Views of Therapy*, edited by Yvonne Bates (2006), includes several compelling case descriptions of emotional and financial manipulation of clients by their therapists. There have also been collections of case studies by practitioners who wish to draw attention to, and foster debate around, practice issues such as the use of integrative approaches to therapy (Stricker and Gold 2006), the role of spirituality in therapy (Richards and Bergin 1997), counselling people with disabilities (Blotzer and Ruth 1995), combining psychotherapy with drug treatment (Beitman 1991) and therapy with older people (Knight 1992).

Box 1.1

Exploring the counselling and psychotherapy case study evidence base: where to start?

For counselling and psychotherapy practitioners and students who wish to become more research-informed, it is fairly easy to know where to start. Excellent general overviews of current research findings are available in Cooper (2008), Lambert (2004), Timulak (2008) and Tryon (2002), and in the series of research reviews published by the British Association for Counselling and Psychotherapy. More specific searches can be conducted through PsycInfo and other on-line bibliographic search tools. It is harder to access case-based knowledge about counselling and psychotherapy, which is often ignored in systematic reviews. One of the aims of the present book is to draw attention to high-quality 'exemplar' therapy case studies. Miller (2004) includes an appendix that lists a large number of therapy case studies. There are two journals that specialize in therapy case study reports: *Clinical Case Studies* and *Pragmatic Case Studies in Psychotherapy*. The latter is an on-line journal, and therefore readily accessible. In addition, the *Counselling and Psychotherapy Research* journal and *Psychotherapy Research* have published several case studies, and the American Psychological Association (APA) has published edited collections of therapy case studies on a range of topics.

Extending and enhancing the interpretability of large-scale outcome studies

In relation to evaluating the effectiveness of different therapies, it is widely recognized that large-scale randomized controlled studies have a unique value, in being able to demonstrate clear links between specific causal factors (e.g., the type of therapy being provided) and outcomes. However, the meaning of the results obtained from large-scale studies may sometimes be difficult to interpret, because they consist of generalisations over a large number of cases. It can therefore be useful, when conducting a large-scale study, to build in the possibility of carrying out subsequent in-depth single case analyses in order to explore the meaning of any contradictory findings that may emerge. A good example of this use of case study methods has been within the Vanderbilt I study, carried out by Strupp and Hadley (1979), in which the effects of psychotherapy on socially isolated young men were evaluated. In a series of cases studies that were carried out following primary analyses of the outcome data, Strupp (1980 a, b, c, d) compared the process of therapy that occurred in pairs of good outcome and poor outcome cases that were seen by the same therapists. A further example of this use of case study methods can be found within the Sheffield outcome study of the effectiveness of time-limited psychotherapy for people with work-related depression (Shapiro and Firth 1987; Shapiro and Firth-Cozens 1990). The publication of case studies from this project (Firth-Cozens 1992; Parry et al. 1986) made it possible to illustrate and explore in detail the way that therapy was helpful for this client group. An advantage of these 'research-based' case studies is that a great deal of information is available on the case. Also, it is possible to determine how typical the case is, in relation to other cases included in the main study. In contrast to the Vanderbilt and Sheffield research programmes, there are many large-scale studies that have yielded results that remain hard to interpret, in the absence of accompanying case analysis. One of the reasons for the enduring influence of these particular programmes of research is that they have provided a combination of group and case analysis which, taken together, offer an opportunity for readers to arrive at a comprehensive, critical understanding of the results that were obtained.

The use of case studies in training

Possibly the most widespread use of case studies has been as a method of illustrating and communicating knowledge and understanding of an approach to therapy to those who are interested in learning how to practise it (Kutash and Wolf 1986; Wedding and Corsini 1979). This use of case study evidence can vary a great deal in its level of complexity and detail; some authors make use of brief case vignettes, while others offer lengthy extracts of case material. A further way in which case studies are used in counselling and psychotherapy training is in the assessment of competence of trainees. In most training courses students are required to submit a case study of their work with a client, as a means of demonstrating their capacity to provide an effective therapeutic relationship, deal with professional and ethical issues arising in the course of the therapy, implement appropriate therapeutic interventions and engage in critical reflection on practice. Case studies are unique, as assessment tools, in enabling examination of the extent to which the student has been able to integrate component elements of competency into a coherent whole.

Developing competence in case formulation: the practical application of case study skills

Box 1.2

Within most approaches to counselling and psychotherapy, it is usual for the therapist to arrive at a *case formulation* following a period of assessment, or within the first few sessions of therapy (Eells 2007a; Johnstone and Dallos 2006). This formulation typically consists of an analysis of the nature and severity of the client's problems, the factors that have caused these problems and which currently maintain them, the strengths or limitations of the client and his/her life situation in relation to addressing the problems and the possible therapeutic interventions or strategies that might be of value in helping the client to overcome his or her life difficulties. The formulation may be arrived at through informal personal reflection on the part of the therapist, or may be produced in a more formal manner (e.g., following a standard protocol). The formulation may or may not be explored with the client, and may or may not form the basis for a therapy contract. Although there exist different styles of case formulation, associated with different therapy traditions, there is a growing consensus that accurate and valid formulation plays an important role in therapy. Tracey Eells and his colleagues have studied the skills used by therapists in arriving at formulations, and the ways in which practitioners can be trained to produce good quality formulations (Eells and Lombart 2003; Eells et al. 2005). Their findings suggest that many experienced practitioners have difficulty in generating plausible and practically useful conclusions on the basis of case information, but that brief exposure to basic principles of case analysis can enable them to become more competent in relation to these tasks. The growing literature on case formulation in counselling and psychotherapy provides a concrete example of how the inclusion of case study methodology and research within both basic training and continuing professional development can make a direct contribution to clinical effectiveness.

The distinctive contribution of case-based knowledge

Within the field of counselling and psychotherapy the case study is a flexible method of inquiry that has been used for a multiplicity of purposes, encompassing evaluation, theory development and education. However, there are other research methods, such as randomized trials, surveys and qualitative interview studies, that also play an important role in the development of theory, practice and training in therapy. What is the distinctive contribution that is made by case study research, in contrast to these other methodologies? There are four factors that help to explain why case studies have been, and remain, critically important in relation to the task of building a knowledge base for therapy. First, case studies offer a form of *narrative knowing*. Second, they provide an efficient way of representing and analysing *complexity*. Third, case studies generate knowledge-in-context. Finally, case studies are an essential tool for understanding *practical expertise in action*. These ideas are explored in the following sections.

The case study as a form of narrative knowing

Jerome Bruner, one of the most influential figures in contemporary psychology, was responsible for introducing the distinction between narrative and paradigmatic ways of knowing. Paradigmatic knowledge consists of abstract, general laws or general 'if–then' statements. There are many examples of paradigmatic knowledge in the field of psychotherapy, such as Sigmund Freud's theory that 'oral' traits in adult life are the result of patterns of feeding in infancy, Carl Rogers' formulation of the 'necessary and sufficient conditions' for positive personality change, or statements that cognitive-behavioural therapy (CBT) is the most effective approach to working with panic disorder. By contrast, narrative knowing consists of stories that are told about various aspects of everyday experience. A story, or narrative, consists of a sequence of events ('I did this then she said that …') that allow the person to organize experience in a way that reflects human purpose and intentionality ('… and then I walked out *because* …'), and also to evaluate it (the 'moral' of the story). Bruner (1986, 1990) pointed out that psychology had constructed a science that was based on paradigmatic knowledge, and had increasingly ignored the role of narrative knowledge. Just as people in their everyday lives draw on a mix of abstract rules and rich narrative accounts, a balanced approach to scientific and professional knowledge in the social sciences and psychology also requires a combination of both types of knowing (Polkinghorne 1995). One of the central arguments for an important role for case study research in counselling and psychotherapy, therefore, is that it provides a source of narrative knowing that is needed to complement the findings of studies that generate abstract or paradigmatic knowledge. It is not that one form of knowing is better than the other, but that human sense-making (in any field of endeavour) requires both of these modalities to exist in creative interplay.

The case study as a means of representing complexity

One of the key choice-points in designing a research study is to decide where to position the investigation on a dimension of *simplicity–complexity*. On the whole, *extensive* research studies, such as surveys or practice-based outcome studies, collect a small number of observations from a large number of subjects or participants. Although in principle it is possible in such research to collect many observations from each participant, very large sample sizes are required in such studies if multivariate analysis is to have any hope of yielding statistically significant results. In practice, therefore, extensive studies with large samples tend to focus on 20 or fewer observation or measurement points for each participant. In *intensive* research, such as case studies and many qualitative studies, there can be several hundred observations or measures collected for an individual participant. What this means is that case studies are well placed to capture, describe and analyse evidence of *complex* processes. This feature of case study research in counselling and psychotherapy is clearly attractive and valuable to many researchers, since many readers of large-sample extensive studies bemoan the fact that these studies usually over-simplify what happens in therapy. On the other hand, complexity also presents a challenge or danger for researchers and research audiences – too much complexity can become chaotic and meaningless.

Contextuality as an essential feature of case study research

A case study involves investigating an entity within its natural context. This approach can be compared with what happens in laboratory experiments or in analogue studies in counselling and psychotherapy, in which a controlled situation is created in order to make it possible to test hypotheses about cause–effect linkages. In surveys, large-scale naturalistic studies and randomized trials, the investigation may be based in a real-world context, but there is typically little information collected or reported about contextual factors. Yin (2009: 18) defines a case study as:

> … an empirical inquiry that investigates a contemporary phenomenon in depth and within its real-life context, especially when the boundaries between phenomenon and context are not clearly evident.

The key idea here is that, in any intensive study of a specific case, the closer the 'case' is examined, the less certainty there is about the boundaries of the case, in terms of information that may be relevant to an understanding of the case. For example, in counselling and psychotherapy case study research, there often arise questions concerning the therapeutic impact of events and experiences that were not part of the actual therapy approach that was delivered. There are also many theoretically and practically inter-esting questions about when the case begins and ends (At the final therapy session? Six months following the final therapy session?). In analysing the factors that influenced outcome in a specific therapy case, it may become apparent that improvements in the client's condition may have been due to getting a new job, or to conversations with the assistant who carried out research interviews. Because the aim is to arrive at a comprehensive understanding of a single case, by creating a rich data set, many of these 'fuzzy boundary' factors are observed and recorded, and become relevant in the analysis. By contrast, in studies with large numbers of participants, there is no scope for such factors to become part of the data set, or to play a role in analysis. In some therapy case studies, the researcher or author makes a specific effort to collect information about the context in which the therapy takes place. However, even when the researcher or author does not prioritise contextuality, the fact that there is more space in a case study to describe the client, the therapist, and therapy, means that readers are provided with a more in-depth understanding of the context of the case.

Describing and analysing practical expertise in action

A further distinctive aspect of case study research arises from reflection on the question: 'What is a case?' (Ragin and Becker 1992). The word 'case' has a wide range of applications within the English language. For example, in sociology, a single factory or neighborhood community may be treated as a 'case' for research purposes. In counselling and psycho-therapy, the concept of a 'case' has a different meaning – it refers to some kind of treatment episode in which a person (or family group) receives help from a therapist. Therapy cases are therefore concerned not only with what happens in the life of the client or patient, but also with the application of professional knowledge on the part of the practitioner. If there was no practitioner involvement, we would not describe what went on as a *therapy* case, although it might be classifiable as, for instance, a case of depression or a case of post-traumatic stress disorder. The American psychologist Dan Fishman has argued that the systematic study of therapy cases can be used to build a *pragmatic* evidence base, consisting of information on the assumptions, strategies and interventions that practitioners use when working with different types of clients. In an important book, *The Case for a Pragmatic Psychology*, Fishman (1999) argues that psychology (and by implication counselling and psycho-therapy) have attempted to create a body of knowledge around positivist, experimental studies that are detached from everyday practice. His pro-posal for a pragmatic alternative makes use of research techniques from traditional psychological research, such as measurement tools, but inte-grates them into a postmodern, pluralistic approach to inquiry, that seeks to generate critical, reflective knowledge about what works in practice. Fishman (1999) points out that, in therapy as in other occupations, expert practitioners follow a cycle of assessing a situation or problem in terms of their conceptual framework, devising a plan of action, monitoring the effectiveness of their intervention and modifying their actions in the light of feedback. Having completed a case, the practitioner takes the practical knowledge of what worked (and didn't work) that he or she has gleaned from that case, and applies it to subsequent cases. Within the career of any individual practitioner, however, he or she will work with a limited number of cases. For Fishman (1999), good quality pragmatic case studies play a crucial role in the development of effective practice by allowing practitioners to gain access to a wider set of exemplar cases.

Narrative knowing, complexity, contextuality and the generation of pragmatic knowledge can be seen as representing distinctive features of case study research in counselling and psychotherapy. It is not inevitable that these characteristics are found in all therapy case studies. It is pos-sible to conduct counselling and psychotherapy case studies that lack narrative impact, eschew complexity, neglect to address contextual factors, and make little contribution to pragmatic professional knowledge. The point is that, unlike other methodological approaches, case studies at least have the potential to yield knowledge and understanding that is imbued with these values.

The case study tradition in other occupations and disciplines

Box 1.3

For anyone interested in carrying out case research, or using case studies in teaching, it can be helpful to be aware that there exists a substantial literature on the methods and applications around case-based knowledge in other disciplines. Sources of information about these alternative traditions of case study research can be found in Bromley (1986), Byrne and Ragin (2009), Gerring

(Continued)

(2006) and Yin (2009). There are many aspects of case study inquiry that have been developed much more fully within these other professional and academic communities, than within psychology, counselling and psychotherapy. Within law, for example, an understanding of how complex case data can be analysed, and what counts as evidence within a case analysis, are routine accomplishments for practising lawyers and judges. Educational researchers have been interested in how case-based evidence can influence policy-making. Medicine and management studies have devised creative applications of case study analysis to help students to develop problem-solving skills. For the most part, counselling and psychotherapy case study researchers have made only tentative connections between their own work, and these wider domains.

Box 1.4

The case study tradition in medicine

Case studies are widely accepted within medicine as having scientific as well as educational value. The *British Medical Journal* operates a special *Case Reports* section, to promote the publication of this type of article. An important part of the rationale for this initiative is an appreciation that large-scale randomised trials are capable of missing vital evidence – for example, decisions to withdraw drugs from the market because of harm are usually made on scientific evidence coming from spontaneous case reports (or case series) rather than randomised controlled trials. The author guidelines for *BMJ Case Reports* invite contributions under the following headings:

- reminder of important clinical lesson;
- novel treatment (new drug/intervention; established drug/procedure in new situation);
- findings that shed new light on the possible pathogenesis of a disease or an adverse effect;
- learning from errors;
- unusual presentation of more common disease/injury;
- myth exploded;
- rare disease;
- new disease;
- novel diagnostic procedure;
- unusual association of diseases/symptoms;
- unexpected outcome (positive or negative) including adverse drug reactions.

Although these are medical model categories, it is not difficult to see how they are translatable into issues and topics that make sense within the field of counselling and psychotherapy (and which are rarely captured in the current literature).

Conclusions

Case-based evidence represents a form of practice-based evidence that has been central to the development of knowledge in counselling and psychotherapy. The fact that a wide range of applications of case study methodology can be found within the counselling and psychotherapy literature, shows that this is a methodology that plays a crucial role within the field. This chapter has considered the question: Are case studies necessary? The evidence suggests that case studies are indeed a necessary part of the overall literature: case studies fulfil a number of important functions, and they generate a unique type of knowledge. But, this answer leads in turn to further questions: How is it possible to do case studies well? What is best practice in case study research and inquiry? How is it possible to assess whether a case study is plausible and credible, or biased and worthless? The following chapter begins to address these issues, by reviewing the movement away from clinical case studies based solely on therapist notes, toward a more systematic and rigorous approach to generating and analysing case-based data.

Topics for reflection and discussion

1 In what ways have case studies influenced your own practice as a therapist? Take a few minutes to reflect, and write brief notes, around the following tasks. Identify three cases that have influenced the way that you think about therapy, and work with clients. Try to identify cases based on different types of evidence: e.g., personal cases from your own practice, clinical case studies, research-based cases. For each case, note down what you have learned from the case in terms of principles for practice.

2 Identify an area of practice in which you are familiar with current research evidence. This could be an issue around the effectiveness of counselling or psychotherapy for a particular client group, or a therapy process issue such as the role of empathy or the working alliance. Look at one or two sources that review the evidence in relation to the area that you have selected. Alternatively, choose an area of research that is reviewed in Lambert (2004) or Cooper (2008). To what extent, and in what ways, do the texts you have looked at incorporate case study evidence into their reviews? What are the implications, for therapy theory and practice, of the ways that these reviewers have dealt with case-based knowledge?

Recommended further reading

The two books that most clearly explain why case study knowledge is an essential part of the evidence base for counselling and psychotherapy theory, practice and training are:

Fishman, D.B. (1999) *The Case for a Pragmatic Psychology*. New York: New York University Press.
Miller, R.B. (2004) *Facing Human Suffering: Psychology and Psychotherapy as Moral Engagement*. Washington, DC: American Psychological Association (particularly Chapter 6).

Issues around the significance of the simplicity–complexity dimension, and the role of context in counselling and psychotherapy research, are explored in:

Russell, R.L. (ed.) (1994) *Reassessing Psychotherapy Research*. New York: Guilford Press.
Seikkula, J. and Arnkil, T.E. (2006) *Dialogical Meetings in Social Networks*. London: Karnac.

The development of systematic methods and principles for collecting and analysing case material

Most of the counselling and psychotherapy cases that have ever been written up are based on information derived from therapist notes and recollections, that have then been interpreted and analysed solely by the therapist. These case studies can be fascinating, informative and persuasive. They convey the sensibility of the therapist, in terms of a finely tuned awareness of the possibilities and process of therapy, and provide rich evidence of how the author thinks about his or her work. This kind of case study can be hugely useful for trainees, and also for more experienced practitioners, who wish to learn about what is involved in adopting a certain perspective in relation to clients. However, these case studies do not provide reliable evidence about what actually happens in a case, because they are not able to supply data that can be subjected to any kind of independent scrutiny. In addition, there is good reason to believe that the information that is provided in a typical clinical case study may be constructed around selective remembering and reporting on the part of the therapist–author. The history of case study research in counselling and psychotherapy can be viewed as a struggle between a desire to retain the valuable qualities of traditional therapist-generated clinical case studies, while introducing some elements of methodological rigour.

This chapter tells the story of how this struggle has played out over the past century, and what it has left us with today. The chapter consists of two main sections. First, a historical account is offered, of the emergence and development of methods of systematic case study inquiry in counselling and psychotherapy. The aim of this section is to explain why different case study approaches have been devised, and their strengths and weaknesses. The second part of the chapter reviews some of the basic methodological principles that inform all approaches to systematic case study inquiry.

The development of systematic methods of case study research in counselling and psychotherapy

The starting point for the clinical case study tradition in psychotherapy was a series of psychoanalytic cases published by Freud, describing his work with clients such as Dora (Freud 1901) and the Rat Man (Freud 1909). Freud typically saw several patients each day, and spent the evening writing detailed notes. He later used these notes as the basis for his case study publications. Subsequent generations of psychoanalytic and psychodynamic theorists have continued to use a similar strategy for writing case study reports (e.g., Casement 1985, 1990; Hargaden and Sills 2002; Malan 1979). However, it seems fairly clear that there are several important limitations of this approach, in relation to the aim of producing an adequate account of what might have happened in the therapy that these clients received:

- it is impossible to recall everything that happened in a therapy session: it seems inevitable that important information may have been lost;
- writing a retrospective account of a session introduces the possibility that the writer has reconstructed events in line with his or her pre-existing assumptions;
- there is an absence of other perspectives – for instance, the views of the client regarding the helpfulness of the therapy;
- there is no way of checking whether the interpretation of the material that has been collected is rigorous, systematic and comprehensive.

One of the most significant critics of the clinical case study approach has been the psychoanalyst Donald Spence (1989, 2001), who has argued that the methodology of the clinical case study leads to a process of 'narrative smoothing', in which aspects of therapy are selectively recalled, in line with the therapist's pre-existing theoretical framework or personal interests, while contradictory evidence is overlooked. The tendency for contemporary therapy writers to publish case examples or vignettes, rather than full-blown case studies, serves to exacerbate these difficulties, because only selected segments of case material are presented. The development of critical perspectives on the traditional clinical case study report has resulted in this kind of analysis having little credibility outside of the immediate professional group to which a case study author is affiliated. It has also had the result of motivating a search for more systematic methods of case study inquiry. From the 1960s, several influential writers argued that it was essential to develop greater rigour in the use of case studies in research (Bolgar 1965; Dukes 1965; Leitenberg

1973; Shapiro 1961). Key contributors to the development of systematic methods of case study research in counselling and psychotherapy include Edwards (1998), Galassi and Gersh (1991), Hill (1989), Schneider (1999), Stiles (2005) and Turpin (2001). The methodological developments that have taken place in counselling and psychotherapy case study research as a result of this debate have led to the evolution of five distinctive types or 'genres' of case study investigation: *single subject* designs, *theory-building* case studies, *pragmatic* case studies, *hermeneutic single case efficacy* studies, and *narrative* case studies.

Freud's case of Dora: an illustration of the methodological inadequacy of the clinical case study method

Box 2.1

Ida Bauer was one of the first patients to be treated by Freud. In the case of 'Dora', published several years after the end of therapy, Freud used this material to develop and explain his theory of hysteria (Freud 1901). Ida/Dora was a young woman from a prosperous middle-class family, who presented with a wide range of debilitating symptoms: difficulty breathing and speaking, sensation of choking, fainting spells, depression, avoidance of social contact and threats of suicide. She described an emotional crisis that had been precipitated by the attempt of a family friend, an older man, to seduce her. Freud interpreted Dora's problems as arising from her own repressed sexual desire toward this man. Because of Freud's fame, and the influential role that this case has played in the evolution of psychoanalytic thought, the Dora case has been re-analysed by many writers, including some who were able to locate information on the case that Freud chose not to include in his original publication, or was not available to him (see Bernheimer and Kahane 1986). Some of these later writers, such as Eriksen (1986), offered ways of re-interpreting the Dora case within a psychodynamic framework. Other writers, such as Billig (1997), have analysed the case from quite different theoretical perspectives. Most of these authors have come to the conclusion that Freud spectacularly missed the point in his interpretation of Dora's experience. In his conclusion to a comprehensive review of the literature on the Dora case, Mahony (1996: 148–9) stated that:

> The case of Dora has an array of negative distinctions. It is one of the greatest psychotherapeutic disasters; one of the most remarkable exhibitions of a clinician's published rejection of his patient; spectacular, though tragic, sexual abuse of a young girl, and her own analyst's published exoneration of that abuse; an eminent case of forced associations, forced remembering, and perhaps several forced dreams, forced remembering of dreams, even forced remembering of forced dreams. Without any stretch of the imagination of the case, the published history, and the subsequent reception can be called an example of continued sexual abuse.

(Continued)

What are we to make of this? It is easy to read the Dora case, now, as an illustration of Freud's mistaken approach to understanding female sexuality. But the massive attention that has been devoted to the case also makes it possible to understand the case as an illustration of the profound limitations of the traditional clinical case study method. Because Freud has been so influential within the field of psychotherapy, and because he placed such emphasis on the Dora case, it has been possible to unpick his account of the case, statement by statement, and find it wanting. However, in principle, one must assume that any clinical case report could be unpicked in a similar fashion. The lesson of Dora is that a radically different approach to case study inquiry in counselling and psychotherapy needs to be found, if therapy case studies are to have any chance of being regarded as sources of reliable evidence about what actually happens in therapy.

Box 2.2

The development of a rigorous approach to psychoanalytic single-case research: the psychotherapy research project of the Menninger Foundation

The Menninger psychoanalytic sanatorium, in Topeka, Kansas, was for many years one of the leading centres of psychoanalytic practice in the USA, offering a combination of inpatient and outpatient treatment for patients who typically had severe and chronic problems. In 1954, under the directorship of Lewis Robbins and Robert Wallerstein, the Menninger Foundation initiated a psychotherapy research project based on comprehensive case studies of 42 people receiving psychoanalysis or psychoanalytic psychotherapy. These case studies were based on analysis of therapist session notes, along with data from a range of psychological tests and interviews (with the patient and family members) conducted before therapy, at the end of therapy and at three-year follow-up (Wallerstein 1986, 1989). Some patients were followed up for as long as 30 years. This project generated a large number of research books and articles, which are summarized in Wallerstein (1986). For each participant, an individual case analysis was carried out by a team of researchers, in relation to a set of research questions concerning the process and outcome of the therapy they had received. Following this initial analysis, themes were identified on a cross-case basis. The case summaries included in Wallerstein (1986) provide a unique insight into the psychological conflicts experienced by middle- and upper-class Americans in the post-war years, and the role that psychoanalytic therapy played in helping many of them to move on in their lives (or not). The findings of the study challenged many of the theoretical ideas prevailing in psychoanalytic circles at that time, and contributed to a shift in psychoanalytic practice in the direction of more collaborative and supportive ways of working with clients. The Menninger study remains a unique achievement in the history of psychotherapy research.

Single subject or 'n=1' studies

The most striking contrast to the kind of literary, interpretive clinical case studies produced by Freud and his colleagues, can be found in the 'single subject' case study approach developed initially within behaviour therapy. Just as experimental psychology sought to develop a scientifically rigorous alternative to introspection and psychoanalysis, the early behaviour therapists sought to devise a method for studying single cases that was as far as possible from the subjectivity that was associated with psychoanalytic case reports. In making sense of these developments, it is necessary to recognize that most of the pioneering research into behavioural laws of learning, carried out by Pavlov, Skinner and Watson in the early 20th century, was based on a case study approach. For example, Skinner would set up an experiment in which the behaviour of an individual pigeon in a cage could be observed as it responded to different contingencies of reinforcement. The results from such a study would usually include a graph of how the frequency of some aspect of pigeon behaviour (such as pecking at a lever) changed over time as the reinforcement schedule was altered. The analysis of these studies mainly consisted of visual inspection of the trajectory of the line on the graph.

It made perfect sense for the pioneers of behaviour therapy, such as Joseph Wolpe (1958) to adopt this methodology when evaluating their efforts to apply behavioural principles in work with individual human clients or patients. In their clinical work, an observable and measurable target behaviour would be identified, and the frequency of this behaviour would be monitored during a pre-therapy or pre-intervention baseline period. The behaviour would continue to be monitored during the period when the therapy was being delivered, and during a follow-up phase. When the target behaviour consisted of a clear-cut observable problem, such as frequency of handwashing, or school attendance, this approach could claim to yield tangible, objective evidence of change resulting from therapy, particularly if the baseline period was long enough to demonstrate that the problem had been stable before the therapeutic intervention had been introduced. This method could readily be extended to analyse the impact of different therapy techniques in the same case. For example, a client with an anxiety problem might receive relaxation training for three sessions, followed by work on maladaptive cognitive beliefs for another three sessions, so that the differential effectiveness of these contrasting cognitive-behavioural therapy (CBT) interventions could be assessed.

This approach to case study research in psychotherapy became known as the 'single subject design' or 'n=1' (where 'n' indicates the number of experimental subjects) study (Barlow and Hersen, 1986; Barlow, Hayes and Nelson, 1984). The terminology is significant: behavioural and CBT researchers see themselves as operating within the experimental tradition, with its emphasis on objectivity and measurement. This form of case study has made a major contribution to the success of behaviour therapy and CBT over the years. This is because it is relatively easy for ordinary practitioners to collect (or ask clients to collect) the kind of daily or weekly behavioural data that can be used in a single subject design. In many instances, behavioural and CBT therapists would be making use of these observations in their routine therapy practice. What this has meant is that the behavioural/CBT therapy tradition has had an accessible and flexible methodology for evaluating and reporting the effectiveness of innovative therapeutic interventions. It is no surprise, therefore, that the history of CBT has been characterised by a steady accumulation of new techniques and interventions.

In recent years, there appears to have been a downturn in the use of single subject case studies within the CBT community. There appear to be two reasons for this current crisis. First, the increasing emphasis in CBT on defining change in terms of shifts in underlying cognitive schema, of reductions in symptoms of psychiatric disorders such as depression, means that CBT is less focused on objectively measurable behavioural outcomes. Second, the current political environment, which prioritizes evidence from large-scale randomized trials, may have led CBT researcher-practitioners to believe that it is not worthwhile for them to invest time and energy in publishing case studies (Molloy et al. 2007). In response to these issues, influential figures within the CBT approach have called for renewed attention to be given to the role of single subject research within their discipline (Borckardt et al. 2008; Sharpley 2003, 2007).

On the whole, the potential value of single subject methods has not been acknowledged or embraced by therapy researchers and practitioners from outside the CBT enclave. This would appear to be on the grounds that more relational or insight-oriented approaches to therapy are not organized around discrete behavioural objectives, and so are not amenable to investigation through a single subject approach. The rhetoric of talking about a therapy case as if it were an experiment is also problematic for colleagues from other traditions. The neglect of single subject methods by non-CBT therapy investigators is a pity, because the single subject approach incorporates three principles that have a powerful part to play in any approach to systematic case study research in counselling and psychotherapy. These are: (a) time-series analysis as a means of assessing change; (b) the use of baseline measures to establish the stability of a problem before therapy begins; and (c) a methodology that can be readily integrated into routine practice, thus allowing a very wide range of potentially interesting cases to be trawled. Further discussion of practical issues around how to conduct and publish single subject case studies is provided in Chapter 7.

The aims of case study research

The development of systematic approaches to case study research in counselling and psychotherapy has focused on four sets of questions that may be addressed through the analysis of case material:

- *Outcome* questions: How effective has therapy been in this case? To what extent can changes that have been observed in the client be attributed to therapy?
- *Theory-building* questions: How can the process of therapy in this case be understood in theoretical terms? How can the data in this case be used to test and refine an existing theoretical model?
- *Pragmatic* questions: What strategies and methods did the therapist use in this case, that contributed to the eventual outcome? How were therapeutic methods adapted and modified to address the needs of this specific client? What are the principles of good practice that can be derived from this case?
- *Experiential* or *narrative* questions: What was it like to be the client or therapist in this case? What is the story of what happened, from the client or therapist point of view?

There are elements of each of these questions, in any comprehensive case study. The development of methodological rigour in therapy case study methods has been largely driven by attempts to find valid and reliable ways to answer these questions.

Box 2.3

Theory-building case studies

Another area that has seen a great deal of methodological innovation has been in the domain of *theory-building* case studies. To a large extent, this genre of therapy case study inquiry has attempted to learn from the success of psychoanalysis, in using case studies to test and refine theory, but in a more rigorous manner that draws on the tools and techniques of contemporary counselling and psychotherapy research. Kvale (2001) argued that psychoanalytic case studies have been hugely successful in being able to generate theoretical ideas, and that if psychoanalytic concepts were eliminated from psychology textbooks, little would remain. However, the process by which Freud and his successors used case material to expand their theoretical understanding was far from transparent. Contemporary theory-oriented case therapy study researchers have been committed to finding ways to make their theoretical analyses more externally verifiable, and as a result more credible to sceptical audiences.

Potentially, case study evidence has a substantial degree of significance in relation to the construction of theory in counselling and psychotherapy. Case studies can throw up examples of therapy processes and events that have not previously been identified, and that require new theoretical concepts to explain them. Case study evidence can be used to disprove a theoretical proposition, or to point out the limits of its applicability. Complex theoretical frameworks can be refined over a series of cases, by using each case as a 'testing ground' for the explanatory power of the model. In case study research, generalisability is not achieved through counting ('this statement must be true because it is supported by data from 1000 therapy clients'), but by the development of theory. The key idea here is that what is learned from any case study is not a statistical generalization, but a way of making sense (i.e., a theory or model), and that it is this theoretical construction that can be generalized to other cases.

The strategy that has been adopted by several groups of theory-oriented case study researchers has been, first, to formulate a comprehensive statement of the theory, and to develop ideas around the kinds of events or processes that might be predicted to occur within therapy, if the theory was valid. Then, a rich case record is assembled, that includes all possible information that is relevant to the theoretical concepts that are to be examined. The case data are then analysed using established techniques for qualitative research, or coding systems, in order to determine the extent to which the processes that were predicted by the theory have occurred. Finally, anomalous processes and therapy events are closely examined in order to generate new concepts and models. These new ideas then become part of an enhanced theoretical framework that is tested out in another case. As this inquiry cycle continues, the theory becomes more comprehensively grounded in evidence, and at the same time more differentiated. This whole endeavour is undertaken by a *team* of researchers, to facilitate dialogue and debate around theoretical interpretations of case material, and to forestall any tendency toward premature rush to judgement in favour of individual theoretical prejudices. Using this type of methodology, what may start off as a 'broad-brush' set of ideas gradually becomes more nuanced and differentiated. The rationale for this way of using case studies is explained more fully by Stiles (2007), and several examples of theory-building case studies are reviewed in Chapter 9.

At this point, relatively few programmes of case-based theory-building have been carried out. This may be because therapy writers find it fairly easy to come up with new concepts on the basis of clinical experience, and do not appreciate the added value that can accrue from using systematic case study research to refine their theoretical ideas. It is also likely that few theoreticians have the time or resources to engage in team-based case study inquiry. A further barrier to this type of work is that many therapists have strong personal and professional allegiances to theoretical systems that are already well established, and have no wish to carry out research that may challenge these conceptual edifices. This neglect of the theory-building dimension of systematic case study research in counselling and psychotherapy is regrettable, because almost any carefully analysed case will yield some observations and processes that are of theoretical interest – there are many opportunities for the development of theory that are being passed by. It is also regrettable because many of the therapy case studies that have been published in recent years have tended to lead to theoretical conclusions that are at odds with the assumptions of 'mainstream' models of therapy.

A comprehensive approach to theory-building case study research in psychology: the work of Henry Murray

Box 2.4

The source of many of the ideas that are used in contemporary systematic case study research in counselling and psychotherapy is Henry Murray, whose 1938 book *Explorations in Personality* remains a landmark in the field of personality research. Based at the Psychological Clinic at Harvard University, Murray was trained in science and medicine, as well as being influenced by psychoanalysis and Jung's analytic psychology. His aim was to create a method of research that would be:

> the natural child of the deep, significant, metaphorical, provocative and questionable speculations of psycho-analysis and the precise, systematic, statistical, trivial and artificial methods of academic personology. (Murray 1938: 33–4)

Through collaborative work over a number of years, Murray and his colleagues, who included Robert White and Erik Erikson, derived a set of principles for carrying out systematic case study research:

- use as many different sources of information on the person as possible, for example, questionnaires, observations, interviews, projective techniques and autobiography;

(Continued)

- use a team of researchers, so that interpretation of the material is less likely to be dominated by bias or counter-transference arising from an individual investigator; this also allows the quality of relationship between the subject and different members of the team to be taken into consideration;
- carry out a series of case studies, in which tentative generalizations and conclusions drawn from earlier cases are checked out against later cases;
- integrate quantitative and qualitative measures or observations at the level of theory. Members of Murray's research team took both types of data into consideration when deciding whether or not the pattern of findings from a particular subject confirmed some aspect of their theoretical model, or stood in contradiction to the theory and necessitated its further development and articulation.

Further information on these ideas can be found in Murray (1938), McLeod (1992), or the collection of Murray's writings edited by Shneidman (1981).

Pragmatic case studies

A central thread that runs through the development of case study methods in counselling and psychotherapy is the idea that what practitioners have to say about their work with clients is usually interesting and illuminating. The difficulty with traditional clinical case studies has never been that they lack theoretical or practical relevance, but that they have a tendency toward bias and selective reporting. The single subject design case study method, described earlier, has the potential to introduce a high degree of rigour to the case reports produced by practitioners, but imposes certain constraints that are not appropriate to the routine practice of most therapists. Theory-building case studies are probably viewed as relevant by the majority of therapists, but require too much effort. The answer to this dilemma, proposed by Fishman (1999), is the *pragmatic* case study, which has been designed to address the shortcomings of traditional clinical case studies. In a pragmatic case study, the practitioner is required to collect as much information as he or she can on a case, and to write it up in a standard format. In the *Pragmatic Case Studies in Psychotherapy* journal, each case report is not only rigorously peer reviewed (a process that challenges the author to question his or her assumptions and biases), but is also published alongside two or three expert commentaries. In addition, as an on-line journal, *Pragmatic Case Studies in Psychotherapy* has the facility to publish transcripts, test scores, therapy protocols and other detailed information as linked appendices, thus allowing the reader every opportunity to arrive at his or her own interpretation of the case. The ultimate aim of the pragmatic case study movement is to achieve a sufficient number of good quality published case studies for practitioners to be able to use it as a resource in terms of finding out about 'what works' with different types of client. Further information about the pragmatic case study approach is available in Chapter 6.

The influence on therapy case study research of ideas and procedures from the legal system: 'quasi-judicial' approaches

Box 2.5

Research in counselling and psychotherapy is dominated by the assumption that valid knowledge is generated through the application of *scientific* methods. However, an alternative perspective, which has been increasingly influential among case study researchers, is that it is also possible to generate valid knowledge through *judicial* methods. The legal system has developed a highly sophisticated set of procedures, including rules of evidence, case law and adjudication systems (judges and juries), for determining the truth in cases that involve highly meaningful and complex social events. The application of 'quasi-judicial' methods to case study research in psychology was pioneered by Murray and Morgan (1945), who set up two competing groups of researchers to function as if they were 'prosecution' and 'defence' teams, in developing competing analyses of case material. Levine (1974) pointed out that there were many 'adversarial' features that already existed in psychology research, such as the system of peer reviews, and suggested various ways in which these elements could be extended, for example his idea that research teams should include a professional 'adversary', whose job was to monitor the way that they collected and analysed evidence. Bromley (1986) developed a framework for evaluating the quality of evidence in case studies. In relation to counselling and psychotherapy case study research, these ideas have been put into action by Bohart (2000), Elliott et al. (2009) and Miller (2008). It seems clear that quasi-judicial methods have a great deal to offer in situations such as therapy case study research (and court cases), where multiple sources of evidence need to be taken into account, evidence can be interpreted in different ways, evidence is of variable quality and data analysts may be motivated to arrive at conclusions that meet their own personal needs. It is important to recognize, also, that a great deal of methodological work needs to be done to create appropriate and time-effective procedures for therapy research that is conducted in this way. The use of quasi-judicial methods in counselling and psychotherapy case study research represents a crucial step in the evolution of a systematic and rigorous case study. Case study research has moved on from lone-researcher approaches, to case analysis that uses teams of researchers. The introduction of quasi-judicial approaches now provides a powerful rationale for conceptualizing and organising the efforts of inquiry team members.

Hermeneutic single case efficacy design (HSCED) studies

The hermeneutic single case efficacy design (HSCED) approach to case study research was developed by Robert Elliott (2001, 2002), a leading figure in the humanistic-experiential approach to therapy. The purpose of the HSCED method is similar to that of single case design approach, in seeking to determine whether the client has substantially improved as a result of the therapy that he or she has received. However, rather than relying on time series analysis of a single outcome variable, HSCED works with a rich case record, that includes both qualitative and quantitative outcome and process data, thus making HSCED sensitive to any kind of change that could occur in the client. Analysis of the complex data set that is generated in an HSCED study is hermeneutic or interpretive in nature – the individual researcher or research team systematically interpret the relevance of all of the data that has been collected, in respect of three key questions: Is this a good outcome case? Can the outcome be attributable to therapy, or has it been brought about by some other means? What elements within therapy brought about the client's changes? Inevitably, different items of data will lead to different answers to these questions, so the interpretive approach also includes guidelines for weighing up the relative significance of different sources of information.

In analysing the case data, the researcher adopts first an *affirmative* stance ('What is the evidence that supports an interpretation of good outcome?') and then a *sceptic* stance ('What is the evidence that supports an interpretation of poor outcome?'). In the more recent evolution of the method, the HSCED protocol has been extended to include a more overtly 'judicial' framework, with the use of independent judges who evaluate the arguments for each position. The HSCED method is a fairly recent addition to the range of methodological possibilities open to therapy case study researchers. Its main advantages are that (a) it offers researchers a clear set of guidelines around how to proceed, (b) there is no prior restriction on the type of data that can be used and (c) it focuses on answering important questions around the effectiveness of therapy, and thus makes a contribution to debates around evidence-based practice. The main weakness of HSCED is that it involves the assembly of a rich data set, and then proceeds to reduce this complexity to a simple answer to a single question: Can this therapy be shown to have been effective? Further coverage of this approach can be found in Chapter 8.

Narrative case studies

A further strand of case study research in counselling and psychotherapy are studies that attempt to convey the experience of the client or the therapist. These case studies can be viewed as falling within the qualitative research tradition of *narrative inquiry*, which emphasizes the role of storytelling and narrative as a distinctive way of knowing (see Chapter 1). The aim in this type of case study is to allow the reader to gain a sense of what the therapy was like for either the client or the therapist (or both). Compared to the other strands of systematic case study research in counselling and psychotherapy that have been discussed in this chapter, there has been relatively little methodological innovation within the narrative approach. Some narrative case studies have consisted of minimally edited diary entries kept by the therapist and client (Dryden and Yankura 1992; Yalom and Elkin 1974). Other narrative case studies have comprised autobiographical accounts written by clients (Dinnage 1988). By contrast, the narrative case study published by Etherington (2000) represents the application of principles of qualitative research, in terms of transparency about the way in which the data were collected and analysed. It seems probable that the increasing acceptance in recent years of the value of case study evidence in counselling and psychotherapy, will result in a proliferation of narrative case reports. This is because well-written narrative case studies are intrinsically interesting and informative, for students, practitioners and members of the general public. They also serve as an invaluable heuristic source of ideas for the development of theory and research. In addition, there are plentiful sources of guidelines and examples of how to conduct narrative case studies, that can be used to inform narrative case research in counselling and psychotherapy, for example within the fields of psychohistory (Crosby 1979; Runyan 1981b), life history research (Bertaux 1981; Josseelson 1987, 1996a; Lieblich and Josselson 1997; McAdams et al. 2001) and auto-ethnography (Ellis and Bochner 1996; Speedy 2007). Further discussion of narrative approaches to case study research in counselling and psychotherapy can be found in Chapter 10.

Principles of systematic case study research

The approaches to case study research in counselling and psychotherapy that have been introduced in this chapter can viewed as representing quite distinct methodological traditions within the field of systematic case study inquiry, that have been developed to answer different types of research questions. Nevertheless, there are some general principles for therapy case study research which have emerged from the efforts of researchers to move beyond the traditional clinical case study approach. These principles include:

1 Creating as rich a data set as possible, based on multiple sources of information, including description of the context within which the therapy took place.
2 Engaging the interest of the reader by telling the story of what happened within the case.
3 If possible, using standardized process and outcome quantitative measures that allow comparisons to be made with data from other cases.
4 Provide enough information within the report, or in appendices, so that the reader can make up their own mind about the interpretation of the case.
5 Use multiple analysts, rather than depending on a single perspective on the data. Also, if possible, more than one person should be involved in data collection.
6 Do some kind of time-series analysis, to enable the process of change to be explored in a systematic manner.
7 Critically examine alternative interpretations of the data – be critical and scholarly, rather than using the case study to 'sell' an approach to therapy.
8 Take theory seriously, on the grounds that generalization is based on the establishment of cross-case theoretical principles.
9 Try to find out what the client thinks about the therapy he or she has received, and about the analysis of the case data.
10 Be reflexive – provide relevant information about the author(s), to allow readers to take potential sources of bias into account (Finlay and Gough 2003).
11 Use a standard format (e.g., the one recommended by the *Pragmatic Case Studies in Psychotherapy* journal), to make it easier for future scholars to conduct meta-analyses, and for current readers to find their way around your case report.

These methodological principles describe a set of guidelines for rigorous case study research in counselling and psychotherapy, that allow case reports to be treated as a valid source of evidence in relation to issues of policy and practice. Further detailed examples of how these principles can be implemented in action are provided in the following chapters. An additional set of principles, concerned with the ethical quality of case study research, is discussed in Chapter 4. On the whole, writers on therapy case study methodology have not devoted much attention to ethical issues. However, as will be seen in Chapter 4, many practitioners who are considering writing up their cases are well aware of the ethical and moral implications of publishing information about their clients. The absence of sufficient attention to ethical issues can be understood as having constituted a barrier to involvement in case-based research.

Conclusions

Over 100 years of case study inquiry in the field of counselling and psychotherapy has yielded a substantial number of ideas about how to carry out systematic and rigorous case studies. Out of this literature, there has emerged a growing consensus around how to collect and analyse case data, and how to write case reports. At the present time there exist a number of distinct case study approaches, each of which emphasizes certain research questions and methodological principles, rather than others. It seems likely that the current increased interest in the role of case study evidence will produce new models for case study research, based on an appreciation of generic methodological principles.

Topics for reflection and discussion

1 Choose one 'clinical' case study that is of interest to you. How convincing is the account of the case that is offered in this report, how convincing are the conclusions that are drawn? What would make this case study more convincing?
2 One of the significant advances in case study methodology has been the application of the 'quasi-judicial' metaphor, in which the analysis of a therapy case is regarded as similar to the process of a legal case. What are the similarities and differences between therapy cases and legal cases? What are the advantages, for therapy researchers, of adopting a quasi-judicial framework, and what are the disadvantages?

Recommended further reading

There do not appear to be any available published accounts that examine the historical development of case study research in counselling and psychotherapy.

A brief and engaging introduction to the idea that case studies can be carried out in a rigorous and systematic fashion is:

Sechrest, L., Stewart, M., Stickle, T. R. and Sidani, S. (1996) *Effective and Persuasive Case Studies*. Cambridge, MA: Human Services Research Institute.

An essential critique of the practice of the traditional clinical case study approach can be found in:

Spence, D.P. (1989) Rhetoric vs. evidence as a source of persuasion: a critique of the case study genre. In M.J. Packer and R.B. Addison (eds), *Entering the Circle: Hermeneutic Investigation in Psychology*. Albany, NY: State University of New York Press.

A 4-page summary of Spence's ideas is available in:

Spence, D.P. (2001) Dangers of anecdotal reports. *Journal of Clinical Psychology*, 57, 37–41.

A valuable overview of issues in case study research in therapy is provided by:

Hilliard, R.B. (1993) Single-case methodology in psychotherapy process and outcome research. *Journal of Consulting and Clinical Psychology*, 61(3), 373–80.

This article is part of a special issue of the *Journal of Consulting and Clinical Psychology* devoted to methodological issues in case study research.

There are three books that have developed guidelines for systematic case study research:

Gerring, J. (2006) *Case Study Research: Principles and Practices*. New York: Cambridge University Press

Simons, H. (2009) *Case Study Research in Practice*. London: Sage.

Yin, R.K. (2009) *Case Study Research: Design and Methods*, 4th edn. Thousand Oaks, CA: Sage.

These authors do not specifically focus on therapy case study research, but instead range across the whole field of social science, education and psychology.

Justifying case-based research: the role of systematic case studies in building an evidence base for therapy policy and practice

Often, both students and experienced researchers who propose case-based research studies find that they need to justify their choice of methodology, in the face of criticism from those who are more familiar with other approaches, such as experimental studies and survey designs. The aim of this chapter is to examine the main areas of criticism of case study methods:

1 Case studies are *biased*, and merely function as vehicles for publicizing the pre-existing assumptions of those who carry them out.
2 It is not possible to *generalize* on the basis of single cases.
3 Case studies are merely descriptive, and tell us nothing about *causality*.
4 Case studies are *ethically problematic*; it is impossible to guarantee anonymity to participants.
5 Case studies can provide fascinating, detailed accounts of human experience, but are hard to *summarize* in a form that can lead to an accumulation of evidence.
6 Case studies may be informative for practitioners, but do not generate evidence that is relevant for *policy-making*.

The following sections explain these positions in more detail, and explore some of the ways in which contemporary case study research addresses each of these issues. The questions that are being discussed here have been described by Flybjerg (2006) as 'misunderstandings', which have been widely used within the social and health sciences to justify the neglect of case-based approaches to inquiry. However, an appreciation of how to respond to these critical points of view is not only relevant to the task of justifying case study research in response to sceptical colleagues and audiences. Through the process of addressing these critical statements, it is possible to open up a range of crucial methodological challenges and choice-points that confront anyone who aims to carry out systematic, credible and useful case study research. The chapter closes with a discussion of some of the advantages of case study methods.

Subjectivity and bias in case study research

In the field of counselling and psychotherapy, it is not hard to see the strength of the sceptical claim that case studies are often *biased* in the direction of demonstrating or supporting the pre-existing assumptions of those who carry them out. Most of the case evidence that appears in the counselling and psychology literature consists of brief case vignettes that are used to illustrate the therapeutic approach of the author of the book or article in which they appear. These authors are very unlikely to choose to write about cases in which their approach proved to be ineffective. There is a sense, here, of case study evidence being used primarily as a means of persuasion, as a teaching aid or marketing tool, rather than as a genuine form of inquiry. Because practitioners and researchers in the therapy world have been exposed to so many of these self-promoting case examples throughout their training and professional life, there is an understandable tendency for their sensitivity to sources of self-serving selectivity and bias to be activated when they read actual research-based case studies.

It is important to retain a sense of balance when thinking about the alleged subjectivity and bias of case study evidence. Researcher bias is a problem for all types of research. For example, medical researchers are routinely required to disclose, in published research reports, the source of their funding, and any possible conflicts of interest that may have affected their investigation. Within psychotherapy outcome research, Luborsky et al. (1999) have shown that the theoretical allegiance of those who conduct randomised controlled trials (RCTs) of psychotherapy outcome is strongly predictive of the results of their studies. In other words, researchers who have been trained in cognitive-behavioural therapy (CBT) and belong to CBT professional associations, tend to find that CBT is more effective than other approaches, whereas researchers who have been trained as psychodynamic psychotherapists tend to find that psychodynamic therapy is the most effective approach. The issue of researcher bias is therefore not restricted to case study research.

Any attempt to conduct case study research in such a way that it is accepted as a source of systematic and unbiased evidence needs to address the issue of subjectivity and bias. There are four main strategies that have been developed for dealing with this problem.

- *Researcher reflexivity*: the researcher describes his or her professional background and allegiances, pre-existing assumptions and experience of doing the study, as a means of being transparent about any potential sources of bias. The researcher may also describe some of the new discoveries or unexpected findings that emerged during the study (i.e., examples of instances where pre-existing assumptions were not supported) (Etherington 2004; Finlay and Gough 2003).
- *Making use of independent 'objective' evidence*: a case study that is based solely on notes kept by a therapist is open to many sources of subjective bias, for example through the selection of observations to include in the notes. By contrast, a case study that makes use of sources of evidence that can be replicated by readers can be seen to be less open to bias. For example, asking a client to complete the Beck Depression Inventory (BDI) makes it easier to justify a statement such as 'the client was moderately depressed at the onset of therapy', in contrast to a similar statement based solely on the therapist's perceptions of the client. This is not to say that a BDI score is necessarily always a more valid indicator of depression than a therapist assessment. The point is that use of the questionnaire gives the reader of the research report a clear, and potentially verifiable, evidence-trail back to something that the client actually did at a particular time and place.
- *Making use of multiple researchers*: probably the most effective and widely used strategy in case study research, for transcending the personal agenda of an individual researcher, is the use of multiple researchers. If a case client has been interviewed by more than one person, or the case data set has been analysed by a team of researchers, and time has been allowed for discussion and resolution of differences in a democratic manner, then the final case report will be less likely to be viewed as a wholly subjective construct.
- *Benchmarking against established interpretive criteria*: most systematic therapy case studies include a mix of qualitative material (e.g., interview transcripts) and quantitative data (e.g., questionnaire scores). If these sources are analysed in an idiosyncratic manner, the impression will be conveyed that the researcher is pursuing his or her individual motives, rather than seeking to contribute to a wider understanding. By drawing on agreed standards of good practice in the analysis of qualitative or statistical data, the researcher can overcome this danger. Particularly valuable are the guidelines for the analysis of qualitative data identified by Elliott, Fischer and Rennie (1999), Morrow (2005) and Stiles (1993), and the criteria for analysing clinically significant and reliable change developed by Jacobson and others (Jacobson et al. 1984; Jacobson and Revenstorf 1988; Ogles et al. 2001; Wise 2004).

Taken together, these methodological strategies can go a long way toward reassuring consumers of case study research that they are being offered a reasonably even-handed and rigorous approach to the case being presented. At the same time, it needs to be acknowledged that good case study research requires an empathic, personal engagement with the case material on the part of the researcher. The debate around subjectivity and bias is part of a wider discussion around the roles of relativism and objectivity in research (Rennie 2000, 2001). There is no point in trying to deny that research is socially constructed and organized, and shaped by individual desires. It is also undeniable that people who read research papers are looking for something more than just the individual opinion of the author. The answer, in case study research as in other forms of social inquiry, is to attain an appropriate middle ground between the extreme positions of wholly detached objectivity and personal self-expression.

The problem of generalizability

The one thing that everyone understands about case research is that 'you cannot generalize from a single case'. This proposition can easily be exemplified. A therapy researcher writes up a case study in which it was clearly demonstrated that 'a depressed client has been significantly helped by psychodynamic therapy' (specific statement). This case does *not* imply that 'psychodynamic therapy is effective for depression' (generalizability statement), because it may be that the researcher has found a rare or unusual case, and that if he or she were to collect another 10 cases of depressed people who have received psychodynamic psychotherapy, none of them would report a good outcome. The most that can be claimed from a single case such as this, in terms of generalizable knowledge, would be that 'psychodynamic therapy *can be* effective for depression' or that 'the proposition that psychodynamic therapy is *not* effective for depression has been disproved'. It should be noted that these limited generalizability claims may still be of some significance, for example in arguing against those who would view a psychodynamic approach to depression as wholly worthless.

The problem of generalizability represents a fundamental barrier to the use of case study methods, in the eyes of many researchers (Campbell and Stanley 1963). The argument here is that the aim of systematic or scientific knowledge is always to be able to make general statements about patterns, trends or 'laws' in the reality that we experience, and that case studies, in only being able to yield descriptions or analyses of single instances, are as a result incapable of making a contribution to this endeavour. Being able to respond constructively to the critical issue of generalizability is therefore of major importance to anyone seeking to undertake case study research.

There are a number of ways in which the issue of generalizabilty has been addressed by supporters of the use of case study methods. One response has been to introduce the idea that generalization takes place in the mind of the reader/consumer of the case study. This phenomenon has been described as 'naturalistic generalization' (Stake 1978), 'transferability' (Lincoln and Guba 2000) or the development of 'working hypotheses' (Cronbach 1975). The key idea here is that a practitioner, such as a counsellor or psychotherapist, possesses a rich and complex set of ideas and practices (a 'schema') through which he or she makes sense of their work (Donmoyer 1990). This schema has been built up from a long period of involvement with clients and cases. When a practitioner reads a published case study, the case study report includes a great deal of detailed information about the client, the therapy that was delivered, the context in which the therapy took place, and so on. There exist, therefore, multiple possible points of contact between the case study and the pre-existing schema, and it is at these points of contact that the reader is able to generate new working hypotheses ('the method used by this therapist might be relevant in my work with client X' or 'I realize now how important it is to keep a focus on the client's theory of change'). As a result, the schema of the reader is reinforced in some ways, and extended in others. The generalization that occurs does not take the form of an explicit proposition, articulated by the researcher, but instead is expressed in practical action and 'implicit' knowledge on the part of the reader. Within contemporary psychotherapy case study research, this is essentially the position taken by Fishman (1999) – the generalizable knowledge achieved by case studies occurs through their enhancement of pragmatic understanding and possibilities for action on the part of practitioners. There are, however, some important methodological difficulties associated with the position that generalizability in case study research is achieved in this kind of 'naturalistic' or pragmatic fashion. In discussing the limitations of this position, Gomm, Hammersley and Foster (2000: 102) point out that it has the weakness of 'transferring responsibility to the reader', and provides little guidance to the researcher on how to select or analyse cases in ways that would enhance this kind of transferability. Indeed, Gomm et al. (2000) even question whether there exists any evidence that case studies are any more effective than other forms of writing, such as fiction, in enabling this kind of generalizability to take place. In conclusion, then, it is reasonable to conclude that although pragmatic or naturalistic generalizability offers a plausible account of why practitioners are interested in case studies and provide a ready audience for case study reports, this model does not have much to say about how to ensure that the generalizability that occurs in and through practitioners' schemas is appropriate, well-founded or valid. Taken on its own, therefore, this response to the issue of generalizability provides at best only a partial response to the sceptic.

Box 3.1

Drawing inferences from case studies

Another way of thinking about the issue of generalization is in terms of *inference* – what can we infer from the findings of a case study? In a classic paper, Kazdin (1981) argued that results from well-conducted case studies can 'approximate' the results of randomized trials, and thus make a contribution to the evidence base for counselling and psychotherapy. He suggested that, in the absence of a control group or a large sample, any change that was observed in a client in a case study could be attributed to factors such as:

- the history of the problem (e.g., if a problem has emerged suddenly and recently, it may just as readily suddenly recede; if a problem has been around for a long time, but has been cyclical in nature, any improvement may merely be a result of the cycle repeating itself);
- the maturation of the client;
- the impact on the client of being tested on more than one occasion;
- lack of reliability of the assessment instrument;
- statistical regression to the mean, reflecting the random variation that occurs within any set of measurements.

Kazdin (1981) identified five characteristics of good-quality case study research that addressed these issues, and allowed plausible inference to be made:

- reliable and valid methods for measuring change;
- continuous assessment (e.g., on a weekly basis) of key target outcome variables;
- stability of the problem prior to the introduction of a therapeutic intervention;
- immediate and marked effect on the problem following the introduction of the intervention;
- replication of the pattern of results over multiple cases (preferably clients with different backgrounds).

Although Alan Kazdin was writing from within the behavioural 'single subject design' tradition (see Chapter 7), his arguments apply to any approach to systematic case study research in counselling and psychotherapy. For Kazdin, there are two golden rules for systematic case study research. First, it is necessary to go beyond anecdotal reports, and use measurement strategies that would allow change to be objectively demonstrated. Second, it is essential to establish a continuous baseline of stability in the problem, prior to therapy. If a stable continuous baseline can be demonstrated, this implies that: (a) any shifts that occur once therapy has begun are unlikely to arise from the lack of reliability of the measures being used, and (b) that the change is due to therapy rather than other factors (because there has been sufficient time for other factors to reveal themselves).

A further approach to tackling the issue of generalizability in case study research is to acknowledge that case researchers have a responsibility to place their case analyses within the context of the larger population of cases from which they are drawn. This strategy builds on the simple idea that each case is a 'case of' something. Cases that somehow exist in their own terms, without any reference to a wider population, are unusual or even impossible. Certainly, in the field of counselling and psychotherapy research and practice, it would be hard to imagine a case that did not come already-labelled ('a case of CBT for social anxiety', 'a failure case', 'a long-term case', etc.) in some way. There are three main strategies that therapy case study researchers have used in order to establish a matrix of generalizability for their work.

- Select a case from a larger series of cases, so that the case can be identified as 'typical' or 'exceptional' in some way. Some researchers have chosen to look at 'good outcome' or 'poor outcome' cases (e.g., Watson et al. 2007). Other case study researchers have selected 'typical' or 'average' cases (Parry et al. 1986), that reflect the majority of cases within a larger sample. In this approach, the researcher is in a position to make tentative claims about the generalizability of the findings of the single case to the set of cases that it represents.
- Conduct a case series, in which several cases of a particular type are studied. Examples of this strategy can be found in Hill (1989) and Waters, Donaldson and Zimmer-Gembeck (2008). In this type of research design, the researcher can offer tentative generalizations based on conclusions that are strongly supported across the case series as a whole, as against predicted trends that were not generally supported.
- Use standardized process and outcome measures to collect data on the case. For example, if outcome measures such CORE-OM or BDI are used, it is possible to compare the pre-therapy severity levels, and magnitude of change, with norms collected for these measures. Similarly, using the Working Alliance Inventory to assess the quality of the therapeutic relationship opens up comparison with other studies that have used that measure.

Note that, whatever strategy is employed, it is always necessary to be sure to proceed with caution when claiming generalizability. This is in fact the same situation that occurs with large-scale randomized controlled trials, practice-based studies or surveys: it is never possible to generalize on the basis of one study. For example, a new drug would not be approved on the basis of a single trial, but would require some degree of replication by other research teams. In this respect, each case can be viewed as a single 'study'.

From the preceding discussion, it is clear that the rationale for selecting a case plays a major role in determining the kind of generalizable knowledge that can be claimed. Within the broader case study methodology literature, there has been considerable discussion and debate around the advantages and disadvantages of different strategies for choosing cases. A summary of these possibilities is provided in Box 3.2.

Box 3.2

Criteria for selecting cases for research

In case study research, a great deal of work and effort goes into data collection and analysis in each case that is investigated. It is therefore important to select cases that will have the greatest yield in terms of generalizability and theoretical impact. The main choice strategies for selecting cases in studies where only one case is to be examined are listed below.

- *Typical case*: the case is known to be typical or representative of a number of other cases in a defined population: for example, a typical good outcome case, or a case where the therapist is known to apply a particular therapy approach in a standardized fashion. This strategy enhances the generalizability of the findings of a case study.
- *Extreme case*: the case is known *not* to be similar to other cases: for example, the client may report particularly severe symptom levels, or the therapist may be the most/least effective practitioner within a group of therapists who have been studied. This strategy enhances the heuristic value of a case study, in terms of producing ideas for further research.
- *Deviant case*: some aspect of the case diverges from the expected process or outcome pathway: for example, a good outcome case where there was a poor therapeutic alliance, or a client with severe and chronic problems who made enduring clinically significant gains within only a few sessions of therapy. This strategy enhances the theory-building potential of a case study: for example, a convincing demonstration of how a good outcome can occur in the face of a poor therapeutic alliance could lead to a radical revision of how the therapeutic relationship is understood.
- *Influential case*: the case has received a lot of attention, perhaps through having been analysed before. This strategy increases the likelihood that a

case report will be widely read. It can also contribute to the theoretical value of the case, through comparison with previous theoretical analyses of the same material.

- *Innovative case*: In this strategy a case is selected that represents a new or innovative form of therapy. The aim is to carry out research of heuristic value that establishes possibilities that may be examined in subsequent research.

In studies where a series of cases are being investigated, some further choice strategies come into play:

- *Similar/matched cases*: a set of highly similar cases is analysed, for example to reinforce or test the findings of an earlier case study.
- *Different cases*: additional cases are selected on the basis of factors that are relevant to the generalizability of a finding (e.g., differences in gender, age, social class, etc.).

It is important to recognize that these choice strategies refer only to decisions made on information that is available in advance of the full analysis of the case material. It can often occur that detailed exploration of a case leads to initial assumptions being open to question – for example, a case that on first sight seemed typical, may be understood as far from typical as more is known about it. Also, in many research situations, a case study investigator may have little choice around the case(s) that are available for study, and can only make a *post-hoc* rationalization of the level of typicality of the case that they have investigated. Further discussion of strategies for case selection can be found in Gerring (2006) and Schofield (1990).

A final approach to generalizability in counselling and psychotherapy systematic case study research is to construct general statements by using case analyses to contribute to the development of *theory*. For example, a researcher might use the Prochaska and DiClemente (1982) *stages of change* model (precontemplation–contemplation–change–relapse) in carefully analysing what happened over the course of therapy in a single case, and could discover what appeared to be a new step in the change process (the 'hitting rock bottom' moment). This case study would therefore result in generalizable knowledge by (a) confirming and supporting the main ideas within the model, and (b) suggesting a new idea that could be incorporated into the model for future use. The strategy of using case study inquiry as part of a 'theory-building' approach to generalizability is explored in more detail in Chapter 9.

In conclusion, it can be seen that there are a number of effective answers to the problem of generalizability in case study research in counselling and psychotherapy. There is no reason for any therapy case study researcher to end up in a 'so what?' cul-de-sac, having completed a detailed and throughtful analysis of a case that does not lead anywhere or connect with any other knowledge. Generalizability can be built into case studies through a combination of purposeful case selection, use of standardized measures and theoretical sensitivity. Beyond this, if the case is described well enough, there is the additional possibility of naturalistic/ pragmatic transferability or generalizability on the part of the reader. It seems probable (though not yet demonstrated through research) that the more work the researcher does to establish a matrix for generalizability, the more opportunities the practitioner–reader will have to generalize what they learn from the case to their own area of work.

The issue of causality

One of the weaknesses of the case study method, from the point of view of some researchers, is that it is not capable of being used to investigate causal links between factors. For example, it may be possible to produce a case study of emotion-focused therapy (EFT) or some other approach to therapy, in which the client can be seen to be much better at the end of therapy, compared to the start. However, this kind of study, the critics would argue, can never tell us whether the therapy *caused* the good outcome, because it is impossible, within a single case, to eliminate other possible causes of this result. It is possible, for instance, that the beneficial outcome might have occurred even if the client had never seen a therapist. These critics would suggest that only an experimental study, such as a randomised controlled trial (RCT), can generate well-founded conclusions around causality. If depressed clients are randomly assigned to therapy, or a waiting list condition, and the therapy clients are less depressed than the waiting list clients after six months, then the cause of this improvement must be the therapy, because all other relevant factors have been controlled.

It is impossible to deny the logical force of experimental research. It is clear that randomized trials of counselling and psychotherapy do make it possible to make confident statements about causality (e.g., therapy X is effective in treating symptom Y) that are widely accepted within the professional and research communities, and by the general public. At the same time, it is important to acknowledge that there are important limits to the extent to which randomised experimental studies of counselling and psychotherapy can provide a comprehensive causal account of how and why therapy is effective (or ineffective). There are two main areas in which such studies are causally silent. First, even in a study in which a form of therapy is shown to be more effective than a contrast or control condition, it will still be found that some clients in the control condition will improve just as much as those who have received the therapy. Also, some clients who have received the therapy will not get better. This kind of result implies that there are always causal factors, other than therapy, that are at work and also that on some occasions the hypothesized causal factors (i.e., the therapy intervention) do not yield the effect they are supposed to produce. A further difficulty associated with the causal accounts provided by randomised controlled studies of therapy is that they only allow causal mechanisms to be specified at a *global* level. They assess the effectiveness of therapy-as-a-whole, and have nothing to say about the more fine-grained causal processes that are taking place within the therapy package. Although it is possible to design randomized studies that 'dismantle' therapy approaches, and examine the causal effects of each element within them (e.g., the relative impact of the 'cognitive' and 'behavioural' components of a CBT protocol), these studies are very difficult to carry out (because of the complexity of therapy and the many reciprocally interacting factors that are in play). These considerations have led Elliott (2001, 2002) to describe randomized controlled trials of psychotherapy as 'causally empty': they generate big, inflated causal statements, but there is nothing inside them. It is important to note that these criticisms do not apply to randomized controlled trials carried out within medical science, in which it is possible to generate a detailed and comprehensive account of the causal mechanisms underlying many diseases by studying micro-processes at the molecular and cell levels.

The causal limitations of randomised controlled trials of counselling and psychotherapy act as a reminder that it is always very hard to be sure about casual mechanisms within any area of social life. Human beings are enmeshed in many different types of reciprocal or circular cause-and-effect sequences (example: therapist empathy may cause disclosure of meaningful emotional material on the part of the client, *but* client disclosure and emotional openness makes it easier for a therapist to respond in an empathic manner. So: what is cause, and what is effect? Where does the causal sequence begin?) There are causal factors operating at different levels (biological, psychological, social), many of which are not visible to ordinary observation. Indeed, many people believe that personal will or intention can be a causal factor ('nothing *made* me do X; I did it because I wanted to do it').

In fact, carefully designed case studies can play a central role in identifying and analysing causal factors in therapy (Edelson 1986). The advantage of 'intensive' case studies, in contrast to large-scale 'extensive' studies, is that they create the possibility of collecting a large amount of data or observations around a relatively restricted set of events, thus making it possible to analyse the relative impact of a range of possible causal linkages. However, this is only possible, and will only be convincing to readers of a case study, if the analysis is planned and conducted in a systematic fashion, so that the *evidence* around causality is made explicit. There are two strategies within case study research that can be used to develop plausible statements about causality: time-series analysis, and Toulmin's rules of logical argument (Toulmin 1958).

Time-series analysis requires the regular collection of reliable observations over a period of time. For example, a person may be seeking therapy to deal with a binge eating disorder, and has been asked to keep a diary record of binge eating episodes for a period of three months before they enter therapy. This record shows that the person indulges in binge eating every two or three days, and that this pattern does not shift even during 'good' times, such as being on holiday. The person continues to keep the diary while they are in therapy, and for six months following therapy. During the first six weeks of therapy, the binge eating frequency drops to once every four or five days. After session 7, when the therapist uses a re-experiencing technique to work with early trauma, the binge frequency drops to zero. It remains at zero for three weeks, and then starts to rise again. Following a further session using the trauma re-experiencing technique, the binge eating again disappears, and remains in abeyance throughout the follow-up period. This time-series sequence would be interpreted by most people as providing plausible evidence for the causal impact of the therapeutic relationship (the client seemed to get a bit better once therapy commenced), and strong evidenced for the causal effectiveness of the specific trauma re-experiencing method. This kind of time-series analysis can be applied to many different types of data that can be collected in a case study, for example changes in weekly CORE-OM scores, changes in ratings of the client's depth of emotional experiencing based on analysis of session recordings, and so on. The logic behind this approach to establishing causality is the simple idea that change must be caused by an event that occurs just *before* the change is observed. For example, a billiard ball moves across the table *because* it has been hit by another billiard ball. Similarly, the reduction in binge eating of the client in the previous example was *caused* by the immediately preceding event (the specific trauma intervention). The use of time-series analysis is explored in more detail, in the context of contemporary case study research, in Chapter 7.

Toulmin's rules for logical argument in case studies

The philosopher Stephen Toulmin (1958) analysed the criteria for assessing the validity of arguments that are made by participants in everyday debate. These criteria or rules have been applied to case study research by Bromley (1981, 1986) and Miller (2004). Toulmin (1958) suggested that a well-founded argument consists of six elements:

1 The *claim*. This is an assertion that is made by a speaker or writer. For example, in a therapy case study, a typical assertion may be that 'the therapeutic intervention resulted in change in the level of anxiety being expressed by the client'.
2 The *data* refers to any evidence that relates to the claim. For example, in relation to the claim referred to above, there may be relevant evidence from change in anxiety scores, fewer references to anxiety in the therapy transcript, descriptions of the approach taken by the therapist, the follow-up interview with the client, etc.
3 The *warrant* is the rationale for accepting the data or evidence. For example, the evidence from the anxiety scores is warranted as evidence because it is a validated scale, and it is known that the client completed it seriously.
4 The *qualifier* refers to the degree of confidence in the claim, given the evidence and warranting that is available. For example, a case study researcher using a validated anxiety scale might propose that he or she has a high degree of confidence in the claim that a reduction in anxiety has occurred.
5 The *rebuttal* refers to any counter-argument that might be put forward, that contradicts the claim on the basis of questioning the warrant. For instance, the claim that a change in anxiety has been recorded might be rebutted if the evidence from a post-session interview contradicts the evidence from the questionnaire that was used.
6 The *backing* for the claim consists of a critique of the rebuttal, in order to support the original claim.

The implication of Toulmin's (1958) framework is that, if a claim or statement is appropriately qualified, in a manner that is based on satisfactory data and warranting, and has received backing in the face of plausible rebuttals, then it can be accepted as valid. In the example given above ('the therapeutic intervention resulted in change in the level of anxiety being expressed by the client'), this sequence would need to be fulfilled to support the claims (a) the therapy was delivered, (b) anxiety was reduced and (c) there existed a causal link between the therapy and the anxiety reduction. Clearly, it involves a great deal of work to submit all possible conclusions or claims from a case study to this kind of intensive scrutiny. However, this methodology has been successfully applied in the HSCED approach of Elliott (2001, 2002). It is also implicit in any case study approach that makes use of quasi-judicial methods, since the process of critical or adversarial examination of evidence that takes place in judicial proceedings inevitably involves this kind of close justification of claims.

Case studies are ethically problematic

It is clear that there are special ethical considerations associated with case study research in counselling and psychotherapy. In large-scale, 'extensive' studies, only a limited amount of information is collected on each participant, and the pattern of data on any individual is embedded within the data for the whole sample, and cannot be identified. Furthermore, investigators in large-scale studies are not interested in drawing attention to individual cases. As a result, in large-n studies, there is little risk that the identity of any individual participants will be divulged in research reports that are written.

The situation is quite different in case study research, where the basic aim of the study is to make statements about individuals. It seems likely the ethical sensitivity of case study research makes many practitioners unwilling to engage in this form of inquiry, which has the effect of limiting the number of cases that might be available for research. However, even once a case study investigation has been conducted, it may be that the efforts of the researcher to disguise the identity of the client (or the therapist) by changing some of the facts of the case may compromise the integrity of the data, and the meaningfulness of the analysis.

It is a mistake to view the undoubted ethical sensitivities arising from case study research in therapy as a reason for not undertaking this kind of work. There are many areas of psychological and social scientific inquiry that involve ethical sensitivities, for example studies of criminal behaviour, or research involving children. There are also other methodologies that involve ethical risk, for example double blind randomized trial of drug treatments where some participants receive a placebo and are in effect denied treatment. The solution is to develop ethical procedures that address any issues of risk of harm or breach of confidentiality in participants. The procedures that can be put in place within counselling and psychotherapy case study research to ensure good ethical practice are described in Miller (2004) and in Chapter 4, below.

It is not possible to conduct case study meta-analysis

Some critics of case study methodology argue that case-based research can provide fascinating, detailed accounts of human experience, but are hard to *summarize* in a form that can lead to an *accumulation* of evidence. This critique opens up the question of the contribution that case studies can make to the evolution of knowledge and evidence as a whole. It is never sensible to make decisions on the basis of the findings of any single piece of research, no matter how expertly carried out it may have been. To be of any practical value, the research literature in any applied field consists of sets of studies that are linked together by shared methods, assumptions and sampling strategies. If therapy case studies are not capable of being summarized and subjected to meta-analysis (a technique for estimating the average effect of an intervention over a number of studies) then their value to the research community becomes severely constrained.

There exists a fundamental tension between case study methodology and meta-analysis. Large-n studies, such as randomized controlled trials, are designed in order to answer a limited set of questions, or test a limited set of hypotheses (e.g., 'is therapy X more effective than therapy Y for problem A?'). These studies therefore generate findings that can be readily summarized in terms of fairly clear-cut, simple statements. In case study research, by contrast, while it may be possible to condense the findings of the investigation into a simple statement (e.g., 'therapy Y has been shown to be highly effective for a client with problem A'), the act of making this kind of summary statement eliminates all of the additional information that makes the case interesting and informative *as a case*. If the aim was merely to produce statements such as 'therapy Y has been shown to be highly effective for a client with problem A', it would not be worthwhile to go to all the trouble of collecting detailed case data, other than to be able to use it to justify the claim that 'therapy Y has been effective in this case'.

The capability of counselling and psychotherapy case studies to yield clear-cut summary statements depends on the approach to case study research that is being adopted. Single subject designs (n=1 studies) and HSCED studies are specifically designed to generate conclusions that are similar in form to the conclusions of randomized trials, and which can be used in meta-analysis (Faith, et al. 1996). Pragmatic case studies and narrative case studies seek to do more than arrive at a simple conclusion on a case, and are harder to summarise. However, in principle it is possible to envisage procedures for reliably coding the conclusions of these types of therapy case study research, in a form that could then be used in meta-analysis.

A key issue in relation to summarizing and meta-analysing therapy case study research is that few researchers have yet tried it. Meta-analyses have been published of the cumulative evidence of case studies carried out into aspects of educational practice (see, for example, Scruggs and Mastropieri 1998). However, few similar exercises appear to have been conducted around evidence from therapy case studies – an exception is the meta-synthesis of a selected set of therapy cases carried out by Iwakabe and Gazzola (2009). The absence of case study meta-analyses is important, because the issues involved in carrying out such analyses only become apparent once they begin to be published. For example, the earliest meta-analyses of randomised trials of the effectiveness of psychotherapy look quite different from the meta-analyses that are published today. Also, once meta-analyses begin to be published, investigators begin to conduct and write up their studies in ways that maximize the chances of being included in future meta-analyses.

The criticism that case study research in counselling and psychotherapy cannot generate cumulative knowledge is therefore not well founded. In principle, the findings of case studies can be summarized and 'added up'. However, this is not happening, because not enough case studies are being published, and the ones that are being published are not being written in a way that would facilitate inclusion in a systematic review.

Case studies do not generate evidence that is relevant for policy-making

The accumulation of research into counselling and psychotherapy that has taken place over the past 40 years has meant that there now exists sufficient evidence to make informed decisions around policy issues. The key policy issues that have been considered by organizations that deliver or commission counselling and psychotherapy services encompass decisions around the approaches to therapy that are offered (e.g., CBT, psychodynamic), the number of therapy sessions that are provided and the level of training and supervision that is required. Debates around these issues have taken place in a policy context within which principles of evidence-based practice (EBP) have been espoused by governments and other health providers in many counties. The key idea in evidence-based practice is that the only treatments that should be offered to patients are those that are supported by reliable and valid evidence from good-quality outcome studies (Rowland and Goss 2000). Within the field of counselling and psychotherapy, the influence of the EBP perspective has meant that evidence from randomized clinical trials (RCTs), the methodology regarded in medical circles as representing the 'gold standard' for evidence, has been given priority over other forms of evidence (e.g., case studies) in relation to decisions around policy issues. Many counselling and psychotherapy researchers have therefore arrived at the conclusion that it is a waste of time to carry out case study research if their goal is to develop evidence that will have an impact on policy.

The hierarchy of evidence — Box 3.3

Many different advisory groups and organizations have developed hierarchical models for assessing the credibility of evidence for the effectiveness of health interventions (Evans 2003). The key idea in such models is that some sources of evidence can be viewed as more reliable and valid than others. A typical hierarchical model is:

Level 1: Conclusions from one or more systematic reviews or meta-analyses.
Level 2: Evidence from at least one properly designed randomized controlled trial.
Level 3: Evidence obtained from well-designed studies without randomization, preferably from more than one centre or research group.
Level 4: Evidence from case studies and qualitative research.
Level 5: Opinions of respected authorities, based on clinical experience, or reports of expert committees.

This kind of model is often used in practice to justify the exclusion of treatments that are not supported by Level 1 or Level 2 evidence. However, evidence hierarchies were never intended to be used in this way, because evidence at Levels 4 and 5 is explicitly defined as worthy of respect. Strictly speaking, evidence hierarchies should be used to motivate professional communities to improve the quality of research evidence that is available, and not as a tool for political control. It is important to acknowledge that there are many counselling and psychotherapy researchers who question the validity of existing evidence hierarchy models, because of the significant methodological problems associated with the use of RCT evaluations of therapy (see Elliott 1998; Rowland 2007; Rowland and Goss 2000; Westen et al. 2004).

In reality, the situation is somewhat more complex that this. In the UK, decisions around treatments that are acceptable within the National

Health Service (NHS) are made by the National Institute for Health and Clinical Excellence (NICE). At the present time, NICE guidelines do not appear to recognize the role of case study evidence. However, they do acknowledge the value of evidence from qualitative studies, which indicates that the NICE system is flexible enough to be willing to consider the contribution of methodologies other than RCTs. Also in the UK, the Medical Research Council (MRC) has published a set of guidelines for the evaluation of complex interventions (MRC 2008). Counselling and psychotherapy can be considered as complex interventions because they are typically delivered over an extended period of time and encompass several 'active ingredients'. The MRC guideline explicitly recommends that the evaluation of a complex intervention should be regarded as a multi-stage process, in which different methodologies need to be employed to collect evidence in order to be able to plan a well-designed RCT, and also subsequently to assess the generalisability of RCT findings in real-life situations. The MRC guideline specifically highlights the role of single subject case study designs (which it describes as 'n-of-1 trials') for two purposes. First, case studies enable the researcher to 'investigate theoretically predicted mediators of … change' (p. 11), in order to 'identify the active components of an intervention' (p. 25), in advance of designing an RCT. Second, this type of case study can be useful at the stage of assessing the generalizability of an intervention in terms of variations in its effects on individual clients or patients. It may be worth mentioning that the inclusion of single subject design case studies in the MRC guideline for evaluation of complex interventions does not reflect any special pleading on the part of psychologists or psychotherapy researchers – the examples of this method that are provided in the guideline are in fact drawn from osteoarthritis research, and studies of the effectiveness of drugs.

The implementation of evidence-based practice and 'empirically supported therapies' (EST) has been a source of considerable debate in the USA. However, within this discussion there has always been a role for case study evidence. For example, the criteria for categorizing a therapy approach as 'empirically supported', in respect of a disorder, were defined by Chambless and Hollon (1998: 18) in the following terms:

1 Comparison with a no-treatment control group, alternative treatment group, or placebo (a) in a randomized control trial, controlled single case experiment, or equivalent time-samples design and (b) in which the EST is statistically significantly superior to no treatment, placebo, or alternative treatments or in which the EST is equivalent to a treatment already established in efficacy, and power is sufficient to detect moderate differences.

2 These studies must have been conducted with (a) a treatment manual or its logical equivalent; (b) a population, treated for specified problems, for whom inclusion criteria have been delineated in a reliable, valid manner; (c) reliable and valid outcome assessment measures, at minimum tapping the problems targeted for change; and (d) appropriate data analysis.

3 For a designation of efficacious, the superiority of the EST must have been shown in at least two independent research settings (sample size of 3 or more at each site in the case of single case experiments). If there is conflicting evidence, the preponderance of the well-controlled data must support the EST's efficacy.

4 For a designation of possibly efficacious, one study (sample size of 3 or more in the case of single case experiments) suffices in the absence of conflicting evidence.

5 For a designation of efficacious and specific, the EST must have been shown to be statistically significantly superior to pill or psychological placebo or to an alternative bona fide treatment in at least two independent research settings. If there is conflicting evidence, the preponderance of the well-controlled data must support the EST's efficacy and specificity.

In a further paper, Chambless et al. (1998) specify that a series of at least nine case studies is necessary in order to achieve the status of 'well-established' treatment, and at least three case studies to be deemed as 'probably efficacious'. These criteria specify a number of requirements that reflect current thinking about research rigour (e.g., the use of treatment manuals, valid outcome measures). However, they do not discriminate against the use of evidence from systematic case studies, and suggest that a series of at least three case studies is all that is required in order to establish a treatment as 'possibly efficacious'. The American Psychological Association Task Force on Evidence-Based Practice (2006: 274) similarly takes a positive stance in relation to case-based evidence. The emphasis in the North American policy statements is to accept that case studies have a valid role in counselling and psychotherapy research alongside other methodologies – different research designs are best suited to investigate different types of questions. Examples of case-series that have contributed to the development of evidence-based practice in recent years include Fisher and Wells (2008) and Waters et al. (2008).

So far, this section has reviewed the arguments around the potential contribution that case study research can make in relation to the formulation of evidence-based policies in counselling and psychotherapy. The conclusion that emerges is that many authoritative policy-making groups have accepted, within their guidelines, that case studies do have a valuable contribution to make. However, this potential has not been fulfilled in practice. At the present time, it is not possible to identify any therapies that have been officially approved on the basis of case study evidence, because there does not exist sufficient good-quality evidence that can be put forward. This situation can be contrasted with other fields, such as management studies and education, where case study evidence has often had a decisive impact on policy and practice (see Yin 2004).

The advantages of case study methods

For anyone embarking on case study research, or reading case study reports, it is essential to be able to take a balanced and informed position in relation to criticisms of this method. However, it is also important to be aware of the *advantages* of case study methods, in contrast to other methods used by counselling and psychotherapy case study researchers. Some of the distinctive features of case study research were discussed in Chapter 1: the case study as a form of narrative, contextualized knowing, the case study as a means of representing complexity, and as a way of describing and analysing practical expertise in action. These features describe the qualities of case studies as a form of knowledge. In addition to these qualities, there exist some further aspects of case study research that are of particular relevance in relation to the field of counselling and psychotherapy.

1 *Developing a critical perspective.* The conclusions of large-n studies provide statements about group-level phenomena. Logically, these statements need not necessarily apply within any individual cases that are part of a larger sample. For example, an RCT may find that CBT is much more effective than psychodynamic psychotherapy for clients with social anxiety. Within the sample of clients, however, there may be one client who received psychodynamic psychotherapy and showed very high levels of gain, and another who received CBT and deteriorated. There are critical 'truths' that may emerge at the case level that bring into question the generalized truths that are generated in group-based research. These critical truths are often of great heuristic value in stimulating further research, and thinking about practice.
2 *Flexibility.* Case studies represent a highly flexible means of carrying out research. There is no requirement to recruit a large cohort of participants. Outcome and process factors can be investigated within the same case.
3 *Analysing and reporting innovative practice.* A case study, or series of case studies, is an excellent means of testing the value of a new intervention or therapy technique.

4 *Learning from unusual cases.* Large-n studies inevitably involve gathering together samples of 'standard' clients, defined in relation to pre-set inclusion and exclusion criteria. By contrast, case studies enable the impact of therapy on clinically rare configurations of problems and disorders to be investigated.

5 *Integration into training and practice.* Funding for research into counselling and psychotherapy is never easy to find. However, students and trainees need to learn about how to work with cases, and carry out case formulations, and so are motivated to learn about case study methods and collect case data so that they can produce high-quality case reports. Similarly, groups of therapists can be brought together into practice networks to carry out case-based research. Programmes of case study research can therefore be constructed with minimal funding.

These features of case study research can be viewed as a set of positive reasons for carrying out this kind of inquiry. As with any research, the design of a study will depend on the questions being asked, and the resources that are available. There are some research questions that are best addressed through large-n studies, and others that are best suited to case-based research. There are some research topics for which resources can be found to allow a large-scale controlled study to be set up. There are other research topics that would never be able to attract sufficient levels of funding to enable such an approach to be realistically considered.

Conclusions

This chapter has discussed the various objections that can be made to the use of case study methods in counselling and psychotherapy research, and in other fields of inquiry. It has been seen that each of the critical perspectives that were discussed highlighted real areas of challenge for those who carry out case study research. At the same time, though, it was apparent that effective solutions and answers to these methodological issues have been worked out by case study researchers. It seems reasonable to take the view that opposition to case study methods is grounded in an outdated view of case study methodology, which does not take sufficient account of more recent advances in this field. For those who care about conducting case study research, the message is that it is essential to be mindful of these methodological developments when planning and carrying out studies.

Topics for reflection and discussion

1   When reading a case study, how do you decide on whether what you are learning might be generalizable to your own practice? Can you recall instances when you were reading a case study report and were clear in your own mind that what it was saying was either highly relevant to your practice, or not relevant at all? What are the criteria you use to make this kind of judgement? What are the implications of these criteria for the design and reporting of case study research in counselling and psychotherapy?
2   Should case studies be included in evidence reviews? Reflect on research reviews that you have read, or locate and read a review of a therapy topic that is of interest to you. How could case study evidence be incorporated into the review? What difference might it make to the credibility of the review, or its conclusions, if evidence from case studies were to be included?

Recommended further reading

A valuable overview and discussion of the issues explored in this chapter, and a clear rationale for why case study research is essential, can be found in:

Flybjerg, B. (2006) Five misunderstandings about case-study research. *Qualitative Inquiry*, 12(2), 219–45.

This article is essential reading for anyone who thinking about embarking on case study research.

A useful source for thinking through the issues involved in case selection is:

Schofield, J.W. (1990) Increasing the generalizability of qualitative research. In E.W. Eisner and A. Peshkin (eds), *Qualitative Inquiry in Education: The Continuing Debate*. New York: Teachers College Press (reprinted in: Gomm et al. 2000 – details below).

The role of case studies in relation to evidence-based practice policies is discussed in two papers:

Edwards, D.J.A. (2007) Collaborative versus adversarial stances in scientific discourse: implications for the role of systematic case studies in the development of evidence-based practice in psychotherapy. *Pragmatic Case Studies in Psychotherapy*, 3(1), 6–34. http://pcsp.libraries.rutgers.edu

Edwards, D.J.A., Dattilio, F. and Bromley, D.B. (2004) Developing evidence-based practice: the role of case-based research. *Professional Psychology: Research and Practice*, 35, 589–97.

For readers who wish to move beyond the practical challenges of doing case-based research in counselling and explore the wider social science and philosophical literature on case methodology, the key sources are:

Bromley, D. (1986) *The Case-Study Method in Psychology and Related Disciplines*. Chichester: Wiley.

Byrne, D. and Ragin, C.C. (eds) (2009) *The Sage Handbook of Case-Based Methods*. Thousand Oaks, CA: Sage.

Gerring, J. (2006) *Case Study Research: Principles and Practices*. New York: Cambridge University Press.

Gomm, R., Hammersley, R. and Foster, P. (eds) (2000) *Case Study Method*. London: Sage.

Moral and ethical issues in therapy case study research

4

the physician takes upon himself duties not only towards the individual patient but towards science as well; and his duties towards science mean ultimately nothing else than his duties towards the many other patients who are suffering or will some day suffer from the same disorder. Thus it becomes the physician's duty to publish what he believes he knows of the causes and structure of hysteria, and it becomes a disgraceful act of cowardice to neglect doing so, as long as he can avoid causing direct personal injury to the single patient involved. (Freud 1901: 8)

Case studies involve a higher degree of moral risk than other research methodologies. When a client in a large-scale therapy study, such as a randomized trial, completes a questionnaire, he or she provides a set of disparate bits of personal information, which cannot readily be connected into a meaningful picture of the person's life because of the absence of an underlying storyline or social context. In addition, in studies with large samples the researcher has no particular interest in individual participants, and will usually report findings in terms of average scores across the group as a whole. In large scale studies, individuals are not recognizable or identifiable. Their friends, colleagues and families are not recognizable either – any statements that the participant makes about significant others is buried in anonymous statistical data. Moreover, if a participant reads the report of the study, he or she is very unlikely to learn anything about himself or herself, or to find out how the researcher interpreted his or her own individual problems and coping strategies. All of these factors are different in case study research. For a client in a case study, his or her *life* is being examined. More than this, it is the most troubling, embarrassing or shameful aspects of that life that are being most closely scrutinized. In the account of that life that may be published in a case study, it is not only the person that may be identifiable, but also information about their family members and other acquaintances. In reading the case study, the client may be confronted with personal truths and experiences that they might prefer to lay aside. Worse, they may be confronted with what they regard as distortions of their personal truth. Finally, they may discover what their therapist *really* thought about them. All of these possibilities are embodied in a document that is in the public domain, and which may be read (and perhaps misunderstood or misrepresented) by anyone, at any time.

The moral and ethical issues associated with counselling and psychotherapy case study research apply mainly to the experience of the client, who is normally the main focus of the study. However, they can also apply to the therapist, whose working practices are being uniquely exposed. And a parallel set of moral and ethical issues arise for case study researchers, who can be faced with crippling moral dilemmas in the process of their investigations.

The aim of this chapter is to examine the moral and ethical issues involved in case study research in counselling and psychotherapy. The chapter begins by outlining the key ethical principles that inform social research, then moves to an exploration of the contours of moral risk that are present within the territory of therapy case study research. The chapter concludes by considering the strategies that can be employed to address these ethical considerations. The underlying assumption that informs the approach taken in this chapter is that ethical research is good research. Attending to ethical and moral issues is not merely a matter of passing the tests set by ethical review boards and committees. Instead, effective attention to ethical issues is a necessary part of creating a moral space in which effective inquiry can take place, in which all participants feel safe enough to make the maximum contribution to knowledge and understanding. Conversely, research that is not sufficiently ethically grounded, may lead to guardedness and a reluctance to share information, on the part of everyone involved.

Basic moral and ethical principles

It is generally accepted, following Beauchamp and Childress (1979), Kitchener (1984) and other authoritative sources, that ethical decision-making in counselling and psychotherapy practice and research should be informed by five moral principles that are fundamental to social life in modern democratic societies: *autonomy, non-maleficence, beneficence, justice* and *fidelity*.

Autonomy refers to the right of every individual to freedom of action and freedom of choice, in so far as the pursuit of these freedoms does not interfere with the freedoms of others. In relation to research, this principle implies that a research study is only ethically sound if each person taking part in it has made an autonomous decision (i.e., has not been coerced or induced in any way) to be involved. In practice, this is achieved through the procedure of *informed consent.*

Non-maleficence refers to the instruction to all helpers or healers that they must 'above all do no harm'. *Beneficence* refers to the injunction to promote human welfare. Both these ideas emerge in the requirement in research design that any harm to the client is minimized (non-maleficence), that participants are informed in advance about any possible harm, and that the study should make a positive contribution to the greater good (beneficence), for example by not being trivial or scientifically worthless.

Justice is primarily concerned with the fair distribution of resources and services. Kitchener (1984: 50) argues for the special significance of justice for counselling and psychotherapy in writing that:

> psychologists ought to have a commitment to being 'fair' that goes beyond that of the ordinary person. To the extent we agree to promote the worth and dignity of each individual, we are required to be concerned with equal treatment for all individuals.

In relation to research, the principle of justice implies that researchers should be mindful of the role of research in working in the interests of oppressed or minority groups.

Fidelity relates to the existence of loyalty, reliability, dependability and action in good faith. Lying, deception and exploitation are all examples of primary breaches of fidelity. The importance in research of maintaining *confidentiality* in research, and respecting the researcher–participant research contract, reflect the importance of fidelity.

Box 4.1

Dilemmas in applying ethical concepts and principles in case study research

Principles of moral action are never straightforward to apply in practice. It is possible to identify a long list of desirable moral qualities and principles, that few people would argue against. It is quite another thing to decide on what is the most morally justifiable course of action in any particular situation. The following examples illustrate some of the potential moral and ethical conflicts that can arise for case study researchers.

A therapist works for several years with a client diagnosed with early onset Alzheimer's disease, and throughout the therapy keeps careful notes, recordings and assessment data. By the end of therapy, the therapist realizes that the data that she has collected constitute a potentially unique account of the role of psychotherapy in enabling a person to adjust to cognitive impairment and other issues associated with dementia. The therapist is faced with the following dilemmas:

- Is the client, in the later stages of Alzheimer's, able to give genuine informed consent (the principle of *autonomy*)?
- Does the close relationship between client and therapist mean that the client is being implicitly coerced into agreeing to the therapist's wish to publish (*autonomy*)?
- How much weight should be given to the therapist's wish to use the case study to argue to make therapy more available to people diagnosed with dementia (*social justice*)?
- How much weight should be given to the therapist's sense of acting with *courage*, in pursuing the publication of this case?
- Could it *harm* the relationship between the client and some of his family members to describe his struggles to come to terms with their reactions to the progress of his illness?

A client who has suffered from recurrent depression throughout her life has been recruited to a project based in a university research clinic, that involves collection of comprehensive process and outcome data, leading to inclusion in a case series to be published in book form (so that each case can be reported in detail). The research team at the clinic have carefully explained what is involved, and the client has signed ethical consent forms before the start of therapy, at the end and at follow-up, agreeing that her therapy data could be used within the book, and she has agreed with the researchers how her identity will be disguised. Now, at the final stage of the process, the client has been asked to read and comment on the draft chapter on her experiences. She realizes that:

- viewed on paper, the case report is much more revealing than she ever thought it might be (*harm*);
- she only agreed to go along with the study because it was the only chance to get high-quality therapy without either paying a fortune, or being on a lengthy waiting list, and because she was too depressed to stand up for herself (*autonomy*);
- what has been written is a compelling and convincing analysis of this particular form of therapy, and it would be a huge blow to the researchers (whom she likes and respects) if it were not to be included in the book (*justice, fidelity*).

How best should these situations be resolved? Note: these scenarios reflect dilemmas where case study researchers have acted with maximum integrity and transparency.

Taken together, these moral concepts represent a comprehensive and complex network of injunctions that informs ethical decision-making in case study research in counselling and psychotherapy. However, they do not, in themselves, provide clear-cut guidance for case study researchers about how to proceed in specific instances. This is because, as in any area of applied ethics, it is necessary to interpret and evaluate the implications of abstract principles in concrete practical situations, by developing 'case lore', precedents, examples of good practice and sets of guidelines. Because of the relative neglect of systematic case study methods in counselling and psychotherapy research (and in adjacent areas of research such as psychology), over the past 30 years there has been little work on the specific ethical challenges arising from case study investigations. The following sections of this chapter examine the literature that currently exists in the domain of ethical issues in counselling and psychotherapy case study research, and then provides some preliminary guidelines regarding practical procedures that might be undertaken by case study researchers.

Ethical guidelines from the Pragmatic Case Studies in Psychotherapy journal

Pragmatic Case Studies in Psychotherapy seeks in part to publish systematic and scholarly case studies of psychotherapy. A very important ethical obligation on authors in such publication is protection of the privacy of those clients who are the subjects of the case studies by effectively disguising their identity … The editors expect that an author has taken 'reasonable steps' to disguise a client's identity. Consent by the client to the publication of the case study as written is an added plus, but not required. Moreover, even with consent, the author is required to disguise the client's identity in order to reduce any harm that could come to the client because of disclosure of their identity. The issue of how to disguise a client's identity while preserving the important parts of a case's 'clinical and contextual reality' is a question that will evolve with experience and will certainly deserve early and ongoing discussion in case-study-method articles in PCSP. Examples of disguise that would not seem to alter context in a major way in many clinical situations is to change the age of a client by a few years (e.g., from 68 to 64); to change the client's ethnic origin from one geographic area to one that is similar (e.g., from one Asian nationality to one that is relatively similar in culture); to change a client's profession (e.g., from lawyer to accountant, both of which are white collar and require similar types of education); and/or to change a client's religion, while retaining the degree of religiosity or spirituality. The decision as to what characteristics to disguise is in part a conceptual decision, based upon separating those factors

Box 4.2

that are crucial to the clinical reality of the case as opposed to factors that are more peripheral ... Other means of protecting confidentiality and reducing potential harm may involve case hybridization where elements of two or three similar cases are combined; publication under an author pseudonym; or posthumous publication a sufficient number of years after the death of the client. Another procedure for enhancing the effectiveness of client disguise involves having the author submit a statement from a colleague in the same geographical area indicating that the information revealed in the case would not be likely to reveal the identity of the client. The advantage is that knowing the geographical area and the base rates of various problems in that area, the likelihood that identity might be deduced would be clearer to a local person than to those who would apply a hypothetical or national standard. (For example, the identity of a case of polygamy in Utah would be a lot harder to deduce than one in Vermont.) ... Editorial appraisal of a manuscript will include a thorough examination of the protection of confidentiality in the cases reported in an individual publication. Changes requested in manuscripts may be specifically for reasons of protecting confidentiality. In many clinical contexts, co-workers, co-therapists, and supervisors are also familiar with a case being reported and may provide an additional check on the degree to which the client's identity has been effectively concealed. (For a thorough discussion of the confidentiality issues raised by case study reports, see R.B. Miller (2004), *Facing Human Suffering: Psychology and Psychotherapy as Moral Engagement*. Washington, DC: APA.)

Source: http://pcsp.libraries.rutgers.edu/index.php/pcsp/about/submissions# authorGuidelines

Research into ethical issues in case study research in counselling and psychotherapy

Historically, research ethics have been viewed as a topic within the broader fields of moral philosophy and law. Within these domains of inquiry, the advancement of ethical understanding has been built on the analysis of concepts, and working through of the implications of specific cases. In recent years, however, there has been a movement in the direction of supplementing conceptual analysis of ethical issues by carrying out empirical research into the ethical beliefs that people hold, and the ways in which ethical practices are experienced by those who are affected by them. For example, within the area of ethical practice in counselling and psychotherapy, there have been studies of client beliefs around confidentiality and client responses to informed consent procedures. The studies that have been published in relation to ethical issues in case study research in therapy have focused on three questions:

- How do clinicians negotiate consent with clients around the publication of case reports?
- What is the impact on a client of being a participant in a case study?
- What is the impact on a therapist of writing a case study?

The body of research that is summarized below is fragmented, meagre and lacking in methodological rigour. For the most part, the evidence that exists in this area consists of first person accounts or small-scale personal research projects, carried out by therapists who are worried about the moral implications of their publication of client case reports. There is clearly a need for further research into this set of issues. Nevertheless, these studies have a valuable story to tell, which has major implications for those engaged in case study research.

Negotiating consent

Lipton (1991) carried out a survey of 15 psychoanalytic colleagues, about whether they asked clients for permission before using clinical material for papers or presentations. All of them stated that they would only use case material if the identity of the client could be effectively disguised. Most of them reported that they preferred to use material from cases that were complete. Permission from the client was requested around half of the time, and tended not to be requested where the therapist believed that the client was unlikely to read the professional literature (i.e., would never come across the case study, and was therefore not likely ever to be harmed by it). However, there were many instances where the client's relatives or friends had then read the case study, and informed the client. (Note: this implies that attempts to disguise the identity of the client had not been effective.) Lipton (1991) also found that many psychoanalysts believed that their clients unconsciously wished for their therapist to write about their case (as a sign that the therapist cared deeply about them). Gavey and Braun (1997) carried out a survey of attitudes and practices around informed consent in over 300 counsellors and psychotherapists who had published case study reports, and received 64 replies. Eighty-six per cent of the respondents believed that it was 'essential in all circumstances' to seek formal consent to publish material on a client who was currently in therapy, with 25% believing that consent was necessary when a past client was being written about. When asked to respond to a hypothetical scenario about whether a current client being asked for consent would feel able to refuse, over one-third of participants in the survey stated that they believed that it was unlikely that the client would feel free to decline consent. In a study of more than 120 psychoanalysts who had published client case material, Kantrowitz (2006) found a similar lack of consensus over procedures for obtaining consent.

The impact on the client

In the survey of psychoanalysts carried out by Lipton (1991), informants reported that, when a case report had been published without client consent but the client had subsequently discovered the paper, clients almost always expressed a negative reaction. These informants believed that this negative response could usually be resolved through further therapy. Lipton (1991) described two examples in his own practice of client responses to case reports for which they had given permission to publish. In each of these cases, the client exhibited a strong negative reaction, shaped by their underlying pattern of psychological difficulty. For one client, the publication triggered feelings about an unreliable father; for the other client, the publication reminded him of his deficiencies, and reinforced his low self-esteem. In both cases, the disturbance caused by the case publication generated material that was worked through in on-going therapy. Lipton (1991) also observed that these clients both re-read the case reports at later periods of personal crisis, which triggered a further round of negative reaction. These findings, from the survey carried out by Lipton (1991), and from his discussion of experiences with his own clients, suggest that, for a client coming to terms with the publication of a case study may require further therapy. This finding underscores the depth of emotional impact of reading a case report, and raises issues around situations in which further therapy may not be available. Kantrowitz (2006) interviewed 11 patients who were not analysts, and 18 patients who were analysts, about their experience of having details of their therapy included in a publication. Reactions ranged from negative (mainly hurt) through to positive (had learned about self through reading the case report). In a review of published accounts of client experiences of reading their case reports, Furlong (2006) similarly found that clients reacted in different ways to reading case reports of their own therapy, on a spectrum from highly positive to highly negative. This review identified several instances where clients sued their therapists following publication of case reports, but were not successful because the court found that the therapist had been acting in good faith in attempting to disguise their client's identity. Furlong (2006) observed that:

> Based upon my perusal of anecdotes in the literature pertaining to the negative reactions of patients who believe they have recognized themselves in published articles, what upsets patients is not exclusively, nor even necessarily, what they read about themselves, but what they assess or intuit – directly or indirectly through the material presented – of their analyst's internal life. (Furlong 2006: 760)

The suggestion here is that reading their case study triggers questions for the client about the nature of their therapist's interest in them, and how the therapist thinks about the work. These questions have the effect of leading the client to re-evaluate, and perhaps doubt, the nature of the working relationship or alliance that has existed between their therapist and themselves. Other studies (Graves 1996; Josselson 1996b) have found that case study participants have been deeply affected by personal information that was *missing* from the case report that had been written about them – details of incidents and experiences that had been hugely significant for them, but which their therapist did not seem to have noticed, or to have considered important enough to write about.

The impact on the therapist

It is usual for therapists to engage in considerable emotional turmoil over whether to write about their clients, and what to write (Gabbard 2000). Therapists are concerned about the possible impact on the client of publication, or even of asking about potential publication. They also worry about whether they may be exploiting clients for their own professional advancement and gain. Finally, therapists agonize about the extent to which they are revealing themselves in what they write. Graves (1996: 73) observed that:

> the hurdle is the intensely self-revelatory nature involved in my writing about my work as an analyst. This writing exposes, more than I like, my mistakes, blind spots, and other limitations, not only my strengths and capabilities.

Josselson (1996b: 69–70) has described her own experience as a case study author as marked by 'dread, shame and guilt':

> the dread that I will have harmed someone ... guilt ... from knowing that I have taken myself out of relationship with my participants ... and been talking about them behind their backs and doing so publicly ... and shame that I am using these people's lives to exhibit myself, my analytic prowess, my cleverness. I am using them as extensions of my own narcissism and fear being caught, seen in this process.

In contrast to these negative aspects of writing about clients, there are some therapists for whom the experience of publishing case studies is viewed more positively. There are some accounts of therapists looking on such publications as a form of self-supervision. Kantrowitz (2006) interviewed several psychoanalysts who intentionally used published case reports on on-going clients as a therapeutic technique, on the basis that the written word would convey certain therapeutic messages in a particularly powerful manner, and function as a type of 'transition object' for clients. These therapists anticipated and relished the negative reactions of their clients to their case reports, as grist to the therapy mill. (Incidentally, Kantrowitz (2006) had some misgivings about the wisdom or effectiveness of this strategy.)

This review of studies of the experiences and attitudes of clients and therapists around the process of producing therapy case studies is necessarily selective, for reasons of space. The literature on this topic is dominated by reports written by psychoanalytically oriented therapists (Gabbard and Williams 2001; Galatzer-Levy 2003). In some respects this psychoanalytic emphasis represents a weakness in the case study ethics literature, since it would clearly be of value to know about how clients and therapists feel about their involvement in other types of therapy case study inquiry. On the other hand, a psychoanalytic perspective is one that is particularly sensitive to the relational dynamics of case study publication, and aspects of this process that may not be readily available to conscious awareness (on the part of both therapist and client).

There are perhaps three central conclusions that can be drawn from the studies that have been discussed. First, these studies have identified multiple dimensions of ethical sensitivity, which are linked in complex ways to the personality and adjustment of clients and therapists, the stage in therapy when the case study is written, and the process of informed consent that has been employed. There is little evidence, from client or therapist accounts, that disguising the identity of the client is sufficient in itself to deal with the ethical issues arising from therapy case-based research. Second, the research suggests that there is a lack of consensus within the professional community about how to handle the ethical implications of case study research. For example, some case study writers believe that informed consent should be essential, while others disagree. Third, when writing a therapy case study, it is necessary to be mindful of the potential impact on the client, as well as the meaning that the study may have for professional readers. As one case study writer put it, the key for him was to focus on 'keeping the patient as my audience' (Graves 1996: 78).

Strategies for the ethical conduct of counselling and psychotherapy case study research

The core ethical issues, in relation to case study research in counselling and psychotherapy, are:

- obtaining informed consent from clients, in relation to being a subject of a therapy case study;
- maintaining confidentiality;
- avoiding harm to case study participants.

The nature of these issues, and the advantages and disadvantages of different strategies for dealing with them, are discussed in the following sections.

Informed consent

The standard practice in counselling and psychotherapy research is for clients to read an information sheet in advance of taking part in a study, and sign a consent form. The information sheet usually specifies: the aims of the study; what the person is being asked to do, in terms of completing questionnaires, being interviewed, etc.; the possible risks associated with participating in the study; what to do if anything harmful occurs; how the data will be stored, and for how long; how confidentiality will be guaranteed in any research reports; who to contact if there are any problems; who has given ethical approval for the study to take place. The person needs to be given a suitable period of time to make their decision on whether or not to take part, should be provided with an opportunity to ask questions and is given a copy of the informed consent information sheet as a research 'contract' to keep for future reference. There should be no inducement or pressure involved in the consent – for example, the person should receive therapy whether or not they agree to take part of the research, they should be free to withdraw from the study at any stage without jeopardizing their therapy and the benefits of taking part must not be exaggerated. In research situations of particular ethical sensitivity, the procedure of *process consent* is often applied (Grafanaki 1996, 2001). Process consent means that the initial consent is reinforced and revisited at regular intervals. For example, if the study involves recording therapy sessions, the therapist may ask for permission to record at the start of every session, and remind the client that the recorder may be turned off at any stage. A further example of process consent (also referred to as *rolling consent* or *provisional consent*; Simons 2009: 103) would be to make recordings, and then ask for additional consent at the end of therapy to use them for research purposes (on the grounds that the person will have no idea at the start of therapy what the recordings might include), or to ask the client to delete sections of interview or session transcripts that he or she does not want to be included in the research data.

In relation to case study research, the procedure of obtaining informed consent generates a number of critical ethical issues:

1 *When should consent be sought?* Winship (2007) makes a useful distinction between *prospective* case studies (where the study is planned before therapy commences) and *reflective* case studies (where the idea for the case study only emerges during therapy, or following termination). In relation to prospective studies, the practice of process consent, where the person agrees in principle, at a pre-therapy meeting, to take part in a case study (by allowing data to be collected), while knowing that final agreement will take place later, once the therapy is complete, is ethically sound. In this situation, maximum autonomy is offered to the participant – he or she has as much control as possible over what is happening. The implication here is that best practice in case study research involves routinely using a consent procedure with all new clients, even if only a few of them will eventually be written up as published cases. In relation to reflective case studies, the action of seeking consent *during* therapy is more ethically problematic, because the client is in a less autonomous position, in the sense that they have developed a relationship of trust with a therapist, and may wish to please the therapist by agreeing to take part in the study, or fear rejection by the therapist if they decline. Seeking consent *after* the completion of therapy is also ethically problematic, because the very act of contacting the client may cause harm, by restimulating memories of the therapy, or being viewed as holding out the possibility of a different type of relationship with the therapist. Careful consideration therefore needs to be given to alleviating the risks associated with seeking research consent during therapy, or after therapy has been completed. A compromise position may be to ask for consent at the final session, for permission to make contact at a later date for a further discussion around taking part in case study. Another factor to take into consideration, if consent is sought during therapy, is the nature of the new contract. Does it merely consist of proceeding as before, but with the possibility of using data for a case study? Or does it consist of the introduction into therapy of additional data collection procedures? Clearly, the latter implies a more serious intrusion into the on-going therapy process, with greater possibility for harm.

2 *Who should negotiate the consent?* In many published case studies, the whole research or inquiry process, including seeking consent-taking, is carried out by the client's therapist. This practice in not ideal, from an ethical perspective. The therapist–client relationship is generally viewed within the profession as being boundaried and 'special', with a great deal of caution being expressed over any unavoidable dual relationships. There is a broad consensus that the ideal arrangement is for a therapist to be solely a therapist for the client, and eschew any other type of relationship that may intrude on confidentiality, the process of therapy, etc. Where other relationships are unavoidable (for instance, in small rural communities), therapists find themselves devoting a lot of care and attention to how to handle the boundary issues that emerge (Lazarus and Zur 2002). So, in order to ensure that the client receives the best possible therapy, if a case study is being envisaged, it is helpful if someone else (e.g., a colleague) takes responsibility for the management of the consent process. The other advantage of such an arrangement is that the client then has an independent person to consult, if he or she has any questions or complaints about the research.

Confidentiality

It is standard practice in counselling and psychotherapy research to provide a guarantee to the client that research information will be stored securely, with personal details separate from any participant information. Typically, participants are also told that research data are destroyed within a specified time of completion of the study. It is usual to let research participants know that individuals will not be identifiable in any reports arising from the study, and that any information that is contributed to the study will be used only for research purposes. In some ethically sensitive areas of research (e.g., where the informant may be disclosing information about illegal or abusive behaviour that they have observed), the researcher needs to let the participant know about the conditions under which confidentiality might be limited. All of these confidentiality procedures apply in case study research. However, in case study research there are particular issues around the requirement that individuals will not be identifiable, because of the large amount of detailed personal information that may be included in a case report. In addition, there are issues around the potential identification of people other than the case study subject (e.g., family members or work colleagues). It is possible to address these issues through the use of a number of strategies:

- *Disguise.* Information about the case participant or other people described in the case study can be altered to make it more difficult to identify them. It is relatively straightforward to change details such as name, age, occupation and place of residence. It is somewhat harder to change the details of the person's story so that it is not recognizable. The main difficulty with the use of disguise as a means of ensuring confidentiality is that it is fairly easy to alter information so that general readers will not be able to identify the case participants. It is much harder to achieve a level of disguise that will safeguard the case in respect of readers who are family members, friends or work colleagues. If the case is disguised sufficiently that these significant others would not be able to identify the client, the question is raised about whether what is published can actually claim to be a fair representation of the case.
- *Deleting information.* A further form of disguise is to omit segments of the case material, identified by the client or by an independent consultant, that may be particularly sensitive in terms of confidentiality.
- *Constructing a composite case.* If the researcher has studied several cases of the same type it can be possible to combine features of each case to create a composite case, which accurately reflects the therapy outcome and process that has been studied, while safeguarding the identity of participants.
- *Using a case series.* If a series of cases have been studied, it is possible to write about them in such a way that only a limited amount of information is provided on each individual case participants. In effect, the limited space that is available for reporting each case makes it easier to omit confidentially sensitive information.
- *Delayed publication.* Some therapy case reports have been published only on the death of the client or patient. Clearly, this strategy does not deal with the question of potential confidentiality breaches around the interests of significant others, and in fact may make it harder to address such issues because the client is not available to advise on how best to alter information to protect family members, etc.

On some occasions case study participants may not want their identity to be concealed, because they wish to use the case study to tell their story in an open and transparent manner. In these situations it is essential to support the person in making an informed, reflective choice, based on a realistic appraisal of the potential consequences of publication of a case report in which they can be explicitly identified.

Consideration needs to be given to the decision-making process around the use of disguise or deletion in case study reports. If possible, it is good practice to invite the case participant to indicate the information that he or she would wish to be changed or deleted, and to suggest the kinds of changes that would satisfy them, for example in relation to alterations in age or occupation. If the case participant is not available to engage in this kind of consultation, it can be valuable to use a third party to audit any changes that might be made by the researcher.

Avoiding harm

There are three main forms of harm that can arise for clients who take part in therapy case study research:

- intrusion on the therapy process;
- the impact of reading the case report;
- negative consequences of breaches of confidentiality.

There are two forms of risk of *intrusion on the therapy process*. First, there is a generalized risk that may arise when a client agrees to take part in a research programme, and then becomes worried or inhibited throughout the course of therapy by fears around the security of the information that they are providing, or around whether they are being manipulated in some way for research purposes. For the majority of clients, this kind of negative experience can be avoided by offering opportunities to ask questions about the research study, at any stage in the research process. There is evidence that the majority of clients in research studies describe their participation as enhancing the therapy they receive (Marshall et al. 2001). However, it is probable that there is a small minority of clients who are highly sensitive around any kind of research procedure. A second type of intrusion on the therapy process occurs when the therapist alters his or her behaviour as a result of knowing that their work with a client may be published as a case study. This knowledge may motivate the therapist to try harder, and make better use of supervision, which would probably be to the advantage of the client. A more problematic consequence arises if the therapist starts to focus on aspects of the therapy process that they believe may be of particular interest for the case study analysis. For example, if a client engages in some effective dream work in the early stages of therapy, and the therapist decides that the case might be worthy of publication, there may be some pressure exerted on the client to continue to produce dream material, even when the natural course of therapy may have moved into another type of work. In respect of the risk of intrusion arising from a shift in therapist stance, it is essential that the therapist's clinical supervisor should be informed about any case study inquiry that is being undertaken, and should be willing to challenge the therapist on the effect of the case inquiry on the way that he or she might be working with their client.

There is evidence, reviewed earlier in this chapter, that it can be harmful for some clients to read case study reports in which they are featured. From a therapist perspective, it can be argued that the disturbance experienced by a client of reading their case report has potential therapeutic value, in raising issues that had not been sufficiently worked through in the therapy, and which may now be resolved through further therapy. From this perspective, it could be argued that any upset arising from reading a case report is ultimately beneficial, because it leads to the person facing up to personal issues that have previously been avoided. However, this position carries little weight from a moral or ethical point of view. The ethical principle of autonomy implies that any decision to extend or re-enter therapy must be one that the client makes for himself or herself. It is not ethically acceptable to plan a research study around the possibility that participation in the study may result in the need for further treatment. It is not easy to devise ways to deal with this particular ethical dilemma. There are many instances in which clients appear to appreciate reading their case reports, and report that they have benefited from the experience. It does not seem justified, therefore, to devise case study research protocols that eliminate client reading of case reports. Such a policy would, in addition, make it impossible to make use of client collaboration around disguising and other confidentiality procedures. There would appear to be two potentially valuable strategies for dealing with the possibility of negative client reactions to reading their case reports. One strategy would be to give careful consideration to the way that the report is written. In some therapy approaches, such as Narrative Therapy (White and Epston 1990) and Cognitive Analytic Therapy (Ryle and Kerr 2002), clients receive letters from their therapists. There is evidence that clients find these letters helpful. In most instances, these letters include information that might well be part of a case study. It may be useful for research into case study ethics to look at the forms and structures of writing that are most or least likely to be viewed as facilitative (or personally hurtful and destructive) by clients. A second strategy for reducing potential damage associated with reading case reports might be to ensure that the case is audited by an independent reader before being sent to the client, and that the client then has an opportunity to meet with this reader (or that the client actually reads the report in the presence of this independent person). It seems likely that one aspect of the 'shock' of reading a case report, for some clients who have agreed to take part in case studies, is that the report represents an unmediated exposure to a different 'voice' of the therapist, one that is saying a lot more, saying different things and addressing a different kind of audience. It may be that the involvement of a third party could be a useful way to allow the client to gain some distance from their memories of their therapist's 'voice-for-me' and appreciate why the report has been written in a particular way. The provision by the therapist of a covering letter to the client could serve a similar purpose. In situations where the case analysis is conducted by a research team that does not include the therapist, some further considerations may apply. The research team may not know the client well enough to be able to anticipate how the client may respond to reading certain passages. Also, the views and experiences of the therapist may be incorporated in the report, but transformed or edited by the researchers in a manner that may be confusing for the client.

Negative effects of breaches of confidentiality can occur when a case study report is read by people who can identify the client and are influenced by what they have learned about this person. For example, an employer or director of a training programme may discover through a published case study that someone they are employing or considering for acceptance into training has a history of mental health problems, or is gay, lesbian or bisexual. These are factors that may result in a failure to be promoted, or to be accepted into training, depending on the circumstances. These areas of personal information are ones whose disclosure is generally accepted in most societies as being at the discretion of individuals. Unintended disclosure through a case study publication may be directly harmful for the person in terms of income, employment and career development. In other spheres of life unintended disclosure may have repercussions for relationships between family members, or between work colleagues. These risks underscore the requirement for careful handling of disguise and deleting procedures during the process of preparing a case study for dissemination. In considering the issue of unintended disclosure of personal information in case study reports, it is important to keep in mind that the authorship of the report can provide clues to the identity of the client. A reader of a case report may think 'I know someone who saw that therapist' or 'I know someone who attended that counselling centre', and thereby be sensitized to seeing through the disguise that has been built to defend the identify of the case study client.

The distinction between 'procedural ethics' and 'ethics in practice'

The discussion so far has demonstrated the complexity of ethical issues associated with case study research in counselling and psychotherapy. In seeking to make some sense of this complexity, in terms of identifying guidelines for practice, it is useful to make a distinction between 'procedural ethics' and 'ethics in practice' (Guillemin and Gillam 2004). Procedural ethics refers to the ethical procedures that are required by institutional ethics committees and boards, in terms of participant information sheets, consent forms and the like. By contrast, ethics in practice, or 'microethics', refers to the moment-by-moment ethical decision-making that takes place in interaction with research participants, 'the difficult, often subtle, and usually unpredictable situations that arise in the practice of doing research' (Guillemin and Gillam 2004: 262). In counselling and psychotherapy case study research, microethical issues arise when talking with a client about whether they might be willing to be involved in a case study, or about their response to a case study paper that has been written about their therapy. Another example refers to whether or not to ask a client in the first place – is he or she at a point where they could meaningfully say 'no'? The intricacies of ethics in practice are demonstrated very clearly in the transcripts of discussions between Kim Etherington and two clients, about the basis on which they might want to work together on producing a joint case report (Etherington 2000). It seems reasonable to categorise virtually all of the psychoanalytic and other research and writing on case study ethics, reviewed earlier in this chapter, as being concerned with *ethics in practice* rather than with formal procedural ethics. The tendency within the psychoanalytic community, responsible for most of this literature, has been to avoid establishing clear-cut procedural rules, and to retain as much of the ethical process as possible within the discretion of the analyst.

From an 'ethics in practice' perspective, three main strategies have been suggested as necessary to ensure that morally justifiable decisions are made. First, Etherington (2000) proposes that the process of ethical decision-making should be as collaborative as possible. It is only through an open sharing of all aspects of the decision to publish that the client can feel truly safe and respected. Second, Guillemin and Gillam (2004) propose that researcher *reflexivity* is a necessary element of microethics – the researcher needs to be aware of his or her own needs and motives, and to pay attention to what is happening during 'ethically important moments' when moral choices become crystallized ('should I push the client a little more to agree, or should I back off?'). Finally, Ellis (2007) argues that the practice of research should be informed by a *relational ethics* in which the researcher is mindful of the responsibilities that arise from being in relationship with another person. Ellis (2007) shares some compelling stories of her own failure, early in her career, to respect the relationships that she had formed with research informants. From *her* point of view, in her interactions with these participants, she was acceding to the requirements of the ethics procedures that had been approved by her university. On the other hand, from *their point of view*, she was betraying friendship ties in the way that she wrote about them. These three characteristics of effective ethics in practice – collaboration, reflexivity and mindfulness of relationships – are not at all easy to separate out from each other, but can be viewed as facets of an essentially person-centred attitude.

Both procedural ethics and ethics in practice are necessary in counselling and psychotherapy case study research. No matter how tightly defined a set of ethical procedures might be, bad things can still happen to clients and therapists, if ethically important moment are not handled well enough. This implies that case study researchers need to be sensitive to the complexities of what can happen around this kind of research. On the other hand, ethics in practice/microethics are ungovernable. There is no way that a body that assumes responsibility for ethical standards, such as a university ethics board, can or should ever accept as an argument that a study will be conducted in an ethically sound manner because the researcher is reflexive and committed to collaboration. It is the duty of the ethics board to ask: 'How can we know that these virtues are being enacted?' It is inevitable, therefore, that ethically acceptable case study research should take place within a structure that ensures that potentially vulnerable participants are safeguarded by an externally verifiable set of guidelines.

A final implication of an acknowledgement that case study research is likely to throw up microethical 'moments' that are not covered by any formal ethics protocol, is that students undertaking case study research need to be provided with adequate support and supervision, because it would be unreasonable to expect them to possess the experience to handle the type of intricate ethical collaboration exemplified in Etherington (2000). This issue is sensitively explored by Ellis (2007), who is clear that if a relational ethical stance is to exist between student-researcher and participant, it also needs to exist between student-researcher and supervisor.

Guidelines for ethical good practice in case study research in counselling and psychotherapy

There are a number of distinctive ethical issues associated with case study research in counselling and psychotherapy that are not explicitly addressed in the existing codes of research ethics that have been published by professional bodies such as the American Psychological Association or the British Association for Counselling and Psychotherapy, or within the author guidelines of relevant journals. The following *Ethical Guidelines for Case Study Research in Counselling and Psychotherapy* are intended to provide a tentative framework for those involved in case study research.

1 The conduct of all case study research and inquiry in counselling and psychotherapy (including clinical case studies) should adhere to the research ethics codes of the professional groups to which the authors of the case reports are affiliated.

2 Authors of therapy case studies should be transparent about the ethical procedures that have been conducted in relation to their studies, and provide details of these procedures within all case publications.

3 The ethical procedures used within any case study project must always be subject to expert external scrutiny, in the form of an institutional approval committee or board, or an equivalent consultative process.

4 It is advised that, wherever possible, prospective informed consent for in-principle case study participation should be obtained from clients before the commencement of therapy, and then at all further stages of the inquiry cycle up to and including the final release to publish (*process consent*). The person who undertakes the informed consent procedure must not be the therapist conducting the case.

5 In situations where prospective informed consent is not feasible (e.g., decision to conduct a case study made following commencement of therapy) alternative consent procedures must be approved by an appropriate institutional approval committee or board, or an equivalent consultative group, and include the involvement of an independent consultant who will undertake all negotiations with the client.

6 In situations where informed consent is not possible (e.g., the client is not contactable) at least two independent expert consultants should audit all aspects of the inquiry process, as advocates of the client.

7 Good practice in case study research involves providing the client with an opportunity to comment on a draft of the case report, and to stipulate the deletion or disguising of material for confidentiality purposes. Good practice involves encouraging the client to make a personal statement about the case report, to be included in the final published version.

8 Clients must be offered support, from an expert independent consultant as well as the researcher and/or therapist, at the point at which they are invited to comment on the draft report. If possible, this support should continue to be available to the client for a period of 5 years following publication of the study.

9 In case study research where the principal investigator is not the therapist for the case, the therapist should undergo an informed consent and release process similar to that of the client.

10 In case study research where the therapist is the principal investigator, the therapist must engage in clinical supervision or personal therapy with the explicit contracted aim of examining personal factors associated with the case study work, as a means of ameliorating the impact of these factors on (a) the client, (b) bias within the case report and (c) the well-being of the author.

These guidelines are informed by a quasi-judicial approach to case study research (see Chapter 2), in advocating various forms of 'witness protection' for case study participants. The guidelines that are presented here must be regarded as offering no more than a preliminary effort to construct a template for good practice in this area of therapy research. To establish some future version of these guidelines as an authoritative source of guidance will necessarily involve further discussion and debate within professional associations and the research community, and empirical and conceptual research that subjects these ethical principles to critical test.

Conclusions

The message of this chapter, however, is not merely that personal and professional virtue is a requirement for morally responsible case study research, but that an organized *collective* approach is necessary. If therapy case study research is to thrive, the profession as a whole needs to be willing to identify the principles and standards of ethical good practice that are to be followed, and to carry out research into the effectiveness of different types of ethical procedure. At the present time, there appears to be a lack of consensus within the professional community regarding what is or is not acceptable in relation to case study research. This vagueness is undermining the case study cause, because it means that individual researchers need to possess high levels of courage, resilience and confidence/competence in order to pursue case study projects. We need to make it morally easier for students, practitioners and new researchers to engage in case study work. Although there are moral and ethical challenges associated with case study research, these issues are arguably less severe than the ethical dilemmas arising from carrying out a randomized trial in which clients may be denied treatment. However, there have been several decades of debate that have hammered out ethical safeguards that enable 'trialists' to proceed with confidence. A similar process is necessary in respect of case study methods.

Topics for reflection and discussion

1 *Entering the experience of a client in a case study* – Readers of this book
   are likely also to be readers of at least some counselling and psychotherapy
   case studies. In order to develop an appreciation of the experience of a
   therapy client who has been the subject of a case study, select three
   published case studies that have been of interest to you (preferably studies
   that represent different genres of case study research), and read *slowly*
   through each of the studies, *as if you were the client.* Try to enter the
   emotional frame of reference and worldview of the client as you read, and
   allow yourself to be aware of any fleeting thoughts, feelings or fantasies that
   arise as you read (these subtle reactions would probably be much stronger
   for the actual client). As you read, consider the following questions:

   • What was the process of consent-giving that I went through, in advance
     of this study being published? How adequately did that process prepare
     me for what I am now reading?
   • What are the statements in the report that jump out at me? What makes
     these statements so significant for me?
   • How does this study make me look? What might other people in my life
     think, if they were to read it?
   • What do I now think and feel about my therapist?
   • What have I gained or learned, as a result of this case study?

   It is useful to take notes of your reactions to the case study. Once you have
   completed the task of imaginatively identifying the world of a case study client,
   reflect on the implications of what you have discovered for yourself as a
   therapist, and/or as a case study researcher.

2 Imagine that you have carried out a therapy case study, and are now in a
   position to invite the client to read your draft case report. You have decided
   to follow the ethical guideline suggested in this chapter, and have asked a
   colleague to facilitate and support the client through the process of reading
   and commenting on the report, and making suggestions for ensuring
   confidentiality. How would you brief the colleague? How would you expect
   your colleague to approach this task? What training or preparation might
   your colleague need?
3 Most of the literature around ethical issues associated with case study
   research has been generated by writers with a psychoanalytic or
   psychodynamic orientation. How generalizable are the issues and concerns
   that these writers have identified? Are there different issues and concerns
   that might arise in behaviourally oriented 'n=1' studies, or HSCED studies?
4 Nigel is a senior social worker, who routinely consults with colleagues
   around decisions about whether to take children into care, the career
   development of staff in his team and many other issues. Nigel has been in
   intensive psychoanalytic psychotherapy for two years, mainly to deal with

(Continued)

the effect of abusive childhood experiences. As he arrives at the final point of a planned ending to this successful therapy, his therapist wishes to write up the case, and is wondering whether or not to ask Nigel for permission, and then whether or not to ask for his comments on a draft of the paper. What are the main issues here, for both Nigel and his therapist?

5   To what extent might the process of asking clients to approve the publication of case reports eventually result in a largely worthless body of knowledge, owing to the fact that therapists had been inhibited from expressing their true perceptions of clients?

6   It has been argued that attempts to disguise the identity of clients undermines the scientific objectives of research, by supplying readers with false information. Do you agree?

Recommended further reading

Further discussion of ethical issues in therapy case study research can be found in:

Gabbard, G.O. (2000) Disguise or consent: problems and recommendations concerning the publication and presentation of clinical case material. *International Journal of Psychoanalysis*, 81, 1071–86.

Galatzer-Levy, R. (2003) Psychoanalytic research and confidentiality dilemmas. In C. Levin, A. Furlong and M.K. O'Neil (eds), *Confidentiality: Ethical Perspectives and Clinical Dilemmas*. Hillsdale, NJ: Analytic Press.

Gavey, N. and Braun, V. (1997) Ethics and the publication of clinical case material. *Professional Psychology: Research and Practice*, 28, 399–404.

Miller, R.B. (2004) *Facing Human Suffering: Psychology and Psychotherapy as Moral Engagement*. Washington, DC: American Psychological Association.

The 'microethics' of case study research are explored by:

Grafanaki, S. (1996) How research can change the researcher: the need for sensitivity, flexibility and ethical boundaries in conducting qualitative research in counselling/psychotherapy. *British Journal of Guidance and Counselling*, 24, 329–38.

A useful discussion of ethical issues, by a highly experienced educational researcher, can be found in:

Simons, H. (2009) *Case Study Research in Practice.* London: Sage (Chapter 6).

The dilemmas faced by writers of case studies are discussed by:

Etherington, K. (2007) Ethical research in reflexive relationships. *Qualitative Inquiry*, 13, 599–616.

Graves, P.L. (1996) Narrating a psychoanalytic case study. In R. Josselson (ed.), *Ethics and Process in the Narrative Study of Lives.* Thousand Oaks, CA: Sage.

Josselson, R. (1996) On writing other people's lives: self-analytic reflections of a narrative researcher. In R. Josselson (ed.), *Ethics and Process in the Narrative Study of Lives.* Thousand Oaks, CA: Sage.

Collecting and analysing case material: a practitioner and student toolkit

One of the key principles of a good quality systematic case study is that it draws on multiple sources of information about the client, the therapist and the process and outcome of therapy. Collecting different types of data enables triangulation across sources. For example, if a case is to be considered as having produced a good outcome, it is not particularly convincing to make such a claim merely on the basis of the therapist's perception of what happened. By contrast, if the therapist's appraisal of outcome is supported by information from a follow-up interview with a client, and by changes in scores on a symptom questionnaire completed by the client on a weekly basis, it is possible to claim that a good outcome has occurred with an enhanced degree of confidence. In addition, each data source has the potential to open up a distinctive perspective on the case. So, it may be that there are discrepancies between the picture of outcome that is generated by analysing weekly symptom scores, and the picture that may be presented by the client in a follow-up interview. This kind of result is invaluable for a case researcher, because it typically leads to a more differentiated and detailed analysis of the case.

Since the pioneering work of Carl Rogers and his colleagues in the 1940s, the field of counselling and psychotherapy research has seen a continuous expansion in the instrumentation of therapy research, with many hundreds of questionnaires, rating scales, observation guides and interview schedules having been developed and published. Within the scope of the present chapter it is not possible to review all of the research tools that have been used in case study research, or which could be used. The aim, instead, is to provide an introduction to a set of basic tools that are readily accessible to practitioners, and require minimal training. The emphasis is on high-quality instruments that are freely available, through the Internet or by directly contacting their copyright holders, rather than tools that are published at a cost by commercial organizations. Clearly, some case study researchers may be based in university departments or clinics in which there is ready access to instruments such as the Beck Depression Inventory (BDI), Outcome Questionnaire (OQ) or Symptom Checklist (SCL-90-R), which require payment for each copy that is used. However, it has been assumed that the majority of readers of this book will be working in settings in which such costs may form a significant barrier to research.

This chapter seeks to describe a basic toolkit or package of data collection and analysis methods that are compatible with practitioner-led systematic case study research. In recent years, various therapy organizations have sought to develop such packages for their members or affiliates and for some readers the easiest way to make a start as a case study researcher could be to join one of these existing networks. Examples of how practitioner research networks operate can be found in Borkovec et al. (2001), Elliott and Zucconi (2006) and Stinckens et al. (2009). The chapter also provides further information on where to find out about specialized scales and interview schedules around specific client problems (e.g., eating disorders, marital problems, work stress, etc.) that may be particularly relevant to researchers working in these areas. Background information on underlying concepts of outcome and process research (e.g., the reliability and validity of scales; estimating clinical and reliable change; advantages and disadvantages of qualitative or quantitative approaches to data collection) can be found in Barker et al. (2002), Lambert (2004), McLeod (2003) and Timulak (2008).

When using any of the techniques introduced in this chapter to collect information that might be included in a published case study, it is essential to seek approval from the client before the start of therapy. Issues around ethical informed consent are discussed more fully in Chapter 4.

A basic practitioner toolkit for a systematic case study

It is possible to identify a set of core data sources that should be seriously considered by anyone embarking on case study research in counselling/psychotherapy.

Therapist notes

There are many good-quality case studies that have been published, in rigorous journals such as *Clinical Case Studies* and *Pragmatic Case Studies in Psychotherapy* (see Chapter 6), on the basis of detailed therapist notes, including near-verbatim accounts of therapy dialogue. It is important to acknowledge, however, that the therapists who produced these case studies clearly made huge efforts to record their observations of therapy in a very thorough manner. If a case study is being planned, it may be valuable to develop a structured format for writing therapist notes, to ensure that essential information is collected after every session. An example of a set of headings that might be used as a structure for thera-pist weekly notes can be found at the *Network for Research on Experiential Psychotherapies* site (www.experiential-researchers.org/index.html).

Outcome measures

It is almost always useful to be able to say whether a case was a good or poor outcome, no matter what kind of theoretical or process analysis is also being carried out on the case material. It is also useful to be able to describe the client's level of functioning in relation to wider norms of problem severity. The easiest way to collect these data is to invite the client to complete a brief questionnaire before therapy begins (preferably on more than one occasion, to enable a pre-therapy time-series baseline to be established), at the start or finish of every session and at follow-up. Although asking clients to complete an outcome questionnaire pre-therapy, and then at the end of therapy is better than nothing, there are significant advantages associated with weekly measurements: there is always a final score if the client chooses not to return, it is possible to carry out a time-series analysis and it is possible to identify points in therapy where the client demonstrates sudden gains (or sudden deteriora-tion). Some widely used open-access outcome scales are listed in Table 5.1. When selecting an outcome scale, there are a number of factors that need to be taken into consideration:

- Does the instrument assess an outcome factor that is relevant to the goals of the case study analysis?
- Has the reliability and validity of the scale been established?
- Do norms exist that can be used for benchmarking and for estimating cut-off points for clinically significant and reliable change?
- Has the instrument been used for other studies with similar client groups or therapy approaches, thus allowing results to be compared?

- Is the questionnaire acceptable to clients (e.g., clarity of questions, cultural sensitivity, length of time to complete)?
- Is the scale sensitive to change, or does it assess enduring personality characteristics that are unlikely to be effected by therapy?

Outcome assessment can be achieved through standardized questionnaire measures of symptom or problem areas such as anxiety or depression, or by using individualized personal questionnaires or target complaints scales, in which the client describes his or her goals for therapy in their own words. It can be valuable to use both methods together, to capture any personal or idiosyncratic dimensions of change, as well as more general problem areas. Outcome data can also be collected through interviews (see below). Further information and guidance on the selection and implementation of outcome measures can be found in Cone (2001) and Ogles et al. (2002). Details of a wide range of assessment instruments that are available can be found in Bowling (2001, 2004) and Watkins and Campbell (2000).

Table 5.1   Accessible outcome measures for practitioner-oriented case study research

Instrument	Factors assessed	Internet source	References
CORE outcome measures (10 or 34 items)	Overall level of psychological difficulties – subscales for *wellbeing*, *symptoms*, *functioning* and *risk*	www.coreims.co.uk/index.php	Barkham et al. 2006; Mellor-Clark and Barkham 2006
Outcome Rating Scale (ORS; 4 items)	Global psychological difficulties	www.talkingcure.com/	Miller et al. 2005
PHQ-9 (9 items)	Depression	www.patient.co.uk/showdoc/40025272/	Kroenke et al. 2001
GAD 7 (7 items)	Generalized Anxiety Disorder	www.patient.co.uk/showdoc/40026141/	Spitzer et al. 2006
Hospital Anxiety and Depression Scale (HADS)	Overall difficulties – *anxiety* and *depression* subscales	www.depression-primarycare.co.uk/images/HADS%20Scoring%20Sheet.pdf	Zigmund and Snaith 1983; Bjelland et al. 2002
Self-Understanding of Interpersonal Patterns Scale (SUIP-R)	Self-understanding of maladaptive interpersonal patterns	www.med.upenn.edu/cpr/instruments.html	Connolly et al. 1999
Change Interview	Client' experience of change	www.experiential-researchers.org/instruments.html	Elliott et al. 2001

(Continued)

Table 5.1   *(Continued)*

Instrument	Factors assessed	Internet source	References
Simplified Personal Questionnaire (PQ)	10-item individualized change measure	www.experiential-researchers.org/ instruments.html	Elliott et al. 1999; Wagner and Elliott 2001
Target complaint rating scale	2-item client self-defined goals/problems	Details available in journal article	Deane et al. 1997
Warwick–Edinburgh Mental Well-Being Scale (WEMWBS)	14-item positive mental health	www.healthscotland. com/documents/ 1467.aspx	Tennant et al. 2007
Perceived Stress Scale	10-item life stress	www.mindgarden. com/docs/Perceived StressScale.pdf	Cohen et al. 1983

Process measures

In most case studies, it is of interest to collect information about the general process of therapy, for example around the quality of the therapist–client relationship, or significant moments of change. In some studies it may be necessary to assess aspects of process that are more theory-specific, such as depth of experiential processing, or levels of therapist empathic reflection. The topic of therapy process encompasses a large number of process factors that have been identified and investigated. Overviews of counselling and psychotherapy process research can be found in Barker et al. (2002), Cooper (2008), Lambert (2004), McLeod (2003) and Timulak (2008). Further information about process assessment instruments can be found in Greenberg and Pinsof (1986) and Toukmanian and Rennie (1992). Within a practitioner case study toolkit, the most useful process tools are probably some kind of measure of the strength of the therapeutic relationship or 'working alliance' such as the *Working Alliance Inventory*, *Helping Alliance Questionnaire* or *Barrett–Lennard Relationship Inventory*. Each of these measures has therapist and client versions, to elicit perceptions of the relationship from both perspectives. These 'relationship' scales allow statements to be made in case studies regarding how the quality of the therapeutic relationship in the case being investigated might compare with norms for clients as a whole. If administered on a regular basis (e.g., weekly or bi-weekly) these scales can also be employed to identify shifts in the relationship (e.g., 'ruptures' in the therapeutic alliance). Another process research technique that is particularly valuable is the *Helpful Aspects of Therapy* (HAT) form, which is completed after each session, and asks the client to describe the most and least helpful or significant events that took place within that session, and rate these events on a scale of helpful–hindering. The *Session Reaction Scale* (SRS) also collects information on the extent to which the client found the session to be helpful or hindering. The *Session Evaluation Questionnaire* (SEQ) is a rating instrument that allows the client to indicate his or her sense of the overall experiential quality of the session – for example, whether it felt 'deep' or 'smooth'. The HAT, SRS and SEQ can be used to assess change in the process, and to provide evidence of whether the process being experienced by the client is consistent with the theoretical approach being used by the therapist (e.g., a client receiving psychodynamic therapy would not be expected to report on the HAT form that the most helpful event in a session was when his therapist gave him some advice). These instruments are also invaluable when session recordings are being made, because they provide the researcher with information about which session recordings (and, in the case of the HAT, where in the session) may be most interesting for purposes of transcription and further analysis. Being able to make this kind of selection can be of great practical value when studying a case in which a large number of sessions have been recorded. Information about open-access process instruments can be found in Table 5.2.

Table 5.2   Accessible process measures for practitioner-oriented case study research

Instrument	Factors assessed	Internet source	Reference
Helping Alliance Questionnaire (HAq-II)	19-item scale: *therapeutic alliance*	www.med.upenn.edu/cpr/ instruments.html	Luborsky et al. 1996
Helpful Aspects of Therapy (HAT) Form	Open-ended descriptions and ratings of most/least helpful events in session	www.experiential-researchers.org/instruments. html	Llewelyn 1988
Revised Session Reaction Scale	24-item scale: *Task reactions*, *helpful reactions*, *hindering reactions*	www.experiential-researchers.org/instruments. html	Unpublished article on website
Working Alliance Inventory – short form	12-item scale: client–therapist agreement around *bond*, *goals* and *tasks* and overall quality of alliance	www.niatx.net/PDF/ PIPractice/FormsTemplates/ Working_Alliance_Surveys. pdf	Hatcher and Gillaspy 2006
Barrett-Lennard Relationship Inventory	64-item scale: *empathy*, *congruence*, *unconditional positive regard*, *warmth*	Available from the author, Prof. Goff Barrett-Lennard, School of Psychology, Murdoch University	Barrett-Lennard 1978, 1986
Session Evaluation Questionnaire	21 items: *depth*, *smoothness*, *positivity*, *arousal*	www.users.muohio.edu/ stileswb/	Stiles 1980; Stiles et al. 2002; Stiles and Snow 1984

When, how and by whom are data collected?

When planning to collect outcome and process data on a routine basis, to make it possible to carry out case study analyses at some future date, it is essential to consider the implications of the practicalities of data collection. In terms of scales, such as the CORE outcome measure or the Helpful Aspects of Therapy scale, which may be administered weekly, some of the options include:

- questionnaire given to client by receptionist, and completed in the waiting room in advance of the session or following the session;
- questionnaire given to client by the therapist, and completed in the therapy room in advance of the session, or at the end;
- questionnaire given to client to take away and complete at home, either mailing it back or returning it at the next session.

In addition to these possibilities, some scales may be available on-line, to be completed on a PC or laptop. In terms of minimizing intrusion on the therapy process, many practitioners might decide to ask clients to complete any questionnaires at home. However, this strategy is likely to lead to a substantial amount of lost data, because clients may forget to fill in the scale, or lose it. Asking the client to stay at the end of a session may not be an appealing option for many clients, who may prefer to be alone with their feelings at the end of a session. In addition, the responses given to scales completed immediately following a session run the risk of being dominated by transient reactions to the session, rather than reflecting more permanent attitudes or changes. On balance, clients will probably feel safer handing a questionnaire back to their therapist than to a receptionist, but may assume that the therapist will read what they have written, and they may therefore use their answers to send messages to their therapist. Whoever is collecting the questionnaire data from the client, it is necessary to be clear to the client about who will read what they have written. There are ethical issues associated with whatever is decided here. For example, some clients may disclose a degree of suicidal risk in questionnaires, that they have not been able to share with their therapist. These are just some of the nuts-and-bolts questions to be resolved when planning a study. There are no definitive right and wrong answers to these questions – for each project that is undertaken, a balance needs to be achieved between the resources that are available, the needs of the research and the needs of clients.

Therapy session recordings

Transcripts of therapy session recordings are the one data source that most effectively provides readers of case studies with authentic insight into what actually happened between therapist and client. Transcripts of sessions capture the lived complexity of the therapy encounter, and can be analysed in many different ways, depending on the aims of the investigation. It is always necessary to be sensitive to the needs of the client around making recordings of sessions, for example by asking permission each time the recorder is switched on, and letting the client know they can ask for it to be switched off at any point, or ask for the recording to be deleted.

The simplest way to record therapy sessions is to use a small digital recorder. Video recordings can be valuable in terms of analysing factors such as body posture, direction of gaze and interactional synchrony. However, video cameras may be regarded by clients as more intrusive, and video data can be time-consuming to analyse, and hard to summarize in a written report. There are different formats that can be used to transcribe audio recordings, depending on the level of detail that is required (e.g., length of pauses, ascending/descending voice tone, etc). However, a great deal can be achieved with simple transcription of verbal content. In terms of analysing transcript material, there is a lot to be gained from just reading the transcript (or listening to a recording), as a means of entering into the process that occurred between therapist and client, and then writing a summary statement of the topics that were discussed in each session. There will always be segments of a transcript that are highly 'quotable', as a means of illustrating key moments within the therapy. Beyond this kind of basic descriptive and exploratory use of transcript data, there exist a number of well-established guidelines for systematic analysis of transcripts, focusing on such areas as metaphor themes (Angus 1996), depth of emotional experiencing (Klein et al. 1986), narrative processes (McLeod and Balamoutsou 2001) and assimilation of problematic experiences (Stiles 2002). An excellent introduction to methods of transcript analysis can be found in Lepper and Riding (2006). Some practitioners who are embarking on case study research projects worry about the amount of data, and corresponding workload, arising from the use of session recordings: for example, if the therapy continues for several months. In this context, it is important to recognize that it is not always essential to listen to, or transcribe, every session. If all sessions have been recorded, it may be sufficient to analyse only those sessions that are theoretically interesting or clinically significant (or even only to analyse segments of these sessions). Indicators of significant sessions can be found in therapist notes, HAT data, interviews with the client or therapist, or sudden shifts in scores on weekly process or outcome monitoring scales. In addition, it is always valuable to look closely at the first session – clients usually tell their story and anticipate the course of the therapy as a whole in what they say during the first 15 minutes of the first meeting with their therapist.

Client and therapist interviews

If possible, it is helpful to interview the client and therapist involved in a case. An interview can be useful for a number of purposes: finding out about participants' experience of therapy, what it was like for them; learning about their reflections on the therapy – how and why it worked or did not work; 'filling in the gaps' where information is incomplete; checking on the researcher's interpretation of the evidence. Over and over again, in the therapy literature, there are examples of studies in which the views of an external observer of therapy turn out to be quite different from the views of those who were there. It is also not uncommon for therapist and client to have different opinions about whether therapy was helpful, and why. Any case study that lacks a straightforward account of the experience of the client and therapist is fundamentally incomplete – there is always a sense on the part of the reader that another story might be told, that it might be possible to configure the data in a completely different way. The most widely used interview strategy is to meet with the client and therapist (separately) either soon after the end of therapy, or within a medium-term follow-up period (3–9 months). An end-of-therapy interview may generate more detailed information about what happened, because it is fresh in the mind of the informant. On the other hand, a slightly delayed interview may allow the person to develop a broader perspective on the therapy. If the therapist also has a role as case study researcher, it is recommended that the interview should be carried out by someone else, to avoid restimulating the therapeutic relationship, and to make it easier for the client to be critical of the therapist.

It is not easy to conduct an effective end-of-therapy interview with a client because the informant may have too much to say, and may have never had a previous opportunity to reflect on their therapy. As a result, carrying out an unstructured end-of-therapy interview runs the risk of generating a large amount of material that is hard to interpret. The Change Interview schedule, developed by Robert Elliott, provides a robust structure that allows the client enough space to explore the meaning of his or her experience of therapy, but also ensures that all of the key areas are covered (Elliott et al. 2001). A summary of the Change Interview protocol is provided in Box 5.2. The questions can be adapted for therapist interviews, and can be supplemented by additional questions that may be relevant to the aims of a particular case study project. For example, if a central aim of a case study was to look at the role of dream analysis within a therapy case, the schedule might be altered to include additional questions about points in the therapy where dreams were explored. It can be useful also to interview the client and therapist before the start of the therapy, or to record any initial assessment or intake interview that may have been carried out with the client. People seeking help can become rapidly socialized into the client role, and it can sometimes be the case in a pre-therapy interview that they say important things about themselves, and their assumptions and hopes about therapy, that later become lost. It can also be valuable, in a follow-up interview, to read back to the client some of the statements that he or she made before therapy, for instance around their problems, or therapy goals, as a means of facilitating further exploration of how they may have changed. Creative techniques that can be used to facilitate client experience, include asking them to draw a picture of their life-space (Rodgers 2006), or draw a time-line of where therapy has entered into their life (McKenna and Todd 1997). Finally, in some studies, a formal diagnostic interview has been implemented at the beginning and end of therapy, if it is considered important to determine whether the client has a psychiatric condition.

The Change Interview

Box 5.2

The Change Interview was developed by Robert Elliott as a qualitative technique that could be used following the end of therapy, to elicit the client's views around the impact that therapy may have had on them. Examples of the topics covered include:

1 *General questions.* What has therapy been like for you so far? How has it felt to be in therapy?
2 *Self-description.* How would you describe yourself? How would others who know you well describe you?
3 *Changes.* What changes, if any, have you noticed in yourself since therapy started?
4 *Change ratings.* For each of the changes identified in section 3: (a) how much have you expected this change vs. were surprised by it?; (b) how likely would the change have been if you hadn't been in therapy?
5 *Attributions.* What do you think has caused these various changes? What do you think might have brought them about? (Include causes from both outside of therapy and in therapy.)

The Change Interview has been used in a number of HSCED case studies (see Chapter 8) and could be applied or adapted for use in any case study research. Further information on this instrument is available at: www.experiential-researchers.org/

Other sources of information

There are many other types of information that may be included in a systematic case study. In some cases there may be 'objective' indicators of change that are highly relevant to the progress of therapy, such as exam results, school attendance, sickness absence from work, hospital visits, frequency of alcohol or drug use, binge eating episodes, and so on. Clients can be asked to keep track of this kind of information in a diary, or it may be possible for the researcher to gain access to official records. In some therapies, there may be artefacts that are created, such as drawings, photographs, sculptures, or poems, that can become part of the case record. There may be referral letters or other forms of communication from outside agencies. Client diaries may be used to collect information on the week-by-week experience of engagement in therapy (Alaszewski 2006; Mackrill 2007, 2008b).

It can be seen that there exists a broad range of sources of information that may be drawn on when collecting data for a systematic case study. Before carrying out a study, it is essential to do some careful planning around the kind of data that will be collected. It is not a good idea to burden the client with too many questionnaires to complete, or interviews to attend. Clients become weary of form-filling, particularly if they regard it as lacking in relevance for them, and may end up answering questionnaires in a rushed manner, rather than using the research instruments to convey their true thoughts and feelings. Also, it is possible for researchers to become swamped with information, and get lost in detail rather than being able to focus in on what is really significant in a case. Finally, although readers tend to be more confident in the veridicality of a case study, if the analysis is based on multiple sources, at the same time they want to be able to follow the story of the case, rather than being caught up in technical detail. It is essential, therefore, to retain a balance when designing a case study investigation. Too few data sources can result in a 'thin' account of the case, and too few opportunities for triangulation across data points. Too many data sources can lead to difficulties in interpreting the meaning and significance of what is found. Whatever data collection instruments are introduced will become part of the therapy itself, and be used by the client in their efforts around meaning-making, learning and change.

Specifying the therapeutic approach that was used in the case

Readers of case studies want to know about what therapy was delivered, and what ideas and models were in the mind of the person delivering the therapy. In the absence of information about the therapeutic approach that was used in the case, it is difficult to make connections between what happened in this case and what happens in other cases, or in the results of large-scale studies. It is rarely sufficient merely to say that a therapist used 'CBT' or was a 'person-centred counsellor', because anyone with any experience of therapy will be well aware that broad labels such as these encompass a wide variety of individual interpretations and schools of thought around what 'CBT' or 'person-centred' might mean in practice. In addition, there is good evidence that therapists are *responsive* to the needs of individual clients, and adapt their practices accordingly (Stiles et al. 1998). It is therefore not sufficient to know whether the therapist identifies with a particular approach, such as CBT or person-centred; what is relevant is to know how CBT or person-centred was delivered *in this case*.

There are several strategies that can be used to specify the therapy that has been delivered in a case. A simple technique is to ask the therapist to give ratings of the relative influence of the therapy approaches that inform their work. For example, Hill et al. (2008) asked the therapist in their case study to use a five-point scale to rate himself on three dimensions: psychoanalytic/psychodynamic, humanistic/person-centred and cognitive-behavioural. This therapist also gave a brief description of his approach, in his own words. This technique is straightforward to use and describe, but yields only a very generalized description of the therapy approach. A more in-depth method for eliciting the therapist's view of what he or she is doing is to ask them to complete a questionnaire such as the *Therapeutic Procedures Inventory* (McNeilly and Howard 1991) or the *Comprehensive Therapeutic Interventions Rating Scale* (Trijsburg et al. 2004). These are questionnaires that include lists of therapy interventions – the therapist indicates which ones he or she has used in the current case. In the *Pragmatic Case Studies in Psychotherapy* journal, one of the main sections that is required in any case study report is titled 'Guiding Conception with Research and Clinical Experience Support.' In this section, the author is asked to write at length about the combination of ideas and concepts, research evidence and clinical practice experience that have informed the therapy that was provided in the case. Beyond these techniques there are two strategies for specifying the therapy that is delivered in a case that are particularly rigorous. The *Psychotherapy Process Q-sort* (Ablon and Jones 1998; Jones and Pulos 1993) is a coding system that can be applied to therapy transcripts to determine the interventions being used by the therapist within each session, and across the case as a whole. Finally, in some studies, such as large-scale randomized trials, the therapists may be trained to deliver a specific therapy protocol, with external assessors evaluating their adherence or fidelity to the protocol by listening to recordings of sessions and rating the level of treatment integrity that was attained (Kendall et al. 2004).

Box 5.3

Analysing case study data: using a 'case book'

In large-sample research, the information that has been collected on participants is usually organized into a statistical database, to enable analysis of patterns of findings across the whole sample and comparisons between sub-groups. By contrast, in single case research, the aim is to identify patterns within data from one participant. Rather than entering case data into a statistical spreadsheet such as SPSS (Statistical Package for the Social Sciences), it can be more helpful to construct a *case book*, which displays the data in chronological order so that the reader can gain a sense of how the case unfolded. Within single case studies it is seldom necessary to use a statistical package such as SPSS to analyse quantitative information – it is usually sufficient to enter such data into a graph, for visual inspection, and to make estimates of clinical and reliable change by arithmetic calculation. The existence of a case book provides members of a research team with a tangible 'object' that they share and work on together, and encourages immersion in the data by reading and re-reading the text, and making marginal notes. The case book also presents the data in a manner that the client may be able to relate to, if he or she wishes to look at it.

Conclusions

The purpose of this chapter has been to offer a review and summary of various ways in which case study data may be collected from clients. In any particular case study project, it is important to select a set of data collection techniques that is acceptable to both client and therapist, and consistent with the aims of the study. A key message that underpins the approach taken in this chapter is that the use of multiple sources of data enhances the credibility of any case study, and expands opportunities for interpretation of the case. The following chapters examine the data collection and analysis strategies that have been developed within different genres or traditions of case study inquiry. Chapter 11 offers a discussion of how groups of students or practitioners can work together in teams to produce high-quality case study reports.

Topics for reflection and discussion

1 Identify a case-based research study that you might like to carry out yourself. What kinds of data would you wish to collect, as part of this study?
2 Reflect on your own counselling or psychotherapy practice. If you were to decide to gather additional data, for case study purposes, what would be the best way to do this, in terms of *by whom*, *when* and *how* the data might be collected? What would be most feasible, within your practice context?
3 Take a few moments to think about your approach to keeping notes on your work with clients. How might this source of information be further developed, in order to make best use of it for case research purposes?

Recommended further reading

A valuable account of how a case study practice research network was established within a therapy training programme can be found in:
Stinckens, N., Elliott, R. and Leijssen, M. (2009) Bridging the gap between therapy research and practice in a person-centered/ experiential therapy training program: The Leuven Systematic Case Study Protocol. *Person-Centered and Experiential Psychotherapies*, 8, 143–62.

A good example of the ways in which multiple sources of evidence can be used in analysis of individual cases is:
Hill, C.E. (1989) *Therapist Techniques and Client Outcomes: Eight Cases of Brief Psychotherapy*. London: Sage.

Further information on the issues involved in using different data collection techniques can be found in:
Barker, C., Pistrang, N. and Elliott, R. (2002) *Research Methods in Clinical and Counselling Psychology*, 2nd edn. Chichester: Wiley.
McLeod, J. (2003) *Doing Counselling Research*, 2nd edn. London: Sage.
Timulak, L. (2008) *Research in Counselling and Psychotherapy*. London: Sage.

6

Documenting everyday
therapeutic practice: pragmatic case studies

The majority of counselling and psychotherapy case studies that have been published consist of descriptive accounts written by therapists about their work with clients seen in routine everyday practice. Many of these case studies have been chosen for publication because they are viewed by their authors as representing examples of their work that might be particularly interesting for colleagues to read about. As Aveline (2005: 138) has put it, this kind of case serves to 'support the dialogue of professional life', by providing a vehicle for practitioners to inform others about the potential value of specific ways of working with different groups of clients, and to receive feedback. The danger is that these case reports can too readily take on the quality of a public relations press release: 'subtle vehicles for boasting about technical mastery and smooth success' (Aveline 2005: 138). The challenge for the profession, therefore, has been to retain the undoubted contribution that can be made by this kind of case study report, while developing methodological guidelines that require authors to write up their case studies in a rigorous and critically informed manner (Messer 2007). The aim of this chapter is to introduce and review these methodological guidelines, and then to discuss some examples of recent case study reports that can be regarded as models for good practice in this area of case study inquiry. The chapter concludes by making some suggestions for some possible further methodological improvements in relation to case studies of everyday therapeutic practice.

The concept of a *pragmatic* case study

It may seem fairly obvious that counselling and psychotherapy practitioners should be able to write up their cases in a straightforward way, and have them accepted for publication. However, there are in fact a number of substantial difficulties associated with this endeavour. First, there are ethical challenges arising from the publication of client material. The extent of these challenges, and strategies for resolving them, are discussed in Chapter 4. Second, it can be hard to condense a vast amount of information that may be collected over the course of many sessions of therapy into an article-length report. Third, it can be tricky to strike a balance between different aspects of the case; for instance, how much space should be devoted to discussion of the theoretical approach that informed the therapy, the client's personality, background and presenting problems, or the therapeutic interventions that were employed? Fourth, what needs to be done to make the report credible and persuasive, rather than a transparent 'vehicle for boasting about technical mastery'?

At this point in time, the best answer to these difficulties lies in the work of the American psychologist Dan Fishman. The major contribution that Fishman (1999) has made has been to go back to first principles, in terms of thinking through the basic rationale for even attempting to produce this kind of case study. The methodological guidelines that Fishman has devised are therefore not only practically useful, in terms of spelling out what needs to be done to write a systematic and rigorous case report of everyday practice. They are also conceptually and philosophically coherent, in describing a perspective on the creation of knowledge that is informed by current debates in philosophy of science, psychology and the social sciences.

In his book *The Case for Pragmatic Psychology* Fishman (1999) argues that the evidence base for psychological practice (which would include counselling and psychotherapy) has for many years been bogged down in an unproductive polarization. On the one side there are those who argue that it is essential to produce general theories of human behaviour, supported by evidence derived from experimental methods, measurement and statistical analysis. On the other hand are those who are influenced by postmodern ideas, who argue that there is no objectively knowable external reality and that all knowledge is socially constructed and shaped by the interests and point of view of individuals and groups who are culturally privileged to make knowledge claims. Neither of these positions is able to generate knowledge that is effective in informing practice. The findings of experimental studies do not translate readily into the complexity of everyday practice, while postmodern inquiry all too often adopts a critical stance in which practice is 'deconstructed', in the absence of tangible suggestions about what might be done to improve services to clients. The solution to this dilemma that is proposed by Fishman (1999: 8) is to adopt a *pragmatic* approach which:

combines the epistemological insights and value awareness of skeptical, critical, and ontological postmodernism … with the methodological and conceptual achievements of the positivist paradigm.

Pragmatism is a philosophical perspective that was developed in the late 19th and early 20th centuries by American philosophers such as Charles Sander Peirce, William James and John Dewey. The key idea in pragmatism is that it is not satisfactory to regard knowledge as consisting of a set of abstract ideas; instead, knowledge is more appropriately understood as a capacity to take effective action within a specific context. This notion has been developed by contemporary philosophers such as Stephen Toulmin and Richard Rorty, who have argued that this capacity to take effective action requires critical analysis of the underlying conceptualizations and assumptions that people use in order to guide their action. What these philosophers are proposing can be viewed as a form of *postmodern pragmatism.* Fishman (1999: 131) offers a summing-up of the implications for therapy research of adopting this perspective:

pragmatism focuses on case studies that address particular practical problems in local and time-specific contexts rather than on the abstract, universal, quantitative knowledge of timeless laws and principles.

The vision here is of a knowledge base that specifies how to get things done, in relation to dealing with social problems and human suffering. Further explanation of the philosophical background to the adoption of postmodern pragmatism as a basis for case study research in counselling and psychotherapy (as well as in other areas of applied psychology) can be found in Fishman (1999, Chapter 5).

In order to make a bridge between postmodern pragmatism as a philosophical stance and the everyday realities of therapeutic practice, Fishman (1999) draws on Donald Peterson's (1991) model of professional activity as disciplined inquiry (see Figure 6.1). In this model, the flow of knowledge and action begins with the problems and goals of the client. The practitioner arrives at an understanding of the client, based on a synthesis of his or her guiding conception (including theoretical ideas, philosophical understanding, political/ethical stance, etc.), along with knowledge of previous cases and with systematic, targeted assessment data about the client's presenting problems, personality, history and life circumstances. From this initial understanding the practitioner arrives at a case formulation of the presenting problems and a resulting treatment plan of how his or her work with the client might proceed. As the therapy does proceed the practitioner monitors what is happening. If the client's

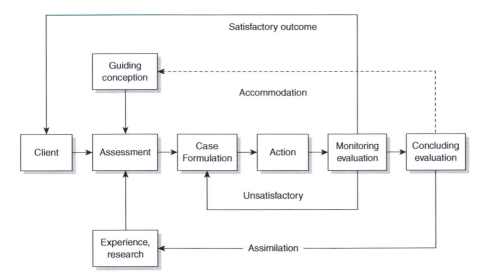

Figure 6.1 *A model of professional activity as disciplined inquiry (Peterson 1991)*

goals are not being achieved, the process returns to further dialogue with the client, leading to reformulation of therapeutic tasks. Also, unsatisfactory outcome may feed back into revision of the original guiding conception. Good outcome is assimilated into the cognitive schema of the practitioner concerning characteristics of effective work, as an image of a 'good case'. The Peterson (1991) model of disciplined inquiry provides a framework for the comprehensive reporting of therapy case studies, that is, a good case study will include information about all of the elements of the model.

When Dan Fishman and his associates set up the *Pragmatic Case Studies in Psychotherapy* open-access, on-line journal in 2005 they adapted the Peterson (1991) model as a template for case study reports (see Fishman 2000, 2005). Articles submitted to the journal need to be structured in terms of the following section headings:

1 Case context and method
2 The client
3 Guiding conception with research and clinical experience support
4 Assessment of the client's problems, goals, strengths and history
5 Formulation and treatment plan
6 Course of therapy
7 Therapy monitoring and use of feedback information
8 Concluding evaluation of the process and outcome of therapy
9 References

A detailed explanation of what might be included under each of these headings is provided in the 'Instructions for Authors' area of the journal website. This format was originally designed, and has so proven, to be flexible enough to accommodate the reporting of cases from a wide range of theoretical orientations – CBT, psychodynamic, family therapy, experiential, humanistic and integrative.

The aims of the *Pragmatic Case Studies in Psychotherapy* (PCSP) journal are: 'to generate a growing database of systematic, rigorous, and peer-reviewed therapy case studies across a variety of theoretical approaches' (journal website). In relation to these aims, there are some further features of the journal that are worthy of note. In recognition of widespread criticism of the methodological adequacies of traditional clinical case studies (see Chapter 2 above) the journal has developed a range of strategies to ensure that the case reports that are published within it are 'systematic and rigorous'. Reports are written in accordance with a standard framework, which ensures that comprehensive and detailed case information is provided. Articles are subjected to anonymous peer review. On publication, each article is accompanied by at least two commentaries, followed by a rejoinder by the author, thus ensuring that readers can view the study from a critical perspective. Finally, the on-line format of the journal means that large amounts of additional supporting material can be provided in appendices. Taken together, these measures ensure that case study articles in PCSP can be regarded as robust and credible additions to the counselling and psychotherapy research literature.

Although PCSP has been established as an open-access, on-line journal with the specific purpose of generating a large database of high-quality case studies, there are other journals that serve a similar purpose. *Clinical Case Studies*, published by Sage, carries articles that are similar to those in PCSP, although it does not explicitly espouse the underlying PCSP philosophy and does not include critical commentaries on the case studies. This type of case study has also been published in *Counselling and Psychotherapy Research*, *Psychodynamic Practice* and other journals.

It seems reasonable, given the major contribution to case study methodology made by Fishman (1999, 2000) and the PCSP journal, to make a clear distinction between old-style 'clinical case studies' and the new 'pragmatic case studies'. Both aim to document and report a therapist's account of how he or she has worked with a particular client, as a means of contributing to the stock of practice-based knowledge. However, pragmatic case studies incorporate an underlying rationale, and set of reporting requirements that introduce a high degree of rigour to this form of case study inquiry. The following section discusses a series of examplar studies as a means of exploring in more detail how pragmatic case studies are constructed, and the kind of contribution they can make to the counselling and psychotherapy literature.

Exemplar case studies of everyday therapeutic practice

In this section of the chapter a series of exemplar studies is discussed, as a means of exploring in more detail how pragmatic case studies are constructed, and the contribution they can make to the counselling and psychotherapy literature.

The case of 'Mr X', an 'incurable schizophrenic' (Karon 2008a)

Bertram P. Karon is a psychoanalytic psychotherapist working in private practice in the USA, who has developed effective approaches to working with clients who are diagnosed as schizophrenic. The very existence of this kind of therapy is regarded by many psychologists and psychotherapists as controversial and questionable – the currently prevailing clinical wisdom and research evidence suggests that the only interventions that are effective with schizophrenia are drug treatment, CBT and long-term in-patient care. The case of 'Mr X', published in *Pragmatic Case Studies in Psychotherapy*, was therefore published as a means of communicating Karon's work to a wider professional community, and as a way of challenging beliefs and assumptions about how best to help people with this kind of problem.

The key features of this case study are summarized in the journal abstract:

Mr X, a schizophrenic, was evaluated by all his psychiatrists as 'incurable' after several years of unsuccessful outpatient and two months of inpatient treatment, both with medications. Electro-convulsive therapy (ECT) was strongly but pessimistically recommended. He was not eating, not sleeping, and continuously hallucinating. He began outpatient psychoanalytic therapy. All medications were stopped. After three days he began eating. After four months he began working at an intellectually demanding job. After two years he could be assured that he would never be psychotic again under normal stresses. But that was not good enough for him. He kept raising new issues: problems in living, difficulties writing his first book, psychosomatic problems, problems in enjoying ordinary pleasures, marital problems, undoing problems he had caused his son. The total treatment took 14 years. More than 20 years after the completion of treatment the patient sent a note indicating his continued professional accomplishments and thanking the therapist for 'giving me my life back'. (Karon 2008a: 1–2)

The information in the abstract clearly signals that the work Karon did with this client resulted in a good outcome, and that the outcome was viewed by the client as attributable to the therapy that he received.

The account of the case that is provided by Karon (2008a) describes how he was contacted first by a friend of Mr X and then by his wife. At this time – 1963 – Mr X was a young university lecturer (not in psychology). The patient had received therapy and medication over several years, but had recently deteriorated to the point where he had been hospitalized. His psychiatrist had categorized him as 'incurable' and recommended ECT. Karon told the wife that X should not be allowed to receive ECT under any circumstances, and asked her to have him discharged from hospital and brought straight to his office. The therapy proceeded on the basis of regular meetings (seven times each week at the start, tapering to weekly after 3 years), some of which were conducted in a restaurant (as a way of working on X's unwillingness to eat). X was told that he could phone Karon at any time. Karon also met with X's wife, and accompanied X to his workplace to support him on his return to work. Arrangements were made for the first two months of therapy for X's wife, or a friend, to be with him at all times.

The case report is based on Karon's notes of his therapy with X (including some verbatim notes of specific conversations), an excerpt from an intake assessment interview conducted by another psychologist, and observations of X reported by family members and others living in the community. The report also includes a description of the therapeutic principles that he employed. Essentially, Karon (2008a) views schizophrenia as a 'chronic terror syndrome', arising from childhood experiences. The symptoms of schizophrenia can be understood as a defence against terror. The therapeutic approach used by Karon (2008a) includes trying to be 'unambiguously helpful' to the client, taking hallucinations seriously and making meaning of them, and conveying a sense of hope. The aims of therapy are to help the person to 'create a livable world' and to internalize the therapist and the therapy relationship as benign images of how to relate to self and others. These ideas are explained in detail in the report, along with supporting research evidence.

The section of the case report that is concerned with case formulation is brief, because:

an explicit case formulation was never part of the treatment ... at each stage, indeed in each session, the therapist deals with what seem most important at that moment, and can flexibly follow the patient into problems of any sort as they arise in the treatment' (p. 14).

The report includes a substantial amount of information about X's life history; some of this data was collected in therapy sessions, with other material being contributed in meetings with X's wife. This information incorporates an account of the childhood circumstances that resulted in X being terrified of close contact with other people. Also in the case report is a description of the course of therapy over a 14-year period, including discussion of the topics that were explored, and setbacks that were overcome. The specific focus on schizophrenic ideas was a stage in therapy that lasted for around two years, with the remainder of the therapy consisting of working through a range of other issues, including psychosomatic difficulties, and marital and parenting issues. Within the case report, Karon (2008a) makes a number of references to points that had been raised by reviewers of the paper, and clearly seems to have inserted further information into the article in response to the issues that they had highlighted.

The publication of the case of Mr X was accompanied by three commentary papers, by experts in the field of psychotherapy and schizophrenia, and a rejoinder (Karon 2008b). Commentaries by Silver (2008) and VandenBos (2008) discussed the case study in a broader context of psychotherapy and mental health policy in schizophrenia. As a colleague and former student of Karon, VandenBos (2008) added some personal observations that confirmed that the way that Karon had described his therapeutic approach was a fair representation of how he generally worked in practice. The commentary by Davidson (2008) adopted a more critical stance, in suggesting that the therapeutic procedures described by Karon (2008a) were not necessarily unique to psychoanalysis, but were similar to therapeutic principles that had been generated in the recovery movement, and in some community-based rehabilitation programmes. Davidson (2008) also suggested that, as a patient with a history of successful life achievements, who had only experienced a 'breakdown' at the age of 30, Mr X could be considered as having a good prognosis, rather than being 'incurable'. All three commentators accepted the essential validity and credibility of the Mr X case study, as a report of a successful treatment of schizophrenia. Davidson (2008) and to some extent VandenBos (2008) questioned whether the therapy that had been delivered could be properly described as psychoanalytic in orientation. In a rebuttal, Karon (2008b) replied to this latter point by reiterating the psychoanalytic principles that had guided his approach.

Overall, the Mr X case represents a good example of the kind of contribution to knowledge that can be made by pragmatic case studies. The case report includes enough unique detail to allow the reader – which can profitably include practitioners, researchers, and students – to gain a reasonably comprehensive appreciation of how this particular therapy helped this particular client. The report includes sufficient discussion of the theoretical, clinical and research background to the case to allow the reader to decide about the generalizability to other, similar clients and about the wider implications of the case. Finally, the commentaries provide a critical context that both affirms the claims made by the author of the case and points to some limitations.

The case of 'B': making sense of the emotional impact of a physical assault (Bichi 2008)

The case of 'B', published by an Argentinian psychoanalyst Estela Bichi (2008), offers an account of a 10-year psychoanalytic psychotherapy with a young woman who had been assaulted on her way home from work:

> B, a 29-year-old divorcee with a 5-year-old daughter, has been working for three months as an educational psychologist in a state institution. Returning home one day in broad daylight, she is assaulted and left in an extremely disturbed state. That is when she asks me for an initial interview, during which she says that this event and her subsequent state of mind are the reason for the consultation. She cannot tolerate the anxiety she feels when she has to leave home to go to work or for other day-to-day purposes. She feels unable to look after her daughter and to provide for the needs, care, and guidance required by a girl of that age, and stresses that this is what torments her most. She asks for and obtains ten days' paid leave from her job, and is recommended to go into therapy. Two days later, at our second meeting, using almost the same words, B repeats her account of the recent episode, in which she was suddenly threatened with a weapon by a young man, to whom, almost paralysed with fear, she handed over her purse and watch, the latter being the most valuable object she says she has so far ever possessed. She adds some information from her history: she lost her father when she was 7 years old and has a younger brother from her mother's second marriage, which took place when she was 11. I sense a pronounced level of distrust in B, which, however, does not cause me to doubt her wish to continue with our interviews. (p. 542)

Like the case of Mr X (Karon 2008a), the case of B tells the story of a good-outcome, long-term psychoanalytic case. However, there are important differences between the way in which these case reports have been constructed and published that highlight important methodological issues in the use of the pragmatic case study approach.

The account of her work with B that is offered by Bichi (2008) is organized in terms of three phases of therapy. Stage 1, the 'nesting phase', of about three months, in which the therapist attempts with some difficulty to create a holding environment in which B might be able to explore the meaning of the highly emotional and chaotic memories and reactions that are around for her during this period. Stage 2, 'trauma, repetition, and historicization', consisted of the identification of a series of earlier traumatic events, and the development of insight into the how the emotional impact of these events had affected not only B's reactions to the recent assault, but had shaped her relationships with men and sense of self-esteem over the whole of her adult life. Stage 3, 'trauma and creativity: a path towards psychic representability', commenced during the third year of therapy. By this stage B had begun to attend art classes, and used examples of her art work, which she brought into therapy sessions, as a means of giving expression to a deepening understanding of a new approach to self and relationships.

The background story to the emotional difficulties that B was experiencing was that her father had died when she was 7. She and her mother had spent some time living in poverty, before her mother re-married. At the age of 16, she had been standing in the street speaking to her boyfriend when she was abducted by three men, probably members of one of the paramilitary groups terrorizing Argentina at that time. She was raped, and left some time later, alone, on a country road. She had never been able to talk about these experiences, which had left her with a profound sense of worthlessness and a mistrust of men. Much of the case study report by Bichi (2008) consists of an account of how she was able to help B to talk about ('symbolize') what had happened to her. This work continued for 10 years, to a point that B described as a 'provisional end' to her treatment. By this stage she had been able to form more satisfying relationships with men, was not overwhelmed by emotion when reminded of past events, was more confident and successful in her professional role and had started a process of making contact with her father's family in Europe.

As a case study published in the *International Journal of Psychoanalysis* the case of B was not required to adhere to the structure demanded by the *Pragmatic Case Studies in Psychotherapy* journal. As a result, the level of reporting of factual biographical information, case formulation, theoretical rationale/guiding conception and other aspects of the case, is less complete. The 'guiding conception' is only sketched briefly toward the end of the paper, which means that it is harder (compared to, for instance, the Karon 2008a case, or other cases published in PCSP) to track the application of the model in the interventions that are described. The only source of information used by Bichi (2008) was her clinical notes, although these did include some verbatim accounts on interchanges in therapy sessions. There is no evidence within the article of any response on the part of Bichi (2008) to reviews of her paper, and the article itself was published without any accompanying commentary. However, there is one facet of reporting in this case report that is particularly noteworthy. Throughout the report, Bichi (2008) consistently offers a closely observed account of her own transference response to B:

> during our third meeting, the presentation of her material becomes more disorderly; she loses the control which I had felt to be somewhat forced, and her intense state of anxiety emerges clearly. I am greatly affected by the incoherence of her words and her disjointed, shapeless, and disconcerting style. Her confusion increases her anxiety, in view of her fear of ending up like her brother, who has serious mental problems. The memory I have of this time is of chaotic countertransference experiences, in the form of impressions and sensations that are difficult to convey, and of the perception of my need to impose order on my own mental functioning, which appeared to be contaminated by B's disorientation and confusion. (pp. 542–3)

> B remains silent for a moment. Then, to my surprise, she picks up her bag, opens it, and takes out a yellowing envelope containing some papers with official stamps. Giving them to me to read, she says: 'This was when I was raped in 1981, when I was 16. I always take them with me wherever I go. I don't know why, but I need to have them by me at all times.' The papers are copies of a police report on her disappearance and of a subsequent statement. The end of the session is approaching, and I observe B's manifestly questioning expression, as she is seemingly making an effort to see how I react to this material, as if expecting a kind of judgement from me. *I feel overcome with surprise, my thought processes virtually inhibited, and I merely add, as we part, that in our future meetings we shall talk about these very important and undeniably painful things that happened to her. I think B has succeeded to some extent in making me too experience the unexpected impact of the traumatic events that befell her. I am indeed overwhelmed by the material of the session, and have to confront my own memories of this period in the history of my country. I am relieved that B is my last patient of the day.* (pp. 543–4; italics in original)

These excerpts underscore the importance, in pragmatic case studies, of being able to write the case in a way that allows the reader to enter the lived experience of the therapy. Both the Karon (2008a) and Bichi (2008) cases accomplish this goal with exceptional skill. However, in describing the countertransference process occurring in the therapist, the Bichi (2008) case adds an important dimension that is largely absent from the Karon (2008a) case (and most other pragmatic case studies).

The case of B has been selected as an exemplar study because it demonstrates that case studies published within the psychoanalytic tradition can contribute to the pragmatic case studies knowledge base. In its emphasis on 'watershed' moments in the formation of the therapeutic relationship, or 'two-person' psychology', the case of B illustrates an area in which the psychoanalytic tradition has something to offer the wider pragmatic case studies literature. However, it can also be said that the reporting of the case of B would almost certainly have been strengthened by adopting the PCSP format, in terms of offering readers a more linear and comprehensive account of the linkages between guiding conception, therapy process and available evidence. It is certainly hard to see that psychoanalytic writers would lose anything by adhering to the PCSP structure, and might stand to gain a broader readership and influence.

The case of Michael: learning alternatives to domestic abuse (Townend and Smith 2007)

The case of 'Michael' provides a pragmatic account of a cognitive-behavioural (CBT) intervention used to help a man to reduce his tendency to engage in violent behaviour towards his wife (Townend and Smith 2007). Michael was a 36-year-old man who referred himself to a specialist service in the UK that offered a structured, individualized CBT programme for perpetrators of domestic abuse. The case report highlights the application of an Interacting Cognitive Subsytems (ICS) (Teasdale and Barnard 1993) model with this client group. This case study, published in *Clinical Case Studies*, differs from the studies discussed earlier in the chapter by being based on a manualized treatment protocol, and by tracking the outcome of the case using two standardized self-report measures (the Aggression Questionnaire and the Rathus Assertiveness Schedule) that were administered pre-therapy, at the end of therapy and at 3, 6 and 9 months follow-up. A follow-up interview was also carried out with Michael's wife, although this was not reported in any detail in the case study.

A particular strength of this case lies in the detailed case conceptualization that is offered:

> Michael would often experience immediate hostile negative automatic thoughts that his second wife could not love him. The thoughts were underpinned by implicational beliefs that she must be saying that she loved him as a ploy toward leaving him and that he would inevitably be rejected because he could never be lovable. Once this implicational level of meaning had been triggered, the global sense of being unlovable and the fear of being rejected elicited an emotional response of fear and anger. This emotional response was accompanied by a physiological response of increased heart rate, sweating, and tensing up of muscles. He then would become preoccupied and ruminate about being rejected. Finally, this would lead to an aggressive behavioral response. These aggressive responses would occur almost immediately in some situations and in others only after a period of rumination. Once the tension had been released by the aggressive behavior, the implicational meaning structure was also further reinforced as his partner withdrew from him, further reinforcing his hostile appraisal of contemporary events. (p. 448)

Although the case report includes a description of the week-by-week structured intervention programme that Michael followed, this information is presented in general terms, rather than being individualized. As a result, it is not possible for the reader to gain much of a sense of how this client engaged with the therapy process, in terms of specific turning points, areas of difficulty or relapse. There are no examples of therapeutic dialogue, or descriptions of how therapeutic techniques were actually delivered. The case report includes some limited information about the early life experiences that may have predisposed Michael to engage in domestic violence.

A distinctive feature of the Townend and Smith (2007) case report, compared to the pragmatic case studies discussed earlier in this chapter, was the use of assessment instruments that were administered at the beginning and end of therapy, and at follow-up. These data provide clear and convincing evidence for change. For example, it is possible to see that Michael's scores on the aggression scale shifted significantly over the course of therapy. At the beginning of therapy his scores were significantly above the mean for the male population, while at the end the scores on all sub-scales were below the male norm. In contrast to the Karon (2008a) and Bichi (2008) studies, the use of standardized assessment measures by Townend and Smith (2007) enabled the latter authors to make claims about the generalizability of their findings – for instance, that before entering therapy Michael was displaying a high level of violent attitudes, and that at follow-up he had markedly improved. In the Karon (2008a) and Bichi (2008) studies the evidence of pre-therapy disturbance, and post-therapy change, is framed solely in terms of evidence that is intrinsic to the case, rather than evidence that could allow comparison with a wider population of cases. On the other hand, with the exception of some corroboration from an interview with Michael's partner, the outcome/change data presented by Townend and Smith (2007) can be viewed as consisting entirely of 'arbitrary metrics' (Blanton and Jaccard 2006; Kazdin 2006). In other words, the measures that were used did not involve any form of direct observation of Michael's actions in everyday life situations, but instead sought to access a hypothetical psychological construct ('aggressiveness'). The Townend and Smith (2007) case report would have been strengthened if examples of actual behaviour change, ideally reflecting shifts in key elements of the initial case formulation, had been included.

In summary, it can be seen that the case of Michael, reported by Townend and Smith (2007), offers readers an informative and valuable account of how it is possible to facilitate relevant cognitive and behavioural change in a man displaying patterns of domestic abuse. The main strengths of this case study are its demonstration of how to 'think CBT', in the context of a detailed and convincing case conceptualization, and in the use of standardized measures to reinforce the conclusion that 'this approach can work'. However, the absence of reporting of the process of therapy, or description of key turning points in the therapy, means that while the study does an excellent job in explaining the *espoused theory* of the therapist, it is less effective in describing the actual *theory-in-use* (Argyris and Schön 1974).

The case of Caroline: therapy for PTSD (Kramer 2009a)

The final exemplar case to be discussed in this chapter is the case of Caroline, a client who was seen by the Swiss psychotherapist Ueli Kramer (2009a). At the time of entering therapy, Caroline was 26 years of age. She had been sexually abused by her maternal grandfather between the ages of 12 and 14, and had developed depression and PTSD symptoms that interfered with the satisfactory development of relationships. She lived with Sylvia, a 40-year-old bi-sexual woman, and worked in a shop. Caroline was ambivalent about entering therapy, because she was not sure whether it was the right course of action for her. The case of Caroline is significant because it represents a well-written example of a pragmatic case study, published in the *Pragmatic Case Studies in Psychotherapy* journal, and also because it highlights the way that single case reports can have the potential to contribute to debate around critical issues of theory and practice.

Caroline received 40 sessions of psychotherapy over the course of one year, at a community therapy clinic. The information on which the case study is based consisted of detailed session notes made by the therapist, the client's scores on a set of standardized, normed self-report measures completed pre-therapy, at session 29, at the end of therapy and at 3-month and 6-month follow-up meetings. The measures used were: General Symptom Index of Symptom Checklist 90-Revised (SCL-90-R); PSS-SR: Posttraumatic Stress Symptoms Self-Report; Beck Depression Inventory; and the Spielberger Anxiety Inventory. In addition, the client returned for a further consultation with the therapist two years following completion of therapy, and was able to report on her continued progress at that point. The case report includes a commentary by the clinical supervisor. The case was written in accordance with the PCSP structure, and includes sufficient detail under all of the headings.

The background to the case of Caroline can be summarized with reference to the sections on client history and treatment goals:

> Caroline's parents divorced when she was 9 years old; they both remarried and had more children. Caroline was sexually abused by her maternal grandfather, from age 12 to 14. Caroline concealed her abuse for two years, until the day she opened up and told her father (at age 14). With no hesitation, he believed in the veracity of the narration, whereas even now, her mother still refuses to accept the facts about her own father. The alleged abuser was brought to justice and convicted by the court; but then, only a few months later, he died of a heart attack. The traumatized adolescent received psychological counseling, an intervention that Caroline reports was not beneficial to her. After her compulsory education, Caroline trained as a secretary and worked for a small local company. Between the age of 17 and 22, she suffered from intermittent depressive episodes, which necessitated antidepressant medication. Apparently, no psychotherapeutic treatment was undertaken during this period. At 19, Caroline had her first erotic relationship with a man, which turned out to be extremely conflictual for her. Her erotic feelings and sexuality were affected by recurrent flashbacks: she had the sensation of seeing her grandfather's eyes in front of her every time she was physically close and attracted to her boyfriend. These disturbing, PTSD-related symptoms made her, after several painful attempts, abandon intimacy and sexuality with her boyfriend, and led to them later splitting up. At the age of 22, Caroline met Sylvia, a 40-year-old bi-sexual, and

started an abusive intimate relationship with her. Sylvia regularly forced Caroline to have sexual intercourse with her, after heavy alcohol drinking. This conflictual relationship lasted 4 years, until the first months of Caroline's psychotherapy. At the beginning of treatment, Caroline had a positive relationship with her father, but a conflictual one with her mother. Caroline's brother was himself in treatment for depression. Caroline came in complaining of PTSD symptoms, including flashbacks, recurrent nightmares, and manifest avoidance behaviors, along with co-morbid, recurrent depression. Caroline reported that she was aware of her symptoms as problems and suffered from them. (p. 6)

[Caroline] was quite clear about objectives for therapy and formulated them to the therapist early in the process: (1) to separate from Sylvia, as this relationship was becoming abusive, and, furthermore, to gain distance from her mother; (2) to be able to live 'less nervously,' without depressive and posttraumatic symptoms, such as irritation and disturbed sleep patterns; and (3) to find an intimate relationship with a man that was satisfying to her. (p. 9)

Caroline was described as being motivated to tackle difficult issues, able to reflect on painful experiences and as having quickly overcome her initial reluctance to engage in therapy.

The approach that Kramer (2009a) described himself as taking with Caroline had three main elements. First, he spent some time carrying out a *plan analysis* of Caroline's hopes, wishes, intentions and goals for her life (Caspar 2007). This procedure yielded a detailed map of Caroline's life plans, organized hierarchically to display the ways in which problematic wishes or goals are nested within higher-order authentic wishes or goals. This assessment technique was used by Kramer (2009a) to guide the construction of a productive therapeutic relationship with Caroline. Although he did not share the details of the plan analysis with his client, he used it to anticipate potentially problematic issues within the therapeutic relationship (e.g., 'avoiding being hurt'), and to address these issues by interpreting them in the light of higher-order non-problematic goals (e.g., 'being more assertive'). In other words, plan analysis provided a structure within which the therapist was sensitized to ways in which the client might undermine the therapeutic relationship and the progress of therapy, and at the same time could build on client strengths.

The second facet of therapy with Caroline consisted of the development of strategies to deal with interpersonal difficulties, for example ending her relationship with Sylvia, and meeting new people. This dimension of the therapy contributed to the lessening of Caroline's level of depression. Third, a major element of the therapy focused on the application of a CBT-based *prolonged exposure* (PE) protocol for eliminating PTSD symptoms (Foa and Rothbaum 1998). The PE approach is based in a behavioural model in which a fear reaction is a classically conditioned response to particular situations and stimuli that are associated with traumatic events, and in which avoidance patterns of behaviour are viewed as operant responses that prevent the fear responses from being extinguished. The aim of PE therapy is to support the client to engage in direct contact with conditioned-fear-eliciting situations so that they can be experienced without accompanying traumatic stimuli and thus eventually be extinguished.

The process of therapy with Caroline proceeded through six distinct stages:

Sessions 1–10:   Establishing a working alliance
Sessions 11–15:   Separating from Sylvia
Sessions 16–20:   A crisis with disturbing eating problems
Sessions 21–23:   In vivo exposure to men in group settings (treating behavioural avoidance patterns)
Sessions 24–26:   Imaginative exposure to abuse-related events
Sessions 27–40:   Switch from imaginative exposure to enhancement of social competence

Each of these stages is described in detail in Kramer (2009a). There were two turning points in the therapy that were particularly significant. At the beginning of therapy Caroline had been able to end her relationship with Sylvia without too much difficulty. However, as soon as this goal had been accomplished, Caroline started to exhibit disordered eating, in the form of a reluctance to eat and regular vomiting. This development surprised Kramer, who had not detected any issues around eating in Caroline's life history or assessment. The therapy therefore focused on eating issues for a few weeks. The loss of Sylvia was interpreted, in the light of the initial plan analysis, as having created a crisis for Caroline in relation to one of her higher-order goals ('search for proximity'). The therapist introduced imaginal activities that allowed Caroline to create an inner 'safe place' that would support her in the temporary absence of proximity in her life, and invited Caroline to keep an eating diary that encouraged her to reflect on the connections between her emotional states and eating patterns. These strategies were sufficient to allow Caroline to eliminate the eating problems, and move forward to commence the PE protocol. The first step in the PE work – homework assignments around approaching men rather than avoiding them – also served as a means of addressing Caroline's 'proximity' crisis.

The next turning point in the therapy arose at session 26. At this time, the PE protocol specified that Caroline should begin to be exposed to abuse-related events that had occurred during her adolescence. The technique recommended by Foa and Rothman (1998) to accomplish this therapeutic task involved talking about the abuse in vivid detail in a therapy session that was recorded, and then taking a recording of the session home and listening to it over and over again. Caroline tried out this procedure once, and became highly upset: 'while listening to the tape at home, she thought of herself as being a 12-year-old child, dangerously vulnerable and helpless, and at the mercy of adults' (p. 13). Therapist and client reviewed the situation together, and decided that the next 10 sessions of therapy would be recorded, and listened to at home, but that these sessions would not necessarily focus on abuse-related events. This revised procedure was carried out, with Caroline using the remaining sessions to work through issues around current social relationships (i.e., to repair the damage to her relationship competence that had been inflicted by the abusive episode in her adolescence).

By the end of therapy, at session 40, and at follow-up, Caroline had become more assertive in her life, and had begun to establish satisfying relationships. There was no recurrence of the eating dysfunction. Her PTSD and depression symptoms had fallen to well within the non-clinical range, as reflected in the standardized self-report measures. These gains were consistent with Caroline's qualitative reports in a meeting between her and her therapist two years after the end of therapy.

The case of Caroline represents an exceptional example of the pragmatic case study approach, in its clarity of explanation of underlying assumptions that guided the therapeutic work, the detail with which specific interventions are described and the use of multiple outcome measures. However, this case is also significant in demonstrating the value of the PCSP policy of inviting expert practitioners to comment on a case. Caspar (2009) offers a commentary that supports Kramer's use of a plan analysis approach. Hembree and Brinen (2009) discuss the position taken by Kramer (2009a), namely, that the complex relationship and self-esteem issues associated with PTSD arising from experiences of recurring child sexual abuse mean that a straightforward CBT exposure strategy may not be sufficient in itself for such clients. They briefly review research on this topic, and conclude that there is no evidence that additional interventions are any more effective than the results that have been obtained by a PE protocol applied alone. Hembree and Brinen also discuss Kramer's (2009a) premise that prolonged exposure is intolerable (i.e., too stressful and threatening) for clients without additional interventions that 'soften' the approach. Again, they offer evidence from controlled studies that this premise reflects a widely held myth about the applicability of evidence-based therapy protocols in everyday practice. In a separate commentary, Muller (2009) similarly argues that Kramer (2009a) did not in fact implement a PE protocol in the manner specified in the Foa and Rothman (1998) treatment manual, probably because he was not sufficiently committed to this model of treatment. Muller (2009: 32) then goes on to emphasise the importance of adhering to empirically validated treatment protocols:

> when a manual is used in a "community" or "real world" setting, we must strive to adhere to the concepts set out in the manual. These specific interventions are prescribed for a reason. When we move too far away from them or modify them extensively, they are no longer empirically supported.

In a rejoinder to these commentaries, Kramer (2009b) – in part citing the commentary by Caspar (2009) – adds some further information about his rationale for diverging from a standard PE protocol, and reiterates his commitment to an approach to therapy based on an *individualized* way of working, that adapts empirically validated methods to meet the needs of individual clients.

The commentaries provided by Hembree and Brinen (2009) and Muller (2009), and the rejoinder by Kramer (2009b), reflect profound differences or schisms that currently exist within the counselling and psychotherapy professional community. Does the availability of intervention packages that have been empirically validated, such as PE, mean that these packages need to be delivered only as intended by their creators? Or does the evidence in support of an intervention imply that it represents a set of techniques and principles from which a therapist might select when designing an 'individualized' treatment plan that is tailored to the unique needs of each client? From a hard-line 'conformity-to-protocol' stance, such as the one that is advocated by Hembree and Brinen (2009) and Muller (2009), how is it possible to explain the excellent outcome that was achieved in the Caroline case? This case also raises questions about the cultural transferability of treatment protocols. PE was developed in the USA, in a context in which brief therapy (less than 20 sessions) is the prevailing option. In Switzerland, by contrast, therapists and clients are able to make use of longer-term therapy. The case of Caroline demonstrates the capacity of pragmatic case study inquiry to 'support the dialogue of professional life' (Aveline 2005: 138) by providing case examples that crystallize the nature of critical choice-points in therapeutic theory and practice.

Reflections on four exemplar pragmatic
case studies

When reading the case reports summarized above, it is essential to keep
in mind that they are not intended to generate conclusions that can be
readily generalized to a wider population. For example, the fact that
psychoanalytic psychotherapy proved to be helpful for Mr X does not
imply that this type of therapy should become the treatment of choice for
people who have been diagnosed as schizophrenic. Instead, the case of Mr
X provides readers an opportunity to engage in 'naturalistic generalization' (Stake 1978), or to develop 'working hypotheses' (Cronbach 1975)
that they can transfer to other cases that they come across (see Chapter 3).
It is also essential to keep in mind that these authors have not been
attempting to develop new theories of therapy. Rather, they have been
seeking to exemplify the way in which a theory, or guiding conception,
can be applied in practice, and to present a kind of dialogue between the
theory and the practice situation (Schön 1983). These pragmatic case
studies were not written from the point of view of the client, and indeed
gave relatively little space for the voice of the client to be heard, but to
try to capture the assumptions and way of working of the therapist.
Finally, these case studies are not placing any particular emphasis on
'proving' that the therapy that was delivered resulted in a good outcome. By contrast, these authors selected cases that they regarded as
good outcome therapies, as a means of providing a secure basis for
explaining how and why their approach was effective. It can be seen,
therefore, that pragmatic case studies occupy a specific place within the
world of therapy case study research, that differs from the case study
approaches described in the following chapters.

A further observation on the exemplar case studies that have been
discussed is that each of them analysed their case material in terms of
stages or *phases* within the therapy. The strategy of using some kind of
time-series or stage analysis to make sense of complex case material is
advocated by Yin (2009) and employed in almost all approaches to case
study research.

Suggestions for improving pragmatic
case studies

One of the reasons for taking four exemplar pragmatic case studies, and
describing each of them in some detail, is to make it possible to consider
what might be *missing* from current good practice in pragmatic case

study methodology. On the basis of the accounts of these case studies provided above, or (even better) on the basis of having read the full articles, what are the questions we would want to ask the authors? Old-style clinical case studies have been around for a long time, but new-style systematic and rigorous pragmatic case studies are still engaged in a process of methodological evolution. What might the next phase of methodological advancement look like, for this type of case study work? Briefly listed below are some possible ways in which pragmatic case studies might be improved.

Author reflexivity

A frequent reaction to reading pragmatic case studies is to wonder 'who is the author?', 'why did the author decide to write about this case?' and 'how did the author, as therapist, feel about the client, or about some of the events that happened in the therapy?' It is common practice in qualitative research to require the researcher to 'own' his or her perspective on the study (Elliott et al. 1999), and this practice could profitably be more developed in the pragmatic case study genre. (Note that with regard to the PCSP journal some discussion of these issues can typically be found in the first section of each case study, titled, 'Case Context and Method'. For a good example of this kind of discussion, also see the 'Concluding Evaluation' section in Ingram's [2009] case study in PCSP.)

More emphasis on the therapeutic relationship

Given that a huge amount of theory and research in counselling and psychotherapy has supported the salience of the therapeutic relationship as a key factor in effective therapy, it is surprising that the authors of the pragmatic case studies presented in this chapter have given so little attention to relationship aspects of their work. In the Bichi (2008) case, the author writes powerfully about countertransference events within the case. In the other cases not much is offered in respect of analysis of the relationship. The absence of discussion of relationship factors inevitably weakens other aspects of the analysis of the case. For example, in the Townend and Smith (2007) domestic abuse case, how important was it, in terms of eventual outcome, that the male client found himself working with a female therapist who was presumably comfortable about hearing him talk about how he hit his wife?

Transparency around ethical procedures

In the Kramer (2009a) and Townend and Smith (2007) cases there is brief acknowledgement that the client gave permission for the case material to be published. However, no detail is provided of how this consent was obtained, and whether the client was able to read a draft report, etc. In the Bichi (2008) and Karon (2008a) cases no information about ethical consent is supplied. Given the considerable ethical sensitivity associated with therapy case study research, and the probable reluctance of many practitioners to publish case reports on the grounds of ethical barriers, it would be helpful if authors of pragmatic case studies were required, by journal editors, to include as much information as possible about the ethical procedures that they followed. In time, this would allow an informed professional consensus to emerge on this topic.

Inclusion of the client's perspective on the case

Many readers of pragmatic case studies will be impressed by the erudite theoretical framework offered by the author of the case, but will nevertheless be left wondering 'what did the client make of all this?' There is plentiful evidence from counselling and psychotherapy research that clients and therapists sometime hold strikingly divergent perspectives on the same case. It would enhance the credibility of pragmatic case studies if clients could be allowed the opportunity to make their own statement of how they felt about the therapy and the way it had been written, in the form of a brief paragraph within the actual case report.

Reporting of contextual factors

The practical value of a case study typically depends on whether the reader can make a connection between the circumstances under which the therapy was conducted, and the circumstances under which he or she sees clients. There can often be a frustrating lack of contextual detail in case reports. For example, in the cases of Mr X and B described above, how did either of them manage to afford such long-term therapy? What kind of supervision or expert consultation was available to the therapist? What were the extra-therapy events and resources that may have contributed to improvement in the client? A case in which there were no financial pressures to limit the length of therapy, a plentiful supply of expert supervision and a cultural environment full of possibility is quite different from the same case where it is a constant struggle for the client to pay for therapy, where the therapist is working virtually alone and the client lives in a high unemployment, depressed region.

Adoption of a dialogical approach

One of the central themes in this book is the idea that it can be difficult for a case study author who was also the therapist for the case to achieve critical distance from his or her experience of working with the client. As a consequence, published case reports can sometimes fail to include information that would be of obvious interest to readers, or is analysed in a way that does not give sufficient attention to alternative interpretations of the material. The use of commentaries in the *Pragmatic Case Studies in Psychotherapy* journal demonstrates the value of publishing a case in a dialogical context. There are many examples in that journal of how commentaries can add a new dimension to the appreciation of a case. However, in PCSP only a limited number of commentaries are published, from writers selected or invited by the editor. It would be important to experiment with on-line open commentary systems in which any reader would be free to take part in a discussion of the case. An example of how this might work can be found on the *Guardian* newspaper website. It might also be helpful for case study authors to engage in dialogue during the production of a paper, for instance by inviting colleagues to comment on drafts of a case report, or by convening a discussion group.

A more focused publication strategy

At the present time pragmatic case studies are published in PCSP, *Clinical Case Studies* and some other journals, on a piecemeal basis. Readers of these journals can find a case study of therapy for PTSD published alongside a study of therapy for schizophrenia and therapy for attention deficit disorder. This publication strategy reflects the way that journals have always operated – articles are submitted and published in order of acceptance. However, this approach is not particularly helpful for readers. Ideally, a practitioner working with PTSD clients might want to be able to read through a batch of relevant case studies, preferably with some kind of overview article attached to them. Currently, databases such as PsycInfo do not seem to be particularly effective at calling up sets of case studies on a particular topic.

Box 6.1

The St Michael's College clinical case study collection

In any field of research and inquiry, it is necessary to move beyond the findings of a single study, and to be able to weave the results of many studies into a broader picture. In the area of pragmatic case studies, the 'single case to database' strategy proposed by Fishman (2000, 2005) is to use the publication of good-quality pragmatic cases to build a database of cases that can be used as the basis for various kinds of meta-analysis. The nearest that has been attained to date, in terms of assembling this kind of database, is the clinical case study collection created by Ron Miller, and lodged in the Durrick Library at St Michael's College in Vermont. This collection consists of more than 350 individual cases, and 125 edited books, catalogued in terms of keywords. Further information on how to access this invaluable resource, and a list of items in the collection up to 2004, can be found in Miller (2004: app. A).

Conclusions

Case studies of everyday practice of counselling and psychotherapy are a means for documenting and analysing professional knowledge. The introduction into this field of a pragmatic, postmodern perspective has made it possible to begin to move beyond the widely acknowledged limitations of traditional clinical case studies, and develop a more rigorous and systematic approach. The primary aims of this chapter have been to review the contribution that pragmatic case studies can make to the evidence base for counselling and psychotherapy, and to discuss the methodological issues associated with this form of inquiry. A further aim has been to encourage greater authorship and readership of this type of case study. For counselling and psychotherapy practitioners, pragmatic case studies can be stimulating, useful, informative and inspiring. Even cases that describe work with client types or therapy approaches that are outside the immediate field of practice of a therapist can yield insights into general therapeutic strategies. It can be particularly interesting to read about therapeutic interventions that are quite different from one's own practice, which may at first glance appear to be profoundly confused and mistaken ... yet are effective.

Over and above any contribution to the published literature, there are advantages for the individual client when his or her therapist writes up a pragmatic case study. The process of writing has the potential to motivate the therapist to be self-reflective, conceptually clear, and in other ways thoughtful in the therapy, and to pay closer attention to the actual, subtle and complex processes taking place. Moreover, peer review of the case study manuscript brings an additional layer of reflectiveness and quality to the therapist's thinking.

At this time there is much to be done to build a database of pragmatic case studies that is sufficiently extensive to be really useful. It is a strange thought that there are more published randomized controlled trials in the literature than there are published case studies. It is essential, therefore, that practitioners should have the courage to write about their work with clients.

Topics for reflection and discussion

1 How successful are the various strategies that have been introduced in the *Pragmatic Case Studies in Psychotherapy* journal to ensure that the case study articles that are published are 'systematic and rigorous'? Read two or three of the articles in the journal and (a) identify the successful methodological strategies that have been employed, (b) reflect on what else might be done to enhance the rigour and validity of these reports.
2 Are there any unique ethical issues arising from on-line publication of psychotherapy case studies? If there are, what might it be possible to do, in order to address these issues?

Recommended further reading

The philosophical justification for a pragmatic approach to therapy case study research is explained in two works by Fishman:

Fishman, D.B. (1999) *The Case for a Pragmatic Psychology.* New York: New York University Press. Chapter 5.

Fishman, D.B. (2005) Editor's introduction to PCSP – From single case to database: A new method for enhancing psychotherapy practice. *Pragmatic Case Studies in Psychotherapy*, 1(1), 1–50. http://pcsp.libraries.rutgers.edu

Evaluating the effectiveness of therapy: n=1 time-series case studies

One of the most important approaches within the field of counselling and psychotherapy case studies has been the tradition of the 'single subject' design. This approach is also known as the 'n=1' or 'n-of-1' study. The terminology that is used to describe this approach ('n=1', 'single subject') reflects its roots in experimental methods – an n=1 study is just like any other experimental study, except that there is only one subject (participant), or that there is a sample size ('n') of one. The key idea in this type of investigation is that the case study is viewed as a vehicle for hypothesis-testing. In a therapy case study, the hypothesis might be that the therapy model or protocol that has been used has been effective in reducing the problem behaviour or symptoms of the client, or that a specific element of the intervention has had an effect. The aim of n=1 studies is therefore to address *efficacy* questions ('is this therapy effective?'). Historically, n=1 studies have their origins in laboratory-based behavioural research that took place in the early 20th century, in which behaviourist psychologists such as B.F. Skinner and Edward Tolman studied the factors that brought about behaviour change in animals such as rats and pigeons. N=1 studies therefore represent an application in the area of therapy practice of a methodology that had initially been developed in a 'pure science' context. N=1 studies have been used in many areas of applied psychology (educational, rehabilitation, sport, neuropsychology) as well as in counselling and psychotherapy.

The intention of this chapter is to provide an outline of the methodological principles that underpin the n=1 case study method before going on to examine some exemplar case studies that have used this approach. The chapter will close with a discussion of the implications of n=1 methods for counselling and psychotherapy case study research as a whole.

Box 7.1

The decline in use of n=1 methods

In recent years a steady stream of writers have lamented the decline in use of n=1 methods in counselling and psychotherapy research (Blampied 1999, 2000, 2001; Borckardt et al. 2008: Molloy et al. 2007; Morgan and Morgan 2003; Sharpley 2005, 2007). These authors have pointed out that fewer single subject case studies are being published in journals that in the past had carried a good proportion of such articles. Three main reasons are put forward to explain this situation. First, the movement in the direction of evidence-based practice has created a climate in which many practitioners and researchers believe that randomized trials are the only kind of research that is worth doing. Second, n=1 methods are not being taught on training programmes, with the result that even when practitioners do wish to carry out this kind of investigation, they lack the confidence and competence to move forward. Third, there has been a shift within cognitive-behavioural therapy away from interventions based on clearly observable and countable behavioural goals toward a form of therapy that aims to produce change within more abstract cognitive structures. The clear message, from these authors, is that a vigorous n=1 tradition represents a necessary element of a comprehensive approach to counselling and psychotherapy research, and that the impetus for a resurrection of n=1 research needs to come from practitioners.

Methodological principles in n=1 case study research

N=1 case studies are based on a number of methodological principles:

- *reliable and valid measurement of outcome variables*;
- accurate *description of the intervention* that is being assessed;
- *time-series analysis* of patterns of change;
- the *logic of replication*.

These principles are discussed in more detail in the following sections.

The use of valid measurement

In n=1 studies it is essential to employ some means of measuring the aspects of the client's behaviour, cognition, physiological functioning or social attitudes that are the target of change (in the behavioural tradition, the term *dependent variable* is used to describe this factor). In other forms of therapy case study research, such as pragmatic or narrative case studies, it may be possible to rely entirely on qualitative descriptions of change. This is not allowable in n=1 studies, where qualitative accounts may play a valuable secondary role in supporting the findings of quantitative analysis, but can never be the central focus of the study. The earliest n=1 studies were based on counting the frequency of specific behaviours (e.g., How many time each day would an agoraphobic patient leave the house? How many time each hour would an OCD patient engage in a specific compulsive ritual? How many panic attacks per week were reported by someone with an anxiety disorder?). This kind of measurement has a number of advantages, in that what is being measured can be agreed by the client and therapist as being something that is clearly highly relevant to the goals of the therapy. More recently, however, there has been an increasing use of standardized instruments, such as self-report rating scale or questionnaire measures of anxiety, depression, PTSD symptoms, etc. These instruments are useful in making it possible to compare a case study client with a wider population. They also allow a broader definition of the outcome factor. For example, having an actual panic attack is only one manifestation of anxiety disorder, and an anxiety questionnaire can enable the researcher to tap into these wider facets of the client's problem. On the other hand, there are disadvantages in using standardized measures. For example, a shift from four panic attacks each week to none is a clear demonstration of the effectiveness of an intervention, in terms of making a tangible difference to a person's life. By contrast, while a shift from a score of 30 to a score of 15 on the Beck Anxiety Inventory is obviously good news it is much harder to know whether the client is now 'better', or has merely learned to assess his or her lived experience of anxiety as more acceptable.

The purpose of valid and reliable measurement in n=1 studies is to make it possible to make statements about what changed, in response to a specific intervention at a specific time. The concept of reliability in psychological measurement refers to the capacity of an instrument to yield the same score under different circumstances. It is useful to think of psychological tests or questionnaires as functioning similar to physical measures of length, such as metre sticks or tape measures. A metre ruler is no good if its accuracy is affected by the temperature, or comes up with a different answer depending on who is using it. Similarly, a behavioural measure is of little value if the score it comes up with is affected by a short-term or temporary emotional state of the person, or by how they feel at that moment about the person who asked them to complete a questionnaire. There are well-defined procedures for evaluating the reliability of psychological measures (this topic is covered in any methods textbook). The issue of measurement reliability is crucially important in n=1 studies because it is essential to be able to know whether changes in the client are a result of the intervention they have received, and not merely a reflection of random variability (i.e., unreliability) of the measurements that have been obtained. N=1 studies represent a challenge to the design of psychological measurement instruments, because the n=1 approach requires repeated measures to be made. However, how reliable is the Beck Anxiety Inventory if a person completes it every day, or even every week over the course of therapy? Surely the meaning of the items in the questionnaire will subtly change over the course of multiple re-readings? This is one of the reasons why clear-cut behavioural measures, such as number of panic attacks, are preferred by many n=1 case study researchers.

Accurate description of the intervention

The aim in n=1 studies is to be as precise as possible about what is caused by what. This position is a reflection of the methodology of the early 'S–R' behavioural psychology, which sought to identify the connections between specific stimuli (S) and specific responses (R) in as much detail as possible. (In the behavioural tradition the factor that is under the control of the experimenter, and which is assumed to be the cause of change, is usually termed the *independent variable*). A good n=1 study tries to go beyond broad-brush statements of the type 'this case shows that CBT was effective in significantly reducing anxiety disorder', to reach a point where it is possible to make statements about which elements of the CBT intervention had an impact on which elements of the pattern of anxiety exhibited by the client (Gresham 1996). In n=1 studies, therefore, it is usual to find a week-by-week description of the interventions and other therapeutic activities that were enacted in each session. Also, n=1 studies often describe the therapy that was delivered as following a specific published protocol, which allows readers to access a highly detailed account of all the elements of the therapy, in terms of precisely what the therapist would have done to deliver each intervention.

Time-series analysis

Accurate description of the intervention, and valid and reliable measurement of outcome variables, are brought together through the analysis of *time-series data*. A time-series analysis involves the construction of a graph that charts the week-by-week change in target behaviour. By identifying the therapy interventions (and extra-therapy factors) that occurred each week, it is possible to analyse the links between interventions and outcomes. Time-series analysis always involves the establishment of a *baseline* against which the effects of therapy can be compared. A baseline consists of a series of measures of the problem behaviour, collected before the commencement of therapy. It is important to note that the requirement to collect several baseline measures, rather than (as in most other types of therapy outcome study) a single pre-therapy assessment, represents one of the most distinctive and powerful features of n=1 methodology. There are three reasons why a baseline series is methodologically more satisfactory than a one-time pre-therapy observation. First, there is higher chance that a single observation could be unreliable – the client might just happen to be feeling particularly good or particularly poorly on that one occasion. By contrast, collecting a series of measures averages out any temporary deviations to the client's state. Second, a single pre-therapy measurement point increases the possibility that the client could engage in impression management ('look how unwell I am') in order to ensure that they are accepted into treatment. In n=1 studies, collecting baseline measures occurs after the client has been accepted into treatment, and is viewed by clients as a routine part of the therapy. Third, if sufficient baseline measures are collected, it is possible to determine whether the problem is stable, or undergoes cyclical fluctuations. The phenomenon of cyclicality of psychological problems presents a critical issue in terms of being able to argue that change may have occurred as a result of therapy. It makes sense to assume that many problems that people bring to therapy are cyclical in nature. For example, a person drinks too much, to the point where his wife threatens to leave him. He then makes a concentrated effort to remain abstinent. This is successful for some months, then he gets complacent and starts to drink again. The cycle resumes ...

A further aspect of any time-series analysis is a *follow-up* period, after therapy has finished. The continuation of data collection for a period of time following the end of therapy is an additional check on cyclicality, as well as a strong test of whether any changes that have occurred are attributable to the mere fact of seeing a therapist on a weekly basis (and as a result gradually disappear once the therapist is no longer on the scene), or represent a more fundamental type of change.

Graphs of two typical n=1 time-series analyses are shown in Figures 7.1 and 7.2. The x-axis (horizontal axis) at the bottom of the graph represents time – weekly assessments that were made. The y-axis (vertical axis) on the left represents frequency of occurrence of the client's main problem – in this case panic attacks. This hypothetical study used what is called an A–B or A–B–A design (A = baseline period; B = period when the intervention is introduced; A = follow-up). It is easy to see from these graphs that the therapy appears to have been successful in the first case (Figure 7.1), but that its effectiveness was less clear-cut in the second case (Figure 7.2). When it is not obvious that the therapy has been effective, on the basis of simple visual inspection, it is possible to draw on various statistical techniques to determine whether significant change has taken place. However, it is not possible to use the kinds of statistical analysis that are applied in 'large-n' studies, such as analysis of variance (ANOVA) or simple t-tests that compare the score at the start of therapy to the score at the end. This is because such techniques make an assumption of *independence* between the pre-therapy and end-of-therapy scores. In a time-series analysis, by contrast, the each weekly score is likely to be highly influenced by the previous measure. As a consequence, it is not possible to make an assumption of independence of measures. The existence of this phenomenon, known as *autocorrelation*, has meant that other statistical techniques have had to be developed for use in time-series analysis. The most straightforward technique that has been devised is the *percentage of nonoverlapping data* (PND) method (Scruggs and Mastropieri 1998). This approach consists of simply drawing a horizontal line on the graph, through the highest baseline data point, and calculating the proportion of data points in the treatment that are higher (i.e., in the direction of anticipated change) than this point. For example, if there are eight data points in the treatment phase, and six of them are higher than the highest baseline data point, then a PND of 75% is recorded. Scruggs and Mastropieri (1998) suggest that a PND score of 90% or greater indicates a highly effective intervention, and an intervention that generates a PND score between 70% and 90% can be considered as effective. A PND score of less that 70% is an indicator of questionable effectiveness. Another fairly straightforward statistical technique that can be used to analyse time-series data is *Simulation Modeling Analysis* (SMA) (Borckardt et al. 2008), which is available as a free download at http://clinicalresearcher.org

A variety of other, more complex statistical methods have also been developed (Morley 2007b). At the present time, there is still debate around the relative merits of different techniques for dealing with the problem of autocorrelation. So far, it does not appear that any of these statistical methods has been widely adopted by n=1 case study researchers:

> although a number of researchers have developed methods of analyzing time-series data possessing autocorrelation, the validity of these methods remains questionable even today … , and the general relevance of statistical inference to single-case data remains a highly controversial topic. (Morgan and Morgan 2009: 228)

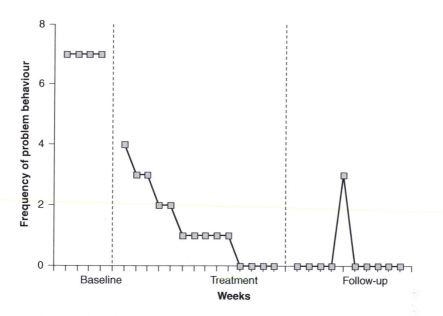

Figure 7.1   *Simple A–B time-series design: good-outcome case*

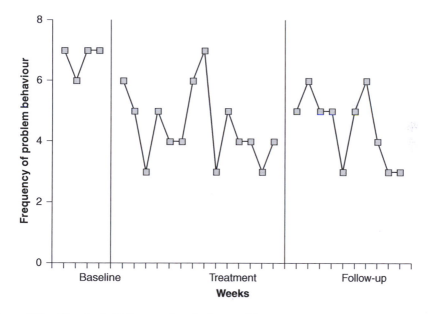

Figure 7.2   *Simple A–B time-series design: ambiguous–outcome case*

Further information about statistical approaches to analysing time-series graphs can be found in Borckardt et al. (2008), Gorman and Allison (1996), Kromrey and Foster-Johnson (1996), Morley (2007b) and Van den Noortgate and Onghena (2003).

Box 7.2

What's in a graph?

The centre piece of most n=1 studies is a graph that displays the change over time of the outcome measures that have been administered over the course of therapy. There are different ways in which this type of visual display can be designed, and these alternatives can make a substantial difference to how the findings might be 'seen' or interpreted. For example, the scale used on the vertical axis (frequency of occurrence of the target outcome measure) can either exaggerate the image of change (if larger-scale intervals are employed) or minimize it (if smaller interval points are used). A useful and comprehensive discussion of graphing conventions can be found in Morgan and Morgan (2009: 84–98). The accurate interpretation of a graph requires sensitivity to the different kinds of information it can convey, such as slope, latency, trend, variability and differences in level (Morgan and Morgan 2009: 211–16). Research has been carried out into the extent to which experts agree on the interpretation of visual data of this type. It has been found that visual interpretation can be susceptible to idiosyncratic interpretation, even when the viewer has received training (Furlong and Wampold 1982). These results have led some critics to question the value of visual representation, and to argue that time-series data should always be subjected to some kind of statistical analysis. However, this critical view has not prevailed. There is a general assumption within the n=1 research community that the goal of this methodology is to be able to identify clearly observable effects, and that where there is ambiguity about whether these effects can be seen in a graph, it probably means that they do not exist. For example, Kazdin (1982) has suggested that visual analysis is a conservative approach to data analysis, because it allows only strong treatment effects to be identified. Practical guidance on how to use Microsoft Excel to generate time-series graphs is available in Dixon et al. (2009) and Lo and Konrad (2007).

The logic of replication in n=1 case research

The concept of n=1 research assumes that single case studies inevitably have limited value, and that the ultimate goal is to achieve generalization through accumulating a series of case reports. The techniques used in n=1 research are designed to make it possible to integrate research into routine practice (at least routine CBT practice) and as a result to be able to generate multiple case studies without too much difficulty. Also, the reporting conventions of n=1 studies do not require researchers to provide extensive detail on each individual case, in the form of case histories and descriptions of the progress of therapy. This means that it is relatively easy to combine cases into a case series. Examples of serial n=1 research projects are described later in this chapter. Further discussion of the logic of replication can be found in Sidman (1960).

Principles of n=1 research: implications
for therapy practice

N=1 methodology is a robust and flexible approach to outcome-oriented single case research that has made a major contribution to the counselling and psychotherapy literature, particularly in relation to the development of behavioural and cognitive-behavioural approaches to therapy. It is a methodology that is built around the simple yet powerful idea of time-series analysis; all other aspects of n=1 methods, such as the use of reliable and valid measures, are driven by the demands of how to do good quality time-series analysis. It was seen in Chapter 6, in the context of discussion of pragmatic case studies, that some kind of 'stage' or time-series analysis makes intuitive sense when faced with the complexity of information that can be generated within a case. On the other hand, n=1 research gives particular priority to the creation of detailed time-series data. It is a methodology in which all other information is subsidiary to the time-series graph. What are the implications of this level of emphasis on the 'chronicity' of a case, in terms of the ways in which therapy practice may need to be adjusted in order to be accommodated within a time-series framework?

Any therapist who is thinking about carrying out a time-series analysis on his or her own work with clients needs to answer the following questions:

- Will I be able to identify with confidence, before therapy begins, the key outcome targets that will be the focus of therapy?
- Do I have access to some means of reliably measuring these outcome variables?
- Can I set up a pre-therapy baseline period of at least three weeks (and preferably much longer) when my client will complete key assessment measures, but not receive therapy?
- Am I comfortable with my client completing an assessment scale every week during therapy?
- Can my model of therapy be broken down into discrete interventions, or a standard sequence of tasks?
- Can I set up a post-therapy series of follow-up measurement occasions?

If the answer to all or most of these questions is 'yes', and particularly if all or most of these requirements are already part of your routine practice, then conducting an n=1 research is feasible, and should be considered. For counsellors and psychotherapists whose approach is not consistent with the implementation of these procedures, n=1 case study research is likely to be problematic. For example, in forms of therapy that are based around an exploratory, meaning-making approach, such as psychodynamic and person-centred, it would not make much sense to identify one, or even a few, behavioural outcomes before therapy has commenced, that could be tracked all the way through treatment.

On the other hand, the movement toward patient-focused (Lambert 2007) or outcome-oriented (Miller et al. 2005) ways of working, in which a generic outcome measure, such as the CORE questionnaire or the Outcome Rating Scale is administered on a weekly basis, begins to make it possible for a much wider range of therapy practitioners to construct n=1 time-series graphs around their work with clients.

Exemplar n=1 case studies

Up to this point, this chapter has discussed some of the general principles of n=1 case study research in counselling and psychotherapy. The focus now shifts to looking at how this methodology is applied in practice, in the context of a set of exemplar studies. These studies have been selected to represent not only the application of an n=1 approach in research on CBT approaches, but also its use in case study research on other therapy approaches.

Tina: a case of hair-pulling (Javidi et al. 2007)

The case of Tina, reported by Zhila Javidi, Malcolm Battersby and Angus Forbes of the Centre for Anxiety and Related Disorders at Flinders University in Australia, represents a good example of an n=1 single case study. Tina was a 29-year-old woman who worked part-time from home and lived with her boyfriend. Tina presented with two main issues: she had a fear of interaction with other people (social phobia) and she pulled her hair out (trichotillomania: TTM). The key information about Tina's difficulties was reported in the case study in the following terms:

> ... her parents died when Tina was 14 years of age, and she developed glandular fever and major depression following her parents' death. An older sibling cared for Tina from the age of 14 onwards. Tina reported that her depression preceded her social phobia, which was subsequently followed by TTM. She had started seeing a psychologist and a psychiatrist from the age of 14 and was prescribed antidepressants that helped to elevate her depressed mood. At presentation, Tina defined her main

problem as panic and anxiety with symptoms consisting of tension, 'butterflies' in the stomach, blushing, shakiness and dry mouth. These episodes occurred in social and family situations such as her appointments with .... other authority figures, and any confrontational situations with friends and siblings. She also experienced anxiety to a lesser degree in shopping centres, while travelling on public transport and when leaving her home. Tina thought that her social phobia became the main drive for her to pull her hair, as it was a way for her to relieve her anxiety and to release emotional pain and frustration in dealing with others. Tina's main fear was of being criticised or judged by others, especially people in authority, and family members for her inability to achieve life goals or complete activities (e.g., going for a job interview). The client specified that at the time her TTM commenced, she was not concerned about her appearance or, later on, the lack of hair on her scalp. At initial interview Tina ... was wearing a hat and there was no hair on her scalp ... her hair-pulling occurred whenever she felt unhappy, stressed, anxious, and alone, rejected or low in self-esteem. Tina pulled hair mainly at night when the stress was greatest and she was alone, that is, when she would not be observed. She used tweezers to pull difficult and very short hair from her scalp, and denied pulling hair from other parts of her body. When she began pulling she was usually aware of the act. However, during an episode she would become less aware ... and experienced overwhelming guilt after each hair-pulling episode. (p. 233)

The therapy that Tina was offered consisted of concurrent CBT interventions for social phobia and for hair-pulling. The social phobia was addressed through gradual exposure to socially fearful situations, allied to techniques for confronting her anxiety in these situations. The hair pulling was approached by inviting Tina to feel the urge to pull out hair, and then not follow through this pattern of behaviour. When at home, she was urged to type out the thoughts and feelings that were around for her when she felt the urge to pull hair. Other techniques used in relation to the hair-pulling included *awareness training* and *self-monitoring* (for example, if she pulled any hair, she was to attach each hair separately to her diary and write the reason why she pulled it, looking at her thoughts, behaviours, emotions and physical symptoms) *contingency management* (her partner complimented her when her hair was growing back), and *relaxation training*. These interventions were practised in therapy sessions, and continued as homework exercises. Regular photographs were taken of Tina's head, as a record of improvement and a means of providing progress feedback for her. After 13 sessions the hair-pulling had been eliminated and the social phobia was much improved. These gains were maintained at 4-year follow-up. In addition, Tina described a broadening of her life, including getting married, getting a full-time job, engaging in pleasurable social activities and beginning a university course.

The case report published by Javidi et al. (2007) includes a detailed case formulation and account of the week-by-week interventions that were employed. The outcome data that were collected included:

- client-defined goal and problem statements, that were rated on a 0 to 8 scale at commencement of therapy and 4-weekly throughout treatment, discharge and follow-up sessions;
- standardized measures of avoidance (Fear Questionnaire), depression (Beck Depression Inventory), anxiety (Beck Anxiety Inventory) and level of disability (Work and Social Adjustment scale), also administered at the start and finish of therapy, every 4 weeks during therapy and at follow-up;
- photographs (every 4 weeks);
- end-of-therapy and follow-up interviews.

At a pre-therapy assessment meeting, Tina also received a diagnostic interview. In terms of the client's experience of being involved in a case study, all that was asked of her was to participate in additional data collection every 4 weeks, and to return to the clinic for follow-up sessions. These data collection activities were part of the regular CBT protocol for social anxiety in the clinic attended by Tina. The data collection strategy included methods for collecting individualized behaviourally based information (goals and problem statements), more broad-based measures (e.g., BDI) and opportunities to collect qualitative descriptive accounts of change (follow-up interviews). The case report includes a 'final word' from the client.

The results of this study are presented in the paper as a series of graphs, each of which displays a different outcome dimension (hair pulling, social phobia, anxiety, depression, social disability). These graphs clearly demonstrate differential outcome effects. Behavioural goals around hair-pulling dropped in a linear fashion over the course of therapy and stayed at zero over the follow-up period. Social phobia behavioural goals similarly fell in a linear fashion over therapy, stayed at zero for one year, then climbed again, although not to a level of clinical significance. The fear, depression, anxiety and work disability scales showed more variability, in the shape of a gradual downward trend over the whole four-year period of therapy and follow-up. The authors acknowledge 'underlying psychodynamic issues' that remained for Tina following the end of therapy, but did not specify the nature of these issues.

In this case, extensive baseline data were not collected. Instead, the researchers used the pre-therapy diagnostic interview to establish that Tina's problems around hair-pulling and social phobia had been stable for some years, and did not exhibit cyclical patterns.

The case of Tina offers a valuable illustration of how an n=1 case study approach can be used to document and discuss effective outcomes arising from innovative clinical practice (in this instance, the concurrent CBT treatment of hair-pulling and social phobia by exposure methods). The case report has little or nothing to say about the therapist, the therapy setting, or the therapeutic relationship. Instead, the study is contextualized, in an introductory section and closing discussion, in relation to debates around the kinds of therapeutic interventions that are effective in working with people who pull their hair. However, this paper does offer a strong client narrative – the reader is left with a good sense of who Tina is, what her problems meant to her, and how she was able to use CBT to overcome these problems. The success of this paper, as a piece of case study writing, is that it manages to balance a primary focus on the agency of the therapeutic intervention with a counter-plot in which the agency of Tina herself is expressed.

A case series on an innovative approach to depression in women (Randall and Thyer 1998)

Elizabeth Randall and Bruce Thyer (1998) conducted a series of case studies to test the effectiveness of a new approach to working therapeutically with depressed women. Their new approach consisted of a phased combination of individual cognitive therapy with some sessions of communication skills training delivered on a couple basis. The rationale for this strategy was a recognition that, although cognitive therapy had been shown to be an effective treatment for depression, there was also considerable evidence that an absence of emotional intimacy in relationships played a significant role in the development and maintenance of depression in women. The study carried out by Randall and Thyer (1998) consisted of a comparison of outcomes in three cases in which cognitive therapy alone was offered, and three cases in which cognitive therapy was combined with a 'guided dialogue' package. Each client received 18 sessions of therapy. In the combined approach, clients received an initial two sessions of one-to-one cognitive therapy, then alternate sessions of guided dialogue (at which their partner also attended) and cognitive therapy, until six sessions of guided dialogue had been completed. Clients in the combined therapy condition then resumed one-to-one cognitive therapy through to the end of treatment.

Information was collected from clients using the Beck Depression Inventory and the Miller Social Intimacy Scale, which were administered each week. Baseline data were obtained by asking clients to complete these scales at a pre-therapy assessment interview, and to take a copy of the questionnaires home with them to complete in the following week. The therapy then commenced in the third week. No follow-up data were obtained. Clients were women who had routinely applied for therapy at a community mental health clinic. No individual client profiles are provided. However, all clients reported depression scores in the 'severe' range at the outset of therapy.

The results of this study are displayed in a series of graphs, which show that all six clients exhibited clinically significant reductions in depression over the course of therapy. The three clients in the combined treatment condition demonstrated significant improvements in social intimacy, whereas the clients who had received cognitive therapy only did not show any overall change in social intimacy. The social intimacy graphs are displayed in Figure 7.3. These graphs are readily interpretable on a visual basis, and show that guided dialogue (GD) in combination with cognitive therapy (CT) was more effective than cognitive therapy on its own. Anecdotally, the women who had received the guided dialogue training reported to the therapist that it had been the most useful part of the therapy they had received.

The focus of the Randall and Thyer (1998) study is on examining the differential impact of cognitive therapy versus cognitive therapy plus structured couple-based guided dialogue training. The paper omits information that would be of interest to many readers, for example around the experiences of clients. In the concluding section of the article, the authors mention that one client dropped out of therapy during the guided dialogue phase, because the egalitarian orientation of the dialogue training threatened the conventional gender role differentiation that existed in her marriage. (This client was replaced by another client.) This observation seems important, given the goals of the study, and it would have been valuable to know more about this incident and other aspects of the therapy process.

Randall and Thyer (1998) are clear about the limitations of their study, and acknowledge that the results that were obtained must be regarded as 'highly tentative'. Their study provides a powerful example of how a practitioner can use an n=1 case series, in the context of a busy community clinic, to explore hypotheses around the development of an innovative approach to therapy.

Finally, it is of interest to note that at about the same time as the Randall and Thyer (1998) study, a similar case series conducted by Jensen (1994) was likewise examining the effectiveness of combining standard cognitive

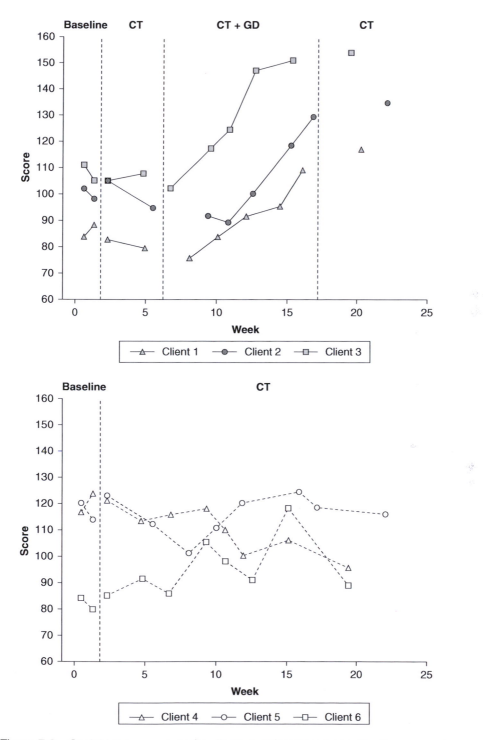

Figure 7.3 *Social intimacy scores for clients 1–3 (combined cognitive therapy and guided dialogue) and clients 1–6 (cognitive therapy only) (Randall and Thyer 1998: 338)*

therapy for depression in women (in this instance, Interpersonal Therapy). Jensen (1994) also found that this combined therapy was highly effective. The idea that depression encompasses a relational dimension that may not be sufficiently addressed in cognitive therapy or CBT will seem fairly obvious to many practitioners. However, more than decade later, the list of 'empirically supported' therapies for depression is still dominated by pure-form cognitive/CBT and interpersonal therapies. No protocol for a combined cognitive-relational therapy for depression has been developed. This situation can be viewed as reflecting the low status in which n=1 studies (and other single case designs) are regarded within the research community – as a mere stepping-stone toward larger-scale studies (which in the domain of an integrated approach to therapy for women's depression, never happened). The Randall and Thyer (1998) and Jensen (1994) studies also demonstrate that an n=1 research design can be applied in the evaluation of non-CBT approaches.

The Randall and Thyer (1998) study is a product of a research process that is readily within the capabilities of any practitioner or clinical team who have developed a high degree of competence or interest in a particular client condition, and have some ideas about the nature of effective therapy for the condition they would like to examine. These studies are *prospective* rather than *reflective*, involving careful advance planning around the recruitment of clients, and the regular administration of relevant data collection measures that can be incorporated into routine practice.

The wider implications for therapy case study research of n=1 methods

The exemplar studies presented in this chapter demonstrate that the n=1 approach provides a practical, flexible and robust methodology for carrying out case studies that are intended to examine the effectiveness of innovative therapy approaches. The n=1 case study framework holds a number of implications for other therapy case study researchers. The practice of establishing a stable baseline allows n=1 researchers to argue with confidence that the changes they have observed in clients are attributable to the effects of therapy, rather than being caused by cyclical fluctuations in client well-being and lifestyle. The combination of time-series analysis, alongside careful description of what happens in each session, provides a powerful means of identifying the effects of different elements of a therapy. The fact that the n=1 case study method has evolved a standard structure for condensing complex clinical data in graphical form facilitates the replication of cases across a series of clients. This capacity to summarize personal information in numerical and graphical terms, across a series of cases, also somewhat alleviates the ethical sensitivity of case-based research – in n=1 studies, the client may not be recognizable, even to him/herself. Finally, the way that regularly administered measures are used in n=1 studies is likely to enhance the learning experience of clients by providing them with opportunities to reflect on their difficulties, and track the way that these difficulties change over the course of therapy.

The exemplar studies that have been reviewed also highlight some limitations of current n=1 case study practice. One of the weaknesses of n=1 case studies is that they are unable to eliminate alternative explanations for any changes that are observed, for example the quality of the therapeutic relationship. To what extent did the clients in the studies that have been explored in this chapter get better because they were able to form a supportive relationship with someone who believed in their capacity to change? Or, more subtly, to what extent were the effects of interventions potentiated by the existence of a supportive relationship (see Borrill and Foreman 1996)? It would not be difficult for n=1 researchers to include process measures, and follow-up questions, that would address this question.

Another issue that appears to be neglected in current n=1 therapy case study research is the question of ethical consent. None of the studies described in this chapter reported whether consent was obtained from clients to publish their cases, or whether clients were able to read the case reports in advance of publication. This is an important issue. While these n=1 case reports did not include interpretive accounts of therapy process, certainly the Javidi et al. (2007) study did include closely described accounts of patterns of behaviour that the client may have found shameful or embarrassing to see in print. As with other types of case study research, greater attention to ethical procedures, and reporting of the consent process, is necessary if the profession as a whole is to achieve a settled consensus on the nature of ethical good practice in case study research.

It seems obvious that, in seeking to establish the utility of new therapy approaches, the majority of n=1 studies will consist of good outcome cases. However, it is also important to learn about apparently good ideas in therapy that do have not yielded satisfactory results. Poor outcome n=1 studies are rarely published (although see Moras et al. 1993 for an example of an apparently promising therapy approach that did not work out in practice).

Conclusions

In conclusion, it can be seen that the n=1 case study method has a great deal to offer, as a practice-friendly method for evaluating the effectiveness of new types of therapeutic intervention. Earlier in the chapter, there was some discussion of the widely held view that the use of n=1 methods in counselling and psychotherapy is in decline. A variety of reasons have been given for this apparent downturn in the publication of n=1 therapy studies. However, the exemplar studies reviewed in this chapter suggest another possible reason. Textbooks of single subject/n=1 methods, written by psychology researchers, introduce readers to a dazzling range of ever-more complex experimental designs that can be applied to evaluate practice. This is confusing. Counselling and psychotherapy researchers, on the whole, do not employ complex varieties of n=1 methodology. They keep it simple. They identify credible outcome measures, track these measures through the course of therapy and follow-up, and then put the data into a visual display. For better or worse, this is not rocket science. But it does provide an effective means of translating practice into knowledge.

Topics for reflection and discussion

1 Imagine that you are a client who is waiting to receive therapy, and have agreed to take part in an n=1 study. You have had a single assessment interview at the therapy clinic, and have been given a self-observation diary, tailored to your particular problems, to complete on a daily basis for a month before the actual therapy commences. What might this task mean to you? What impact might it have on your problems? How might it influence what happened in the first sessions of therapy?

2 Reflect on clients with whom you have worked. In how many of these cases was it possible to identify a goal or target behaviour, at the start of therapy, that remained the focus of counselling throughout your work with this person? In how many cases did a distinctively new focus or problem emerge once therapy had commenced?

3 Identify one type of client difficulty (e.g., depression, anxiety, PTSD) that interests you, in relation to your practice as a counsellor or psychotherapist. Use on-line databases that are available to you to locate at least one n=1 case study that has evaluated a new approach to working therapeutically with that client group. Read this article. What have you learned from it, in relation to your own practical competence and theoretical understanding around working with this client group?

4   What is the 'range of convenience' of n=1 methodology, in respect of research into non-CBT therapy approaches? What might an n=1 study of an innovative variant of psychoanalysis look like? Of Gestalt Therapy? Of client use of a self-help book? If you are successful in imaginatively creating n=1 studies of these modalities, then why are they not being carried out? If such studies are unthinkable, what are the implications for the n=1 method itself? What might it mean if a methodology can be applied to some areas of a discipline and not others?

Recommended further reading

There are several books on the market that offer detailed overviews of n=1 single subject methodology. Particularly recommended, as an accessible text that conveys an infectious enthusiasm for the possibilities of this approach as a means of enhancing practice, is:
Morgan, D.L. and Morgan, R.K. (2009) *Single-Case Research Methods for the Behavioural and Health Sciences.* Thousand Oaks, CA: Sage.

The classic introduction to n=1 methods in therapy research remains:
Kazdin, A.E. (1982) *Single-Case Research Design: Methods for Clinical and Applied Settings.* New York: Oxford University Press.

An excellent overview of various ways in which n=1 approaches can be used in counselling and psychotherapy research can be found in:
Borckardt, J.J., Nash, M.R., Murphy, M.D., Moore, M., Shaw, D. and O'Neil, P. (2008) Clinical practice as natural laboratory for psychotherapy research. A guide to case-based time-series analysis. *American Psychologist*, 63, 77–95.
Math-phobic readers may wish to skip the statistical sections of this article, and should be assured that the paper as a whole makes a lot of sense even if these parts are avoided or skimmed.

Using multiple judges in evaluating the effectiveness of therapy: the hermeneutic single case efficacy design (HSCED)

In the previous chapter, the 'single subject' or 'n=1' tradition in therapy outcome research was reviewed. In that approach, a small number of key outcome variables are identified that reflect the client's goals for therapy. Information on these factors are collected before therapy begins (baseline), regularly during therapy and over a follow-up period. These data are used to draw a time-series graph, which provides a visual representation of the extent to which change has occurred. This methodological approach has proved to be a flexible and robust means of testing and demonstrating the potential effectiveness of innovative approaches to therapy. At the heart of the n=1 strategy is a *simplification* of therapy outcome – the enormous spectrum of emotional, cognitive and relational learning and change that can occur for a client in therapy is condensed into one or two graphs.

The logic of the n=1 design, with its emphasis on quantification, tight focus and observable outcomes, is highly consistent with the practice of cognitive-behavioural approaches to counselling and psychotherapy. Therapists and researchers from other approaches have tended to eschew n=1 case study methodology on the grounds that they are interested in qualitative aspects of therapy that may not be readily captured by existing measures, because they wish to respect the complexity of process and outcome as experienced by the client, and because they believe that the true goals of therapy are often emergent, rather than being identifiable at a pre-therapy assessment interview.

Until recently, this resistance to n=1 methods has meant that practitioner-researchers in humanistic, experiential, psychodynamic and many other non-CBT approaches have not had access to a means of carrying out systematic case studies that evaluate the effectiveness of new ideas and techniques. It could be argued that this absence has been partially responsible for holding back the accumulation of a credible evidence base for these approaches, and slowed down the 'research and development' conveyor belt of innovative therapy 'products'. In contrast, the CBT had been able to use n=1 studies to test new prototype therapies, in advance of scaling up these therapies through randomized trials prior to releasing them on the market.

Over the past 15 years, Robert Elliott, Art Bohart and their colleagues have been involved in developing an alternative to the n=1 design. Their aim has been to retain the fundamental question that n=1 case studies are trying to answer ('has therapy been effective in this case?') but to do so in a way that is congruent with the values and assumptions of all approaches to therapy, including those that favour an exploratory and relational stance. Although Elliott and Bohart are leading members of the humanistic/person-centred/experiential tradition in therapy, their case study method is intended to have wide applicability across any counselling and psychotherapy approach.

The *hermeneutic single case efficacy design* (HSCED) (Elliott 2001, 2002) is a framework for carrying out comprehensive analysis of the outcome of therapy in single cases. The aim of this chapter is to provide an introduction to what is involved in carrying out an HSCED study. The rationale for the HSCED approach is discussed, as a means of setting the scene for an account of the methodological procedures used in HSCED investigations, followed by a detailed account of an HSCED case study. The chapter closes with reflection on some issues arising from the use of HSCED methodology.

The rationale for a hermeneutic approach to single case efficacy research

If the significance of HSCED as a new type of case study approach is to be fully appreciated, it is essential to understand the rationale for this method, as articulated by Bohart and Elliott. For them, HSCED is not merely a matter of 'doing n=1 better', but is grounded in a critical analysis of the assumptions underlying mainstream approaches to research in counselling and psychotherapy, in four key areas: (a) the image of the person in therapy research; (b) the nature of causality; (c) methodical hermeneutics as a means of creating reliable knowledge; and (d) the relevance of 'adjudicational' decision-making procedures developed in the legal system.

The image of the person in counselling and psychotherapy research

The implicit image of the person that underpins mainstream counselling and psychotherapy research studies, such as n=1 studies and randomized trials, is a concept of the client as a passive object on which therapy has an 'impact'. A particularly cogent analysis of this pervasive conceptualization of the person in therapy can be found in the discussion of the 'drug metaphor' in therapy research, by Stiles and Shapiro (1989), who pointed out that most research is conducted as though therapy is a drug treatment, and the aim of investigation is to determine the active ingredients of the drug, or its optimal dose. However, this image of the person is not compatible with an understanding of therapy clients as active self-healers, purposefully collaborating with therapist to construct outcomes (Bohart 2000; Bohart and Tallman 1996, 1998, 1999). Part of the rationale for the HSCED approach, therefore, is to build a method for single case research that recognizes the agency of the client, and provides space and support for the client's intentionality and experience to be taken seriously.

Re-thinking the concept of causality

In counselling and psychotherapy research, the received wisdom is that randomized trials represent the best (or only) means of establishing causal links between therapy interventions and outcomes. If clients are randomly allocated to Therapy A and Therapy B, and Therapy A produces better outcomes, then it has been shown that Therapy A has caused these outcomes (because all other possible causal factors have been dealt with by the randomization process). Elliott (2001, 2002) argues that this way of thinking reflects an inadequate understanding of the concept of causality. He suggests that randomized trials are 'causally empty': 'they provide conditions under which inferences can reasonably be made but provide no method for truly understanding the *specific nature* of the causal relationship' (Elliott 2001: 316; emphasis added). By 'specific nature', what is meant is that, in each individual client in a randomized trial, it is possible to imagine a huge array of in-therapy and extra-therapy events and processes that may have caused the *specific* change reported by this specific client. For example, there may be a client who received Therapy B (which the randomized trial has shown to be less effective than Therapy A) who exhibits more change, and at the end of therapy was more recovered, than the majority (or even all) of the clients who received Therapy A. The logic of a randomized trial provides no basis for constructing a causal explanation for this outcome, because it only produces causal knowledge at a group level, not at an individual level. Similar analyses of the limitations of traditional experimental methods in psychology as a means of generating causal knowledge can be found in Eells (2007a), Sato et al. (2007) and many other sources. The bottom line here is that 'RCTs do not warrant causal inferences about single cases' (Elliott 2002: 2). This is not to dismiss the role of RCTs (Robert Elliott has himself been involved in RCT research), but merely to underscore the idea that an adequate understanding of 'what causes what' in therapy cannot be delivered by RCTs alone.

A further critique of conventional assumptions about causality is made by Bohart and Boyd (1997: 3) in relation to a distinction between 'hard' and 'soft' causality: '... "hard" analysis of causality assumes a kind of mechanistic, linear causal relationship between the application of a technique and outcome. The research goal is to demonstrate such a "hard" if-and-only-if causal relationship'. By contrast, psychotherapy is a complex, nonlinear, recursive, interactive process, that can be characterized as involving 'soft' causality:

> it is meaningless to talk about client-centered therapy 'causing' a change in self-acceptance. Rather the formal properties of client-centered therapy define a set of boundary conditions for a whole set of possible interactions, from which a variety of possible outcomes are possible, including changes in self-acceptance. It becomes much more interesting to study the *individual trajectories* by which individuals 'occupy the space' of client-centered therapy, and engage in that complex interactive process, and subsequently come to the outcomes they achieve, than it is to try to 'manipulate the variables' in order to establish strict linear causal relationships. (Bohart and Humphreys 2000: 5; emphasis in original).

The implication here is that analysis of 'soft causality', in terms of factors such as 'boundary conditions' and 'trajectories', requires extensive use of methods of qualitative inquiry, in addition to the kind of standard quantitative measures used in n=1 studies.

Methodical hermeneutics as a means of creating reliable knowledge

Having established a concept of the person as an active co-creator of meaning and change, and a concept of causal knowledge that necessitates the construction of thick descriptions of the complex and interactive processes that occur in therapy, it is then necessary to address a further question: how to make sense of this kind of information? Clearly, neither statistical methods of analysis, nor visual inspection of n=1 time-series graphs, are likely to be of much assistance. At the same time, well-established methods of qualitative analysis, such as grounded theory (Charmaz 2006; Corbin and Strauss 2008) or Interpretive Phenomenological Analysis (IPA) (Smith et al. 2009) will be much help either, because they have been devised to make it possible to analyse multi-informant sets of interview transcripts, rather than individual cases. The strategy adopted by Elliott (2001, 2002) in response to this dilemma was to adopt a *hermeneutic* approach. Hermeneutics refers to the act of making sense of a complex text through a process of interpretation. Hermeneutic approaches are used in a wide range of disciplines, for example the law (interpretation of the implications of legal cases), theology (interpretation of the meaning of religious texts), history (interpretation of historical documents) and literary criticism (interpretation of novels and plays). Within this broad tradition of hermeneutic inquiry, a number of key principles have emerged. Interpretation is aided by sensitive empathic appreciation of the personality and the cultural context of the creator of the text that is being interpreted. The process of interpretation involves continual movement through a hermeneutic circle or cycle, in which the meanings of segments of a text are considered in relation to the meaning of the whole (and vice-versa). Convincing interpretation is built on analysis of the *whole* of a text, rather than selectively focusing on certain aspects of the text to the exclusion of others. The attitude of the hermeneut should be one of openness and dialogical engagement with the text; rather than impose a favoured interpretation, the inquirer should be open to changing his or her interpretive framework in response to the voice of the text itself. Specific qualitative techniques such as grounded theory or IPA can be viewed as methods for implementing a hermeneutic approach to research and inquiry. Rennie (2000, 2001) has argued that effective qualitative research that yields credible and useful conclusions is based on a process of *methodical hermeneutics*. By this, Rennie (2000, 2001) means a system of interpretation that follows a set of steps that can be explained to others and (at least in principle) replicated by them, and is written up in a manner that is rhetorically consistent with the inquiry process (e.g., allows audiences access to the most important sections of the original text, is transparent around the links between interpretive categories and the root text, explains the presuppositions with which the author approached the text, etc.).

A quasi-judicial analytic framework

A quasi-judicial approach was chosen by Bohart and Elliott as a means of operationalizing methodical hermeneutics in the context of the single-case efficacy research that they wished to carry out (Humphreys et al. 2000). In fact, the notion of a quasi-judicial approach is only mentioned briefly, toward the end of each of the publications that introduced the HSCED method (Elliott 2001, 2002). With the benefit of hindsight, however, it is possible to see that a quasi-judicial inquiry strategy was implicit in the methodological procedures described in these papers.

In HSCED research, the adoption of an adjudicational approach serves two functions. First, it organizes the interpretation of case data in such a way that competing interpretations are held open for as long as possible, thus preventing premature closure of the hermeneutic circle. In the context of an HSCED project, the researcher or research team works up two alternative interpretations of the case data – that it supports a conclusion that therapy was effective in this case (the 'affirmative' stance) and that it supports a conclusion that therapy was not effective (the 'sceptic' stance). The relative merits of each stance are then worked through, to arrive at a final conclusion. The second reason for adopting a quasi-judicial approach is that it draws attention to the need to develop an appreciation of legal concepts such as 'rules of evidence' and 'case lore', which have been thrashed out over centuries of legal debate. For example, in conventional psychological research, a statement is only regarded as valid if it can be shown that the chance of it being false is at a near-zero level of probability ($p<.05$ or $p<.01$). By contrast, in judgments in legal cases, the standard criterion would be 'beyond a reasonable doubt', which is a more relaxed threshold than 'near-zero'. The point here is that the legal system has evolved a highly sophisticated set of rules and procedures for arriving at truth-claims in legal cases, and that these can provide a valuable source of ideas for those conducting single case research in counselling and psychotherapy.

These four principles (the client as an active participant in inquiry; a focus on 'soft' causality; a hermeneutic stance; use of a quasi-judicial framework as a means of structuring the inquiry process) represent a distinctive approach to case study research.

HSCED in action: methodological procedures

How are these methodological principles put into practice? We now turn toward consideration of the data collection and analysis techniques employed in HSCED investigations. The primary aim of this type of case study is to investigate the effectiveness of therapy in specific cases. The key research questions are:

1 Did the client change?
2 Did therapy make a substantial contribution to change?
3 Can causal links be established between therapy process and eventual outcome?
4 What specific events or processes brought about the reported changes?
5 How plausible are non-therapy explanations for the change that has been observed?

In any single case, when each of these questions has been addressed in a rigorous manner, it is possible to determine whether the case represents a good or poor outcome in relation to the application of a specific set of interventions to a client with a specific set of problems. Elliott (2001, 2002) argues that this approach can provide an alternative to randomized trial as a source of valid evidence about the effectiveness of therapy.

It is important to note that the HSCED method grew out of prior work by Elliott and associates using *Comprehensive Process Analysis* (CPA) (Elliott 1983, 1984, 1993; Elliott and Shapiro 1992; Elliott et al. 1994), a structured hermeneutic approach for the analysis of therapeutic processes occurring in significant events in therapy sessions. Readers wishing to carry out an HSCED study are advised to familiarize themselves with this earlier literature, as a means of sensitizing themselves to the type of in-depth multi-perspective style of Elliott's work.

To carry out a single case efficacy study, it is necessary to assemble a rich case record, for example comprising factual information about the client and therapist, quantitative questionnaire measures, process measures administered on a regular basis, end-of-therapy interviews, therapist process notes, transcripts of sessions, etc. The amount and type of information that is available will depend on practical constraints and the goals of the particular study. The key point is that a variety of sources of information are ready to hand, so that interpretations made on the basis of specific client statements or claims can always be checked, and corroborated or refuted, against other statements. Details of the type of measures that can be employed in an HSCED case can be found in Chapter 5 and in the case that is described later in the present chapter. In an HSCED study, the information on the case is collected into a case record or 'case book', which is then interpreted from two competing positions: an 'affirmative' position (looking for evidence to support a 'good outcome' interpretation) and a 'sceptic' position (looking for evidence to support either a 'poor outcome' interpretation, or a conclusion that a good outcome occurred, but was not substantially due to the impact of therapy). The rival interpretations can be carried out either by a lone researcher, who formulates each interpretation in turn, or by separate teams of researchers (Bohart and Humphreys 2000; Elliott 2001, 2002).

Interpretation of case data is facilitated by sets of guidelines that operate as a kind of 'case law', by giving explicit rules for arriving at an agreed interpretation of evidence. For example, Table 8.1 lists some 'plausibility criteria' to guide comprehensive search of the data for evidence that a good outcome may have occurred (Bohart and Humphreys 2000). Table 8.2 summarizes some of the issues to think about when considering non-therapy explanations for outcome in a case study (i.e., developing the sceptic position) (Elliott 2001, 2002). Table 8.3 outlines some of the factors that are relevant to deciding the extent to which changes reported by the client are attributable to therapy (Elliott 2001, 2002).

If a team approach is being used, the two alternative interpretations of the case material (affirmative/sceptic) are presented in written form to the other team. Each team then prepares a rebuttal of the other argument, in the style of Toulmin (1958) (see p. 43 above). There is an auditor involved, in the style of a clerk of the court, whose responsibility is to ensure that participants adhere to the procedures, and to coach inexperienced participants in the use of the interpretive guidelines. The case record, along with sceptic and affirmative arguments, is then sent to a set of judges, who arrive at a view concerning the interpretation of the case.

Table 8.1   Plausibility criteria for interpreting good outcome

Evidence that the client has changed:

Clients note themselves that they have changed
Clients are relatively specific about how they have changed
They report that others have observed them to change
They mention problems that didn't change

Evidence that it was therapy that helped:

Clients themselves report that therapy helped
Describe plausible links to therapy experience
They mention aspects of therapy that didn't help

Evidence that the person did not change:

Clients note themselves that they did not change
They are specific about how their life is still the same
They seem the same in the therapy session

No evidence that it was therapy that helped:

Clients ascribe changes to events in their life
They give unabashedly positive testimonials, but provide few details about how therapy helped
Changes described in the client's life could plausibly account for the client's changes, whether the client sees it that way or not

Table 8.2   Factors to consider when developing a 'sceptic' interpretation of a case

1 Non-improvement:

    (a) apparent changes are *trivial*
    (b) apparent changes are *negative*

2 Statistical artefacts:

    (a) Apparent changes reflect measurement error
    (b) Apparent changes reflect outliers, or regression to the mean
    (c) Apparent change is due to experimenter error (e.g., adoption of a 'fishing expedition' strategy to data analysis)
3 Relational artefacts: apparent changes are superficial attempts to please the researcher or therapist
4 Apparent changes are a result of client expectations or wishful thinking
5 Self-correction: apparent changes are the result of self-help or self-limiting easing of short-term or temporary problems
6 Apparent changes are due to extratherapy events (e.g., a new relationship or new job)
7 Psychobiological factors: apparent changes can be attributed to medication or herbal remedies, or recovery from medical illness
8 Apparent changes can be attributed to reactive effects of research, including contact with research staff

Table 8.3   Factors to consider when examining links between therapy process and outcome

Retrospective attribution:
In post-therapy interviews the client explicitly states that changes were the result of therapy. This attribution can be a general statement (the client is not clear about what it was in therapy that brought about the change), or specific (the client can identify events in therapy that lead to particular changes)

Process-outcome mapping:
The content of post-therapy changes can be linked to specific events, processes or events in therapy

Within-therapy process-outcome correlation:
Specific interventions that are implemented by the therapist (e.g., evidence from therapist notes), or specific therapy events (e.g., evidence from HAT), are linked to client change over the following week

Changes in stable problems:
The client has had a longstanding problem and change is observed soon after therapy commences

In a simpler version of this procedure, a single researcher can follow each of these steps, including taking on the roles of sceptic, affirmer and judge. Whether a team or individual analyst is employed, the ultimate published case report needs to provide a sufficient 'paper trail' to convince readers that a thorough analysis of the case has been carried out.

An exemplar HSCED study

HSCED is a relatively new approach to counselling and psychotherapy case study research. At the time of preparation of this book, although several HSCED projects had been reported at conferences, or are known to be in the process of completion, only three published HSCED analyses are available (Carvalho et al. 2008; Elliott 2002; Elliott et al. 2009).

The case of George: HSCED analysis of the effectiveness of experiential therapy for panic/phobia (Elliott et al. 2009)

The case of George comprises the most fully realised HSCED study that has been published. George had applied to the experiential therapy research clinic at the University of Toledo, Ohio, USA, for help with some difficult personal issues, and was recruited into an HSCED research study. His therapist was Robert Elliott, director of the research programme, one of the founders of process-experiential/emotion-focused therapy (Greenberg 2002; Greenberg, et al.1993), and the lead author for this case study.

The nature of George's difficulties, and their origins in his life history, are summarized by Elliott et al. (2009: 545) in the following terms:

> George was 61 years old at the beginning of his therapy. A married, European-American male, he had some college education and had been a security administrator before he retired. Over the course of his therapy, he disclosed that he had suffered both emotional and physical abuse as a child, at the hands of his mother and a housekeeper. In addition, he recounted an incident in which his uncle had attempted to 'dump' him from a motorcycle while driving on a high-level bridge. He also admitted to a suicide attempt as a teenager, in which he had driven his car into a water-filled quarry. The client was estranged from two of his three children. The one child, a daughter, with whom he had a good relationship, suffered a recurrence of cancer during the therapy. At the beginning of therapy, George reported a strong desire to move to the southwestern United States, and to 'work on old cars, under the shade of a tree'. He was frustrated that he and his wife had to stay in the area while she worked and took care of his aging mother-in-law (who subsequently died during the course of his therapy). George's panic attacks began suddenly, five years prior to this therapy, not long after his retirement. The first attack occurred while he was approaching an expressway bridge. After this, he refused to cross all bridges for fear of further attacks.

He subsequently received several sessions of behavior therapy, which he said made him worse, and he quit when his therapist forgot to inform him that he was going on vacation ... George ... presented with frequent panic attacks, which prevented him from driving over bridges, primarily on the expressway. He also reported fears of heights, flying, excessive speed, and boating. These fears were surprising for him, considering that he had a history of jumping out of airplanes and racing cars. In addition, he described interpersonal difficulties, which he believed were due to his 'abrasive personality'.

A psychiatric screening interview diagnosed George as suffering from panic disorder and agoraphobia. He received 23 sessions of therapy over an 11-month period, and ended because he said he was 'finished'.

A rich case record was assembled, incorporating the following sources of information:

- Standardized self-report outcome measures (Symptom Checklist-90; Inventory of Interpersonal Problems), administered at the beginning of therapy, after sessions 10 and 20, at the end of therapy and at 6-, 18- and 24-month follow-up meetings.
- Simplified Personal Questionnaire – rating scale of client-defined list of problems that he wanted to work on in therapy – completed at every session and at follow-up.
- Helpful Aspects of Therapy form (HAT) – open-ended descriptions of important events in therapy – completed by the client following each session.
- Change Interview – administered after sessions 10 and 20, post-therapy and at follow-up.
- Therapist process notes.

In addition, all sessions were recorded, but these recordings were not used in the case analysis. The adjudication process (affirmative and sceptic cases, and evaluation by judges) was based on only evidence collected up to and including the immediate post-therapy data collection point; the adjudicators did not have access to follow-up data.

It is clear that the rich case record produced by the Elliott et al. (2009) research team included a great deal of information. The key quantitative and qualitative findings provide a mixed picture, in relation to the effectiveness of therapy in this case. The quantitative outcome data provided to the Affirmative and Sceptic Teams are summarized in Table 8.4.

Interpretation of the outcome data in Table 8.4 is assisted by Elliott et al. (2009) through the inclusion for each of the measures and sub-scales of information on the *caseness cut-off* and *Reliable Change Index* (RCI) norms for each factor. Clinical caseness refers to the score that differentiates

Table 8.4   Quantitative analysis of change in the case of George

	Caseness cut-off	Reliable Change Index	Pre-therapy	Session 10	Session 20	Post-therapy
SCL-90-R GSI	0.93	0.51	0.77	0.56	**1.20**	0.57
Interpersonal sensitivity	1.07	0.67	0.67	0.33	**1.22**	0.22
Hostility	1.10	0.80	1.00	0.50	0.83	0.17(+)
Phobic anxiety	0.75	0.46	0.71	0.29	**1.00**	0.14(+)
Inventory of Interpersonal Problems (IIP)	1.50	0.57	**1.96**	1.46	**1.81**	2.27
Controlling	1.07	0.52	**2.14**	**1.14**	**1.71**	**2.83** (−)
Detached	1.35	0.60	**2.44**	**2.20**	**1.70**	**2.70**
Self-effacing	1.84	0.62	1.33	0.89	**2.00**	1.67
Personal Questionnaire (PQ)	3.00	0.53	**4.33**	**5.33**	**5.67**	**4.83** (−)

between the 'clinical' population (i.e., people with serious problems) and the non-clinical or 'normal' population. So, for example, for the SCL-90-R GSI (a 90-item revised version of the symptom checklist; a measure of general psychological symptoms) global/total score (top row of figures) the cut-off is .93 (a score of greater than .93 means that the person has a 'clinical' level of symptoms). The RCI figure indicates the amount of change that needs to be demonstrated on a measure that would allow a confident assertion to be made that real change has occurred. (The importance of this indicator is that small shifts in scores may be attributable to random fluctuations and temporary or situational influences, and can be disregarded.) For the SCL-90-R GSI global or total score (top line of figures), therefore, a shift of more than .51 is required in order to support a claim that change has reliably exhibited. Further explanation of these statistical conventions can be found in Cooper (2008), Barker et al. (2002) and McLeod (2003) and other counselling and psychotherapy research introductory textbooks. The best source of information about caseness cut-off and RCI norms for measures that are used in therapy research studies can be obtained by examining recent outcome studies that have used specific measures, and have reported figures for these indicators.

What does Table 8.4 tell us? On each of these scales, a *higher* score means more severe problems. In relation to the SCL-90, which is a measure of various aspects of general distress or symptoms, George was *below* the clinical cut-off point at the pre-therapy assessment point. In other words, he was not demonstrating a level of emotional distress or dysfunction that would normally be expected in therapy clients. On three of the dimensions of this scale (total score, interpersonal sensitivity and phobic anxiety), he had moved into the clinical range at session 20 (near to the conclusion of therapy) but had moved back into the normal range by the end of therapy. On two of these dimensions (hostility and phobic anxiety), at the end-of-therapy assessment he was reporting reliable positive change (i.e., having started off with a 'healthy' score, he had moved into the 'very healthy' range).

The Inventory of Interpersonal Problems (IIP) is a measure of the extent to which a person is experiencing difficulties in their relationships. In addition to the total score, three factors from this scale are reported: *controlling* (being too controlling in relationships), *detached* (being too detached) and *self-effacing* (lack of assertiveness). On the IIP total score, controlling and detached factors, George reported significant problems at the start of therapy, with scores in the 'caseness range'. At the end of therapy, he remained in the 'caseness' range on each of these variables.

The Personal Questionnaire (PQ) is a particularly important measure in an HSCED analysis, because it reflects the client's personal goals for therapy. The PQ should therefore be highly sensitive to therapeutic change, because it is solely focused on the issues that the client is intending to work on, in contrast to scales such as SCL-90-R or IIP, which include generic items that may or may not be relevant to the client's goals. Also, changes in the PQ should presumably be highly sensitive to events in therapy that involved resolving these problems. In his pre-therapy assessment interview, George used the PQ to identify 6 problems that he wanted to work on in therapy (Elliott et al. 2009: app. A):

- I have a fear of driving on the expressway.
- I'm not able to interact with relatives and acquaintances.
- I have a fear of heights.
- I have a fear of excess speeds.
- My personality is too abrasive.
- I have a fear of boating.

It is worthy of note that George did *not* include an item in the PQ that specifically related to crossing bridges. The PQ data (bottom row of Table 8.4) show that George had moderately high problem ratings at the outset of therapy. However, these ratings were not extreme – the PQ scale ranges from 1 to 7, and George's average pre-therapy rating of 4.33 indicates that he views his problems as being somewhere between 'moderately' and 'considerably' bothering to him. By contrast, many clients use PQ ratings at the start of therapy to express states of desperation and demoralization, and typically use the extreme points on the scale (6: 'very considerably'; 7: 'maximum possible'). At the end of therapy, George's

PQ (4.83) score has deteriorated, but not to a reliable extent (not quite by the .53 point RCI index). In other words, at the end of therapy he still rates his self-defined problems as being in the 'moderately/considerably' troubled range.

Qualitative outcome data were derived from the post-therapy Change Interview (conducted not by the therapist, but by another member of the research team in the clinic). Here, George reported that he could now cross bridges, had a better relationship with his wife, was more tolerant of difficulties and setbacks and was less afraid of flying. He regarded these changes as unexpected (i.e., would not have happened without receiving therapy) and as personally very important for him. The opening section of the Change Interview transcript provided in Elliott et al. (2009: app. A) underscores the contribution that this source makes to the overall rich case record, as well as giving a flavour of the meaning of therapy for George:

I: What's the therapy been like for you?
C: Umm, I think it's sneaky, to tell you the truth [*laughs*]. Because I couldn't figure out where in the world we were going with this to begin with, and I thought, 'What's he want? What's he after? Where are we going? I know what I want but not necessarily what he wants.' And, uh, I find therapy just a little bit disconcerting, because no one ever, just answers a question, all they do is, ask a question as an answer. 'Well,' you know, 'How did that feel to you?' And then you tell him how that—, 'Well, how did that relate, too?' You know, it's back and forth, but it's always a question with a question, and then he answered with a question. And that's unnerving, because that's not the way [*laughs*], that's not the way I live [*laughs*]
I: Not like a regular social ...
C: No, social discourse is— no. But anyway, when I finally figured out that this is how this guy gets to where he wants to go, then it was fine, I had no problem with it, after that. But it just took me a while to get this figured out. Never having been exposed to psychologists that much [*laughs*].
I: So it just took some getting used to.
C: Yeah, it just took some getting used to. And he is a nice man. I've enjoyed our time together, I really have. And he's helped me, to beat the band, I know he has, um, only because he, I don't know if he instilled it in me, or if he reinstilled in me to, be able to do what I used to do, without being, I won't say not apprehensive but not being frightened. I still get apprehensive, I don't think that'll ever go away, maybe it will, I don't know, I don't have that supreme confidence that I used to have, I don't have it anymore.

I think it's a part of just my getting old, and I look back at my mother and my grandmother and that [apprehension] was there with them, I don't think my dad was afraid of anything, but I just didn't inherit that, I guess. There are some things that still, like I say I'm apprehensive. Well, yeah, if you want me to climb a flagpole, there's no way it's going to happen because I'm not going to get that far off the ground [*laughs*]. But, just the normal for me things, it's still the bridge thing, I still have trouble getting over bridges, but I've learned to manage that.

I: So it's still a little bit frightening for you.

C: Oh, yeah, absolutely.

I: But it's manageable now or?

C: Oh, yeah, it's manageable. We just came back from Florida a couple of weeks ago and we had driven out to Key West and ...

I: It's all bridges.

C: I mean you can't get bridgy-er than that. And we done it in a SUV [Sports Utility Vehicle; big American car], which is the worst vehicle ever built. I don't care, I wouldn't have an SUV if you gave it to me, but that's all we could get to rent, and that's what we drove it in, and it was just absolutely awful, but I had to keep telling myself that there are a lot of other SUVs out here, and they're not rolling over on their side and falling in the water.

I: So you were kind of able to talk to yourself.

C: Oh, I have to do that. Yeah, I've got to do that. I keep up this dialogue with myself, and my wife understands that now. She didn't understand that before and she does understand that now, and so consequently she doesn't give you one of those looks [like] 'What is the matter with you?' [I say to myself:] 'Well this doesn't bother you but it bothers me. So I'm willing to let you be bothered by whatever your gremlin is and I'll be bothered by [*laughing*] whatever mine is.' So, we made it out there and made it back, survived the whole thing.

Evidence for connections between what happened in therapy, and changes in George's problems, were studied in a number of different ways. Analysis of the relationship between therapy interventions, recorded in the therapist's notes, and ensuing changes in George's Personal Questionnaire ratings of his problems, found no correlation. Second, an analysis was made of connections between significant therapy events, described by the client on the HAT form, and subsequent PQ changes. No link was found. Finally, the therapy events that George described in the HAT form as being most helpful were identified. Three of these helpful events referred to exploration of different aspects of bridge-crossing, indicating a link between in-therapy events and outcome.

The Helpful Aspects of Therapy (HAT) form: capturing the client's sense of what has been meaningful in therapy

Box 8.1

The Helpful Aspects of Therapy (HAT) form is an effective technique for exploring the client's view of therapy (Llewelyn 1988). The client is invited to use the HAT within 24 hours of each session, to record their recollection of the events in the session that have been most significant and helpful, or most hindering for them, and to rate each item on a scale of helpful/hindering. The therapy events that were identified by George as most helpful were:

Session 4, extremely helpful: 'When [therapist] mentioned that my childhood experiences could have a direct bearing on my problems now. Never thought of it as having anything to with my fear of bridges ...'
Session 6, extremely helpful: 'The part where I talked to my daughter [empty-chair work]. Found out she is one of the bridges I cannot or at least have not tried to cross.'
Session 9, extremely helpful: 'When [therapist] told me to confront my mother [empty-chair work] and tell her how disappointed I was and still am with her. Never did this when she was alive. Should have. It was a relief.'
Session 11, extremely helpful: 'Discover my deep-seated anger. I never knew how much anger could influence how I feel about almost everything I encounter in life.'
Session 16, greatly helpful: 'I found out that before I tackle a problem, I stop breathing. Upon facing the problem of crossing a bridge I made an effort to breathe clear across the bridge and it worked.'

These brief descriptions provide a vivid image of how some distinctively emotion-focused therapeutic activities (e.g., sessions 6 and 9) made an impact on George.

The four postgraduate students, with training and experience in psychotherapy, who served as the Affirmative and Sceptic Teams, were allocated to teams in accordance with the likelihood that they would readily identify with their brief. The two Affirmative Team members (Rhea Partyka and Rebecca Alperin) described themselves as process-experiential and psychodynamic in orientation; the Sceptic Team members (John Wagner and Robert Dobrenski) were cognitive-behavioural in theoretical orientation. The published case report (Elliott et al. 2009) includes a set of appendices available on-line, which include full versions of the arguments laid out by each team.

The affirmative team argued that George explicitly stated in the end-of-therapy Change Interview that therapy had helped him to achieve his main goal of crossing bridges, and also identified other ways in which therapy had been beneficial for him. They noted that the specific problems that had been alleviated by therapy had troubled George for between 2 and 10 years. Although uniform change had not been reported on all outcome measures, the sub-scales that most closely reflected George's target problems (interpersonal sensitivity, hostility, phobic anxiety) did reveal clinically significant change. The Affirmative Team believed that the PQ measure had not been sufficiently sensitive to change, because the researcher who helped the client to construct it had not pressed the client to include a specific 'bridge-crossing' item. The Affirmative Team therefore carried out an analysis of the therapist's notes, and were able to show that the client's descriptions of anxiety associated with bridge-crossing (as reported to the therapist) showed clear signs of improvement over the course of therapy.

The case presented by the Sceptic Team made four main points. First, they pointed out that the client had not shown reliable change on any of the pre-post-outcome measures, and in fact had got worse on two of them. Second, George's ability to cross bridges was not an outcome of therapy, but arose from his own willingness to expose himself to this fear, by making himself drive across bridges. Third, there were contradictions between qualitative and quantitative data. For example, in the Change Interview, George stated that his relationship with his wife had improved. However, the corresponding PQ item had not shown any change. The Sceptic Team suggested that the more positive information in the Change Interview could be explained as a relational artefact – George had wanted to please the female interviewer. Finally, the team believed that 'an overall sense of altruism about participating in the study influenced the client's perceptions of change'.

The Affirmative rebuttal of the case made by the Sceptic Team acknowledged that pre–post outcome measures did not provide a consistent pattern of change, but argued that, since George had focused on a single, identifiable goal for therapy (crossing bridges), the variables being assessed in these measures lacked relevance for the case. In relation to the sceptic claim that George's ability to cross bridges derived from his own efforts, the Affirmative Team replied by pointing to statements in the post-therapy Change Interview in which the client explicitly stated that he could not have made these changes in the absence of his therapist's assistance.

The sceptic rebuttal of the affirmative case argued that the analysis carried out by the Affirmative Team into severity of bridge-crossing anxiety as recorded in the therapist's notes was of little value, since these notes merely reflected the therapist's subjective interpretation of the client's inner state. The Sceptic Team introduced a new perspective in their rebuttal, which was that the client had 'failed to identify any negative changes or aspects of therapy, throwing suspicion on the validity of his self-report'.

The expert judges who agreed to take part in this project were well-known therapy researchers, drawn from different theoretical orientations – Stanley

Messer (psychodynamic), Jeanne Watson (experiential therapy) and Louis Castonguay (cognitive-behavioural). Judges were sent a copy of the case record, along with the briefs and rebuttals that had been formulated by the Affirmative and Sceptic teams. All three judges independently agreed, largely on the basis of the qualitative data, that George had changed. They also agreed, although with less certainty, that therapy had played a role in bringing about this change, but felt that his relationship with his therapist had been important for George. Copies of the complete judges' opinions are available in Elliott et al. (2009: app. F).

The HSCED adjudication process on the case of George was completed in the immediate post-therapy period; the adjudication teams did not have access to follow-up data. The SCL-90-R and IIP follow-data at 6 and 18 months essentially replicated the pattern found at the end of therapy. On the PQ, George's problems had reliably improved at 6 and 18 months, but remained (just) in the caseness range. At the 6-month follow-up, George had requested further therapy, to work on relationship issues. Only two sessions of therapy were completed before he was admitted to hospital for major cardiac surgery. At the 18-month follow-up, he reported that he was able to cross bridges 'at least half of the time'. There was some deterioration visible in George's questionnaire measures at 24 months, in respect of personal problems and symptoms: this change may have been caused by illness that George had experienced around that time.

Conclusions

In reflecting on the case of George, it is essential to keep in mind that HSCED is a newly developed approach to case study research in counselling and psychotherapy. Elliott et al. (2009) describe the publication of their case as an 'experiment', designed to assess the value of HSCED as a means of making 'causal inferences about the efficacy of a novel therapy application'. The account of the case of George that is offered in the present chapter has sought to provide readers with sufficient information about the procedures used in the case to be able to arrive at their own appraisal of the value of this methodology. However, readers are advised to access the original paper and appendices, which contain much additional material.

What is evident from examination of this case is that a thorough interpretive process is being carried out, with many checks and balances to ensure that the final conclusions that are reached are justifiable in terms of the information in the case record. It is clear that HSCED analysis is a time-consuming process and also an *interesting* process, likely to have educational value for all members of the adjudication group, in terms of both informing and challenging their understanding of therapy process and outcome.

Given that n=1 and HSCED studies are attempting to answer the same type of question ('has therapy been effective in this case?'), there are some striking differences between the case of George and the n=1 studies reported in Chapter 7. These include:

- The absence of visual graphic display of the PQ outcome data in the main HSCED case report.
- The absence in the HSCED case of a detailed theoretical account of the therapeutic intervention that was delivered, how it was hypothesized as able to address the client's problems and a case formulation that demonstrated how the theoretical model being used was applied to the specific case being studied.
- The use in the HSCED case of a much wider range of data, including process and qualitative data.
- The inclusion in the HSCED case of the client's personal account of change.

If the case of George had been analysed according to the principles of n=1 single subject research, using visual display of time-series data, it would almost certainly have been recorded as a poor-outcome case, because there was no consistent pattern of improvement across the outcome measures. Only if all the outcome measures other than the phobic anxiety sub-scale of the SCL-90-R had been discarded, could it have been presented as a good-outcome case using n=1 criteria. It seems that the additional information collected through the HSCED process was enough to allow expert judges to set aside conventional ideas about how outcome is determined, and arrive at a different view.

Probably because the n=1 approach has been used in counselling and psychotherapy research for 50 years, authors who write up n=1 case studies tend to pay relatively little attention to methodological issues and procedures, and instead are able to devote more space to reviewing the nature of existing research and practice in relation to the client's diagnostic condition, and explaining how the innovative therapy that they are investigating is an improvement on previous therapy models. What this does, for readers of n=1 studies, is alert them to what they might expect to happen in the case, in respect of change processes. Most of this is lacking in the case of George, with the consequence that the case report gives readers (and maybe adjudicators as well) a lot of information about whether change has occurred, but relatively little basis on which to judge whether the change that occurred was attributable to specific process-experiential/emotion-focused strategies used by the therapist, or to other factors. It might be valuable, in future HSCED studies, to offer a more substantial account of the theoretical basis of the therapy, and how the theoretical model is applied through a case formulation and specific therapeutic interventions.

An intriguing aspect of the Elliott et al. (2009) study is that, by adopting an image of the person/client as an active participant in therapy, and an active participant in interpreting the outcomes of therapy, the research design makes it harder to arrive at a clear conclusion as to whether the *therapy* was the active agent in change. Reflecting on the experience of his research group in conducting HSCED studies, Elliott (2002: 18) observed that:

> the question 'Did the client improve' has turned out to be more complex than we first thought. Our clients often present with a mixed picture, showing improvement on some measures and not on others or telling us that they had made great strides when the quantitative data contradicted this.

The results of HSCED case studies may therefore hold implications for the broader field of counselling and psychotherapy outcome research, in stimulating new ways of thinking about outcome.

In conclusion, it is certain that HSCED provides a valuable addition to the range of single case methodologies that are available to researchers in the field of counselling and psychotherapy. As Elliott et al. (2009) acknowledge, there are many further methodological possibilities to be explored, in relation to the HSCED approach. For example, it would be useful to be able to experiment with implementing the HSCED procedure with judges who were lay people or service users, rather than therapy professionals, or to enact a real-time courtroom-style adjudication proc-ess as proposed by Miller (2004, 2008). As a methodology that is based in a quasi-judicial paradigm for inquiry, there is also much to be learned in relation to the accumulation of relevant case law. For example, in any HSCED study, it seems probable that a Sceptic Team would argue that a client's report of good outcome could be attributable to a wish to please the therapist, the researcher, or both. Presumably, there is some kind of procedure that would enable a more informed view of client compliance to be achieved. At the present time, we do not know what this procedure might look like. It is easy to point to examples in the real legal system of new procedures that have been brought in as a means of introducing additional precision to certain types of argument. In the past, defence lawyers would argue that confessions had been forced by violence on the part of interviewing officers. The introduction of mandatory recording of police interviews has reduced the frequency of this kind of defence plea, while also giving it more weight in some instances. It probably needs at least another productive decade of HSCED research to allow a solid consensus to be developed around the case law and evidential procedures that are necessary for this form of single case methodology.

Topics for reflection and discussion

1 What are the advantages and disadvantages of a quasi-judicial approach to analysing a rich case record? What other approaches might have been employed?

2 Under what circumstances might a researcher who is interested in establishing the efficacy of a new therapy approach, decide to use a n=1 design rather than HSCED (or vice-versa)?

3 It is not unknown for legal proceedings to go wrong, with the result that innocent people are convicted, and the guilty walk free. What might be the main sources of error in a quasi-judicial approach to case analysis? How might these errors be minimized?

4 What might it be like, as a client, to read Sceptic or Affirmative briefs that dispute your account of therapy? What would be the implications of giving the client a greater role in the adjudication process?

5 How might the analysis of the case of George have been enhanced by carrying out an interview with the therapist? What topics might be covered in such an interview?

6 How might the analysis of the case of George have been enhanced by incorporating transcripts of all or some session recordings into the rich case record? Or by interviewing his wife? What else might usefully be included in a rich case record? What are the minimum requirements for a rich case record?

Recommended further reading

Because of the recent development of the HSCED method, relatively few articles have been published on this approach. The key sources are:

Elliott, R. (2001) Hermeneutic single-case efficacy design: an overview. In K.J. Schneider, J. Bugental and J.F. Pierson (eds), *The Handbook of Humanistic Psychology: Leading Edges in Theory, Research and Practice*. Thousand Oaks, CA: Sage.

Elliott, R. (2002) Hermeneutic Single Case Efficacy Design. *Psychotherapy Research*, 12, 1–20.

A stimulating discussion of some further possibilities of quasi-judicial methods can be found in:

Miller, R.B. (2004) *Facing Human Suffering: Psychology and Psychotherapy as Moral Engagement*. Washington, DC: American Psychological Association. pp. 236–41.

Theory-building case studies

Ever since the earliest case studies published by Freud, careful analysis of the process and outcome of single cases has been used as a vehicle for developing and articulating therapy theory. The development of theory is one of the main ways in which it is possible to move, in case study research, from a focus on specific instances or cases, and more general statements that may have applicability across groups of cases or a wider population. It is not sensible to attempt to generalize from single cases on the basis of 'facts'. For example, the fact that one person diagnosed as schizophrenic achieved recovery through psychoanalytic psycho-therapy (Karon 2008a; described in Chapter 6) does not infer that other patients with the same diagnosis will necessarily also benefit from that type of therapy – for all we know, this one case may represent a unique instance. In terms of statistical generalization, all that can be claimed is that psychoanalaytic therapy *can* be effective in schizophrenia – that a good outcome may be *possible*. By contrast, a theoretical model of the process of psychotherapy with schizophrenic patients *can* readily be generalized to other cases. A theoretical model can be tested against other cases, or can inform practice in further cases. The construction of theory therefore represents an important arena within which case study research can make a major contribution to the counselling and psychotherapy literature. Theory is transferrable.

It is also important to recognize that case study methods have a number of advantages, in relation to theoretically oriented research, when compared to other methods. In a large-n extensive study, involving many research participants, only a small number of observations can be collected from each participant. In case study research, on the other hand, a large number of observations are made on one participant. What this means is that case studies are particularly effective in addressing theoretical issues that involve complex interactions between different factors.

The aim of this chapter is to provide an introduction to different ways of using case studies to build theoretical understanding. There is a brief discussion of the concept of theory, then a review of some strategies for conducting theory-building studies. The next section offers a discussion of some exemplar theory-building studies. Finally, there is a discussion of issues associated with this type of case study inquiry.

What is a theory?

In order to appreciate what might be involved in 'theory-building' case study research, it is necessary to give some attention to the concept of 'theory'. What is a theory? What are theories for? Where do theories come from?

There are at least two ways of thinking about theories. First, a theory can be understood as a system of ideas or concepts that somehow reflect or represent an aspect of the world. Usually, the set of ideas or concepts that make up a theory are organized or structured in terms of different levels of abstraction (Rapaport and Gill 1959). There are concepts that describe or categorize concrete observable events. At the other extreme are abstract concepts, that refer to underlying philosophical assumptions. Then in the middle are theoretical propositions, that describe the ways in which observable entities are connected up. The way that theories are structured can be readily illustrated by reference to a well-known theory of therapy. In psychoanalysis, for example, there are many concepts that refer to concrete observable entities, such as 'defences', 'resistance', 'countertransference' and 'interpretation'. The qualities of these entities (e.g., frequency, intensity) can be measured, for instance by counting the number of times a therapist makes an interpretation in the course of a therapy session. The main underlying, abstract philosophical concept that holds psychoanalytic theory together is the idea of the 'unconscious'. This is a concept that is hugely important for the theory, but is hard to define and impossible to measure. The middle level of psychoanalytic theory is occupied by ideas such as attachment theory, anal personality and object relations, which function to bring together webs of ideas that enable predictions to be made (e.g., a person who reports insecure attachment patterns in childhood will engage in a particular type of transference relationship with their therapist, which calls for a specific type of therapeutic strategy …). If a theory is regarded as a set of ideas, then the obvious question that arises is: are these ideas in some sense valid or *true?* Do they reflect what actually happens in the world, or not?

An alternative way of thinking about theories is to view them as socially constructed. From this perspective, a theory can be understood as functioning as a kind of language that people use when talking about certain things. Being able to speak a certain theoretical language binds people into theoretical communities, who view the world in a particular way. Being able to espouse a particular theoretical stance is part of the identity of a scientist or a practitioner. A theoretical language makes certain things happen, it brings some aspects of experience into being, and results in other aspects of experience being ignored. For example, psychoanalytic theory offers a rich language for talking about relationships, whereas cognitive-behavioural theory has a limited relationship vocabulary. An important aspect of any language is that it is always changing – the meaning of words shift, and new words are introduced. This aspect of language implies a notion of a theory not as a static set of concepts, but best seen as an evolving tradition, encompassing creative tension between different language communities within it. If a theory is regarded as a social construction, or a language, or a tradition, the obvious question that arises is: how is this language used? What effects does it have on individuals and communities to talk about things in particular ways?

This account of the concept of theory is hopelessly simplistic. Further discussion of the nature of theory in counselling and psychotherapy can be found in McLeod (2009, Chapter 3) and in additional works referenced in that source. However, this distinction between theory-as-a-structured-set-of-ideas and theory-as-language is crucially important in appreciating the theoretical role of case study research. When carrying out theory-oriented case study research, it is essential to engage with the complex set of ideas that constitute a theory, with the intention of discovering the degree of correspondence between the ideas and the case record. At the same time, it is futile to imagine that this process will generate support for the truth of a theory. This is because, for a social constructionist position (Gergen 1999), any aspect of social life can be described and understood using a multiplicity of languages or meaning systems. The implication here is that while a therapy theory such as psychoanalysis can be refined and articulated through case study inquiry, it will never be possible to use case studies to establish whether psychoanalysis is more valid or true than cognitive-behavioural theory, person-centred theory, or any other framework of ideas. There are many ways to approach the problem of determining 'truth', in the sense of accurately explaining or predicting what happens in the world. A randomized trial can be used to look at whether psychoanalysis or CBT are more effective treatments for certain disorders. Biological research can be used to determine the extent to which the idea of psychoanalysis or CBT are supported in terms of evidence about brain function. But case study research does not work like that. A case is a specific occurrence or event, and any specific event can be viewed through many lenses.

Box 9.1

The role of theory in therapy practice: postmodern epistemology

Textbooks on counselling and psychotherapy are usually organized in chapters in distinct therapy approaches, such as person-centred, psychodynamic and CBT. Research into the effectiveness of therapy similarly reifies these approaches as distinct entities, through studies of the effectiveness of specific approaches. It may appear, from these sources, that therapy practice merely involves the application of one chosen theory to a series of clients. However, a different picture emerges from studies of how counsellors and psychotherapists actually use theory on a day-to-day basis. Polkinghorne (1992) interviewed therapists about their use of theory, and found that, although theories were seen to function as useful models and metaphors that 'assist in constructing cognitive order' (p. 158), there was no sense that any theory could ever capture the complexity of human existence. These therapists were 'comfortable with the diversity of theories' (p. 158) and believed that their theoretical knowledge was necessarily 'unfinished'. Skovholt and Jennings (2004) interviewed a sample of 'master therapists' and found that, even though these practitioners identified themselves as belonging to specific 'theoretical communities', their fundamental curiosity about people led them to read widely, and to be interested in a broad range of theories of human behaviour. Polkinghorne (1992) argues that contemporary therapy is based in a *postmodern epistemology of practice*. Rather than espousing a single 'grand theory', practitioners regard theories as tools that can be used for different purposes with different clients. Therapists are open to acquiring new theoretical tools, particularly those whose relevance has been established through grounding in real-life case examples.

Where case study research comes into its own, in relation to theory, is through the activity that Stiles (2007) has characterized as theory-*building*:

> in any scientific research, observations change theories. They may confirm or disconfirm or strengthen or weaken the theory. More constructively, the changes may involve extending, elaborating, refining, modifying or qualifying the theory … observations *permeate* the theory …. Thus, a theory is not a fixed formula, but a growing and changing way of understanding. (Stiles 2007: 123)

In psychology and social science, and therefore in counselling and psychotherapy, any theory begins as a simple idea, that has emerged in a reaction to other ideas that no longer fit the prevailing cultural *zeitgeist*. At the outset, a theory typically consists of some kind of alternative metaphoric image. Gradually, over the course of time, this image becomes refined and differentiated into the type of complex structured set of propositions described above. For example, in Europe prior to Freud, 'odd' or abnormal behaviour in people was viewed in religious terms, and treated through prayer, Biblical study and so on. Freud's metaphoric starting point (not unique to him) was the image of an illness or a wound – it was as though the person had been wounded or damaged in childhood, and their current 'odd' behaviour could be viewed as residual symptoms of that event. This is a useful notion, but in itself it did not take Freud. By applying his prototype idea to his patients/case, Freud was able to flesh out the theory, in terms of the kinds of wounds that could occur in childhood, the relevance of different ages/stages at which they took place, the ways in which they are 'remembered', etc. This is what is involved in the process of *building* a theory. It is a curiosity-driven journey, a search for new understandings or new 'bits' of the theory, that can arise by asking question such as 'how well does this theory help me to understand this case?' and 'what do I need to add to/ subtract from the theory to make it fit better with this case?'.

In the field of counselling and psychotherapy, virtually all the good ideas (i.e., theoretical developments) have come from practice. There are very few examples of good ideas that have emerged from pure science, laboratory studies. What this means is that practising counsellors and psychotherapists have always used their experience with clients (their cases) as a means of thinking about theory and coming up with new ideas. Theory-building case study research is merely a way of doing this more effectively and transparently.

Basic principles of theory-building case study research

In a later part of this chapter, a series of exemplar theory-building case study investigations will be discussed. These studies make use of many different types of sources of evidence, and different forms of data analysis, including quantitative, qualitative and mixed methods. However, they all make use of a common set of theory-building principles. The key steps that are involved in theory-building research are described below.

Step 1: Develop a theoretical starting-point

Theory-building case study research always begins from somewhere. A researcher will always have some theoretical assumptions and ideas that guide his or her journey of inquiry. It does not make sense to read a case record in the hope that theory will 'emerge' from it. All that will emerge are the theoretical ideas that are in the mind of the reader. A more systematic and effective approach is to sit down, in advance of reading cases, and to work out the theoretical concepts that are being brought to the case, and that it is hoped will be clarified further through contact with the case. It may be that, at the outset, a researcher starts with a vague idea that he or she wishes to pursue. For example, the case study research conducted by Bill Stiles and his associates (described below) began with a model (the assimilation model of the change process) that was already specified in some detail on the basis of the clinical experience and reading of existing theory and research.

It is essential to do as much preparatory theory-building as possible, before starting work on a case. This process can involve several activities, such as personal reflection, reading and consulting with colleagues. In terms of assembling a 'prototype' theoretical model, it is necessary to consider different levels of conceptualization. What is the 'root metaphor' that underpins the theory? What are the specific theoretical propositions that can be formulated? What are the *observable* aspects of the theory? A valuable resource for thinking through the conceptual structure of a theory is Sloman (1978).

Each 'layer' of a theory is significant in different ways. The root metaphor (or metaphors) will usually carry a great deal of implicit meaning, that needs to be unpacked. For example, what does it mean to think about therapy as a process of 'assimilation' or as a type of storytelling? Alternatively, the root metaphor that underpins a theory may not be obvious (what assumptions about human beings lie behind the concept of 'immediacy'?). Is there metaphorical consistency throughout the theory? For example, does a notion such as 'defence mechanism' make sense within a 'storytelling' perspective on therapy? What kind of image of the person does the root metaphor evoke? Is it an image that is consistent with the values position of the researcher? When exploring these questions, it can be helpful to consider the writings of people who have studied the role of metaphor in meaning-making, such as Pepper (1970) and Lakoff and Johnson (1980, 1999).

The 'middle' layer of theory is concerned with 'if–then' propositions, that reflect possible causal connections between factors '*if* the client is able to become aware of the emotion associated with issue, *then* they are ready to give it a name ...', '*if* the person tells a vivid story about a specific problematic event in their life, *then* the therapist is able to make an appropriate intervention ...'. In thinking about theoretical propositions, it can be useful to make a visual map or flow-diagrams of a theory, with arrows indicating possible direction of influence. This kind of preparatory analysis alerts the researcher to possible sequences of events in the case.

'Observable' concepts are particularly significant for theory-building case research, because it is these 'observables' that comprise the 'points of contact' between the theory and the case (Stiles 2007). They constitute the researcher's answer to two questions that are central to the whole endeavour: *'what do I expect to see in the case?'* and *'where in the case would I expect to find theoretically relevant information? (i.e., where should I look?)'*. For example, the assimilation model (Stiles 2002) suggests that certain types of assimilative processing should be observable in the way that a client talks about specific topics throughout the course of therapy.

Wherever possible, the outcome of the process of formulating a preliminary or 'starting point' theoretical position should be written down as a formal statement. This makes it easier to check, at later stages, the extent to which ideas that arise in the analysis of the case may correspond to the concepts in the theoretical statement. It also has an additional benefit in allowing the researcher or research team to 'externalize' the theory, and leave it to one side, as they engage with what the case itself has to say to them.

Step 2: Selection of a case

The choice of case to analyse may be influenced by the aims of the theory-building projects. For example, at the beginning of a series of case studies exploring the process of immediacy in therapy, Kasper et al. (2008) intentionally selected a case in which the therapist was known to favour the use of immediacy, so that they would be sure to have many examples of relevant therapy events with which they could work. For their next case study, Hill et al. (2008) then chose a case that was expected to have a more routine level of immediacy, as a way of testing the general applicability of the model that had been generated from the first case.

Step 3: Construction of a rich case record

The case record should include data that are relevant to the theory, and if possible should include different data sources that can be triangulated to provide a more reliable interpretation of the frequency and quality of factors derived from the theory. A wide range of data collection sources were employed in the exemplar theory-building case studies that are described later in this chapter.

Step 4: Immersion in the case

Theory-building case study research is *discovery-oriented*. The purpose of this kind of study is not to demonstrate that the author is able to apply a particular theory in interpreting a case (which is what is typically expected from case studies written by students and trainees during training programmes), but to push back the edges of the theory, to find the limitations of the theory and suggest ways in which it might be more fully articulated. The goal of demonstrating that a specific theoretical approach to therapy can be applied effectively to certain disorders, is the task of other genres of case study inquiry, such as pragmatic case studies, n=1 single subject studies and HSCED (see earlier chapters). A theory-building case study that merely confirms what is already known is not very interesting.

The requirement to adopt a discovery-oriented stance can be challenging for therapy researchers who are also practitioners. Becoming a therapist may involve years of professional socialization into the language and assumptions of a theoretical approach, and the development of relationships with members of a theoretical community. It can be hard to set aside these ingrained ways of thinking and seeing, and approach a case with an open mind. This is why a period of disciplined immersion in a case is essential. Before attempting to carry out any formal analysis of a case, the researcher or research team should do everything possible to engage imaginatively and emotionally with the material. Useful strategies include repeated reading of the material, reading it from different perspectives (client, therapist) and re-reading after some time has elapsed. It can be helpful to make notes on initial responses to the material – intuitive insights that may be lost when more formal analysis of the case record is undertaken. Flybjerg (2006: 235) suggests that:

> researchers who have conducted intensive, in-depth case studies typically report that their preconceived views, assumptions, concepts, and hypotheses were wrong and that the case material has compelled them to revise their hypotheses on essential points.

The purpose of immersion in the data is allow a sufficient degree of *intensity* to occur, that will allow 'preconceived views' to dissolve.

Step 5: Applying the theory to the case

The next stage of a theory-building case study is to analyse the case in terms of the theory. This can be a qualitative, interpretive process, arising from careful reading of the case. Alternatively, it can be a structured or quantitative process, that makes use of rating scales or coding schemes. Analysing a case can involve a combination of qualitative and quantitative methods. Examples of ways in which theory-building case study researchers have conducted theoretical analyses of cases are provided later in this chapter.

Step 6: Identifying gaps in the theory: applying the case to the theory

Once the case has been analysed, the next stage is to turn this process around, and analyse the theory from the perspective of the case. Stiles (2007: 125) described this activity as 'turning the observations back on the theory in order to improve it'. Here, the researcher is asking questions such as 'does the theory do justice to the complexity of the case?', 'what are the segments or aspects of the case around which the theory has nothing to say?' or 'at what points did I feel frustrated or confused when I was using the theory to code or analyse the case?'. At this point, a theory-building case study project can be viewed as having some similarity to a crime mystery. The detective in a crime novel is presented at the scene of the crime, and then later in interviews with witnesses, with a great deal of information. But there is something missing. A good theory-building case study researcher, like a good detective, needs to be able to go 'beyond the information given', and have a sense not only of what might be missing, but how to go about searching for it.

Step 7: Refining the theory

Once the gap or gaps in a theory have been identified, in relation to a specific case, it is necessary to propose some kind of amendment to the theory that will allow the discrepant information to be taken into account. This process was described by the pragmatist philosopher Charles Sander Peirce as 'abduction' (Peirce 1965; Rennie 2001). Abduction is the logical activity of changing a category or theory, to make it fit some new observations. The new version of the theory needs to be able to make sense of the new observations while still making sense of the past observations upon which it was built. Abduction is a logical process that is different from deduction (deriving a statement a set of premises) or induction (collecting a set of observations that imply the same conclusion). In contrast to deduction or induction, there is always an element of creative thinking involved in abduction.

It is important to note that the authors of theory-building case studies, such as those described in the following sections of this chapter, typically provide little information (or none at all) on how they handled stages 6 (identifying gaps) and 7 (refining the theory). This is frustrating for new researchers, but also understandable. There is no easy formula or protocol to guide a theory-building case study researcher through these stages. Instead, there needs to be a willingness to submit to an emergent, creative process that is familiar to all experienced researchers, but which few choose to write about. Suggestions for how this process might be facilitated can be found in Braud and Anderson (1998) and Moustakas (1990).

Step 8: Testing the revised version of the theory against further cases

As with other types of research, the findings of any one study need to be confirmed by results from other investigations. The metaphor of theory-*building* implies a multi-case approach. Each case study represents a window that gives a new view, a door that enters into a new area, a new room that encloses an array of theoretical furniture, or even a new floor or wing of the building. Good theory-building case study research is best regarded as programmatic – it is only when two or more case analyses are completed that the hard-won insights from each study begin to add up to anything substantial. The big gain in impact, in this kind of work, comes when cases start to be published by researchers and groups outside the initial circle. There are many examples in counselling and psychotherapy theory-building research, where tightly knit groups of like-minded investigators have been highly productive in terms of generating new ideas, and making these ideas work within their own practice. When other researchers begin to be involved, the conceptual framework may collapse, or fragment off into splinter theories. At this point, the key factor seems to be the strength and generativity of the root metaphor and philosophical ideas that underpin the theory. Clearly, the root metaphors that provide the foundation for psychoanalytic therapy have been able to sustain at least three generations of case study inquiry.

These eight steps or stages provide an outline of the general principles of theory-building case study research and inquiry. In the next part of the chapter, a set of exemplar case studies is used to illustrate the ways in which groups of researchers have overcome the substantial methodological challenges associated with putting these principles into practice. These exemplar studies are grouped in accordance with the evidence sources and methodological strategies that they have employed: *therapy transcripts, therapist notes, mixed methods, ethnography, therapist process notes* and *comparison of good- and poor-outcome cases.*

Therapy transcript studies

It is possible to carry out theoretically interesting case study research on the basis of therapy transcripts data. This source of information is attractive for many practitioner-researchers because it involves a minimal level of intrusion on the normal process of therapy.

Refining a theory of assimilation of problematic experience (Brinegar et al. 2006)

The *assimilation model*, developed by Bill Stiles and his colleagues, represents a transtheoretical or integrative framework for understanding the process of change in counselling and psychotherapy. The model suggests that one of the central tasks of any form of therapy is to help the client to come to terms with problematic life experiences. With the help of a therapist, a problematic experience that has previously been too painful to think about or face up to gradually becomes allowed into awareness, named, understood and mastered. An overview of the stages that occur within this process is provided in Table 9.1. The model also suggests that important aspects of personal experience, whether problematic or otherwise, are expressed as 'voices', which are apparent within a person's way of talking. From this perspective, a problematic experience can be observed as a silenced or quiet voice, that tends to be drowned out by the dominant voices within a 'community of voices' that are used by the person. Further information about the assimilation model can be found in two review articles (Stiles et al. 2002) and in studies listed on the home page of Bill Stiles (www.users.muohio.edu/stileswb/).

The development of the assimilation model has been of particular significance for the field of theory-building case study research, because it has intentionally deployed a strategy of using analysis of case studies as a means of refining the theoretical model (Honos–Webb et al. 1998, 1999, 2006; Stiles et al. 1991, 1992; Stiles 2005). A number of alterations

Table 9.1   Stages in the assimilation of a problematic experience in counselling

0   *Warded off.* Client is unaware of the problem; the problematic voice is silent or dissociated. Affect may be minimal, reflecting successful avoidance

1   *Unwanted thoughts.* Client prefers not to think about the experience; topics are raised by therapist or external circumstances. Affect involves strong but unfocused negative feelings; their connection with the content may be unclear. Problematic voices emerge in response to therapist interventions or external circumstances and are suppressed or avoided

2   *Vague awareness.* Client is aware of a problematic experience but cannot formulate the problem clearly. Affect includes acute psychological pain or panic associated with the problematic experience. Problematic voice emerges into sustained awareness

3   *Problem statement/clarification.* Content includes a clear statement of the problem – something that could be or is being worked on. Opposing voices are differentiated and can talk about each other. Affect is negative but manageable, not panicky

4   *Understanding/insight.* The problematic experience is formulated and understood in some way. Voices reach an understanding with each other (a meaning bridge). Affect may be mixed, with some unpleasant recognitions but also some pleasant surprise of the 'aha' sort

5   *Application/working through.* The understanding is used to work on a problem. Voices work together to address problems of living. Affective tone is positive, business-like, optimistic

6   *Problem solution.* Client achieves a successful solution for a specific problem. Voices can be used flexibly. Affect is positive, satisfied, proud of accomplishment

7   *Mastery.* Client automatically generalizes solutions. Voices are fully integrated, serving as resources in new situations. Affect is positive or neutral (i.e., this is no longer something to get excited about)

Source: Stiles et al. (2002)

to the model have been made over the past 20 years as a result of case study analyses. A particularly clear example of the way that the assimilation model team have made use of case study material can be found in a study by Brinegar et al. (2006).

The Brinegar et al. (2006) study reports on two linked case studies that were used to explore a particular aspect of the assimilation model. Each of the studies was drawn from a large-scale York University (Toronto, Canada) comparison of the effectiveness of client-centred therapy and process-experiential therapy for depression. The two cases that were selected were from good-outcome therapies, in which the clients (Margaret and Lisa) reported Beck Depression Inventory scores indicating that they had essentially recovered from depression by the end of 16 or 17 sessions of therapy. Although these clients had taken part in a research study in which they had been interviewed at various points, and completed outcome measures, these data were not used in the Brinegar et al. (2006) study, other than to identify the clients as having had good outcomes. For the purpose of the case analyses, only transcripts of session recordings were used. The aim of the study was to look at what happens in therapy to facilitate movement between stage 3 (problem statement) and stage 4 (understanding and insight) and to develop a more detailed version of the assimilation model, that specified sub-stages between 3 and 4. The Margaret and Lisa cases were chosen for analysis because both clients had passed through stages 3 and 4 of the assimilation process, and the cases were known to include particularly rich data around this phase of therapy. The Margaret case was analysed first, and was used to generate a new model of sub-stages between 3 and 4. The Lisa case was then analysed as a means of checking the validity of the new model in the context of a different case.

In the Brinegar et al. (2006) study, the primary analysis of the case material was carried out by two postgraduate clinical psychology students, Meredith Glick Brinegar and Lisa M. Salvi, with Bill Stiles acting as auditor of their analyses. The analytic procedure in the Margaret case consisted of:

1 *Familiarization and cataloguing.* The researchers immersed themselves in the case by reading the transcript a number of times. They then derived a sequential list of the topics that Margaret had explored in therapy: 'each entry in the catalogue was a restatement or summary of a *client thought unit* (defined as saying something distinct from the previous thought unit). These entries were indexed by session and line number to make it easier to find passages of interest in later stages of the research.' (p. 168)

2 *Identifying problematic and dominant voices.* The researchers (by now very familiar with the case material) reflected on the ways in which the client expressed herself when discussing topics, and identified the different 'voices' that she appeared to be using, and the ways that voices inter-acted with each other.

3 *Excerpting passages.* The researchers went back to the catalogue that they had assembled at Step 1, and located passages of the transcript where the different voices could be detected. This procedure resulted in a set of transcript passages where Voice A was apparent, a set where Voice B was apparent, etc.

4 *Describing the process of assimilation represented across the sequence of passages.* The Assimilation of Problematic Experiences Scale (APES; available at www.users.Muohio.edu/stileswb/) is a set of guidelines for rating the level of assimilation represented by passages of therapy discourse. Each of the passages selected in step 3 was assigned an APES rating. The passages that occurred in the therapy during the stages 3–4 transition were exam-ined particularly closely, to determine whether any sub-stages could be identified.

At each of these steps, the two main researchers carried out research tasks independently, then met to discuss what they had found. Once they had come to an agreement over their conclusions at each step, the auditor (who was also deeply familiar with the material) read and commented on their analyses. The three members of the research team continued their discussion of findings at each step in the analysis until consensus was achieved. At some steps in the process quite striking differences emerged and needed to be resolved. For example, at step 3 of the analysis, one of the researchers identified 58 relevant passages, while the other identified 13.

In summary, the process of analysis of the Margaret case started with immersion in the data, and a preliminary cataloguing of the topics that the client had explored in therapy. Then, a key concept from the theory (the idea of voices) was applied to the material, and different voices were identified. Third, a further key concept from the theory (the characteristics of different stages in the assimilation process) was applied to the case. This allowed a segment of the case material to be identified (i.e., what happened between the first signs of stage 3 assimilation, and the first signs of stage 4). At this point, the 'case was applied to the theory'. In other words, the theory had nothing to say about what happens between Stages 3 and 4. The researchers than 'abducted' some new theoretical ideas, in the form of a set of sub-stages. This whole process provides a clear example of how systematic theory-building case research can be carried out. 'Observable' aspects of the theory are used to divide up the enormous complexity of the case into manageable chunks. Some of these chunks are accepted as either making sufficient theoretical sense, or not, of particular theoretical interest. This then allows a further focusing of the inquiry – the team have now identified a relatively limited set of chunks of data that are not adequately theorized. They then are able to reflect on how the theory needs to be developed further in order to make sense of these sections of the case.

What did Brinegar et al. (2006) come up with? The client, Margaret, was 58 years of age, with depression that was primarily associated with a breakdown in her relationship, along with additional concerns around her adult children leaving home, and caring for her elderly parents. The three dominant voices in Margaret's way of talking about herself were *caretaker, care for me* and *self-doubt.* The *caretaker* voice was dominant in Margaret's life. She took care of other people, by giving them love, cooking meals and looking after their needs. The *care for me* voice represented a silenced part of Margaret. It was problematic for Margaret to express her needs. She was tired of taking care of others, and wanted something back for herself. However, she had suppressed this part of herself for many years. The *self-doubt* voice represented a self-critical part of Margaret, which questioned her capacity to make the right decisions. This final voice was not involved in the analysis of the stage 3–4 assimilation sub-stages.

As early as session 1 of the therapy, the *caretaker* and *care for me* voices were apparent in much of Margaret's speech. In the following excerpt from session 1, the dominant *caretaker* voice is in bold, and the emerging *care for me* voice is in italics:

> **You know, my husband is a very nice person.**
> **He's a very easygoing person you know.**
> *But, I mean he's wrapped up in his job,*
> *and its just that I – I know I don't understand it enough you know.*
> Like I just sort of feel like
> 'Hey, I've been giving, giving, giving to kids and the
> husband for 30 odd years,
> when is it going to be my turn?'

This segment of transcript was rated as late APES stage 2, on the point of entering stage 3 – the opposing voices are differentiated and are almost beginning to be able to talk about each other.

The analysis of therapy segments/excerpts that were rated by the research team as APES stage 3, yielded four sub-stages:

Rapid cross-fire: each voice was fighting for possession of the floor.
Entitlement: the *care for me* voice appeared to feel entitled to speak, and was given more space by the dominant voice.
Respect and attention: the dominant voice began to listen to the needy voice.
Joint search for understanding: the voices began to work together to achieve a mutual understanding.

For reasons of space, it is not possible here to give examples of segments of therapy discourse from each of these stages. The flavour of the *rapid cross-fire* sub-stage is captured in the following excerpt from session 3:

Margaret: **When you've been from my generation,** [*Therapist*: 'Mm-hm.'] **you know that you've always got your husband's supper. It's very difficult to change, like to say, like, '***get your own***' [slight laugh], you know. And, but, I know that he doesn't expect it, because he has said 'If I [come home late?] that's my problem, and if you're in the middle of something . . .',** because *for a long time, if I was in the middle of*

> *something, I did resent it. I felt, well, I had my dinner. He's – he's the one who's ruined the routine, not me. Why should I stop what I'm doing?*
>
> Therapist: Right.
>
> Margaret: **But I still felt I should do it.** [laughs] **Because this is my generation, you know. And, um,** *but I resented doing it.* **So, I kind of, I'm sort of resolving that as I go along.** (p. 170)

A quite different pattern of interaction between the voices can be observed in session 10, in this example of what happened during the *joint search for understanding* sub-stage:

> Margaret: *I just nagged him! I was actually looking for things to nag him about.*
>
> Therapist: Mm-hm.
>
> Margaret: *And I thought, why am I like this? I know I'm contributing to this, sort of, I guess maybe he just gets tired of listening to me and shuts me out . . .* [lines 458–465]
>
> Therapist: And yet, and there are probably things *he's* doing to contribute to the way they are now, but you're saying but there are also things *I* do.
>
> Margaret: **Mm-hm** . . . [lines 473–477] **he was trying to help me you know** . . . [lines 596–597] *it's almost like verbal abuse that I was giving him, and I feel bad* [pause] *but I do it and I can't stop myself . . .* [lines 617–619] **I think sometimes he shuts me out because I'm sure it's very painful for him too, you know.** *Maybe this is just his way of coping, he just shuts me out. And then, of course, I become more frustrated.* (p. 173)

Session 11 of Margaret's therapy was highly meaningful for her. While talking about a family incident that had occurred some years previously, she had a moment of insight in which she realized that she had pushed her husband away when he had tried to help her, and that this event had marked the beginning of their troubles. This memory formed a 'meaning bridge' that allowed the two voices to arrive at a shared understanding of Margaret's marital difficulties and depression in which both voices acknowledged the part they had played: the dominant *caretaker* had refused to be helped, while the weak *care for me* side had failed to speak up for what she needed. This moment of insight was hugely important for Margaret because it made it clear for her what she needed to do differently in her life. From that point on in the therapy the *care for me* voice was able to join the community of voices as an equal member, and Margaret was able to resolve issues in her life in a way that fully acknowledged these two sides of her being. In being able to move on, she became less depressed.

The Brinegar et al. (2006) paper also includes a further confirmatory analysis of an additional case (Lisa) which involves applying the new sub-stage model to that case transcript. The sub-stages were found in the Lisa case record, but not always in the predicted sequence. Brinegar et al. (2006) discuss some possible explanations for this out-of-sequence finding, which would need to be resolved by examining additional cases.

Close attention has been devoted to the Brinegar et al. (2006) study, because it provides an exceptional example of the process of theory-building case study research. The paper is written in such a way that the reader can be clear about what the researchers were trying to achieve, what they did and what they found. Detailed examples from the therapy transcript are used to substantiate 'observable' constructs such as voices and sub-stage discourse patterns. It is of interest to reflect on how the Brinegar et al. (2006) paper is constructed. It is not written as a 'mystery' in which the reader does not learn the answer until the end. Instead, the new sub-stage model generated by the study is presented at the start of the paper, and the remainder of the article is devoted to explaining how this new theoretical formulation was developed. This way of writing the paper has two effects. First, by 'headlining' the ultimate results of the study, readers can quickly learn the message of the study, and are in a position to decide whether they wish to, or need to, work through the detailed account that follows. This is kinder to readers than holding back the 'news' until the end, and taking the risk that readers will be disappointed ('I have worked my way through 6,000 words of this stuff, and is that all it adds up to ... !?'). Second, it allows the authors to create a collaborative relationship with readers, who at several points in the paper are invited by the authors to reflect together on the possible meaning of the study in relation to theory and practice. The paper therefore represents not only a valuable example of how to carry out this kind of research, but of how to write it up.

Other transcript-based theory-building approaches

Other examples can be described of theory-building case studies that have used therapy transcript material as the basis for analysis. Paul Lysaker has developed a theory of psychotherapy for people diagnosed with schizophrenia (Lysaker et al. 2001; Lysaker and Lysaker 2002). The central idea in this theory is that people with schizophrenia have great difficulty in telling the story of their lives. The implication for therapy is the suggestion that what may be particularly helpful is to provide assistance to the person in developing an ability to tell more coherent stories. This theoretical approach to schizophrenia has been developed through a programme of research and theory-building that has included the use of case studies to examine specific aspects of the model (Lysaker et al. 2005, 2007a,b). These case studies have been based on analysis of transcripts of audio recordings of therapy sessions over the course of long-term psychotherapy for schizophrenic clients. Lysaker and his colleagues developed two rating scale instruments for assessing different aspects of the process and content of storytelling during therapy sessions. The *Narrative Coherence Rating Scale* (NCRS) assesses the extent to which the client's way of talking about events in their life contains sufficient details, temporal conceptual connections and plausibility for someone else to understand the stories being told. The *Scale to Assess Narrative Development* (STAND) evaluates the prevalence in the narrative of certain key content themes: illness, agency, self-worth and social connection. The assumption behind NCRS is that the stories told by schizophrenic clients will be low in coherence at the outset of therapy, and will gradually become more coherent. The assumption behind STAND is that over the course of successful therapy, clients will be less likely to characterize themselves as 'ill', and more likely to describe themselves in terms of themes of agency, self-worth and involvement in society and relationships. The NCRS and STAND are administered by independent raters who read a transcript and make judgements on the level of each factor (detail, temporal connect, plausibility, etc.), based on criteria laid down in a scoring manual. The level of agreement between rates is assessed using a statistical calculation of inter-rater reliability. The two sets of ratings are then either averaged (if the level inter-rater agreement is sufficiently high) or there is further discussion until an acceptable level of agreement can be achieved.

A further example of the use of therapy transcripts as a vehicle of theory-building case study research is my own work on narrative aspects of the process of therapy. This research has employed an approach to transcript analysis that is based solely on qualitative methods, and has produced four case studies (Grafanaki and McLeod 1999; McLeod and Lynch 2000; McLeod and Balamoutsou 1996, 2000) and a number of theoretical papers (McLeod 1999, 2002, 2004 a,b, 2005). This research started with a vague theoretical notion that the way the client told his or her life-story, and the way the therapist responded to this story, was important in therapy. The case studies, and theoretical reflections associated with them, were driven by a need to develop a conceptual framework that would let me understand this kind of process in therapy. In relation to the current chapter, the most significant aspect of this body of work was the attempt to devise a method for qualitative narrative analysis of therapy transcripts (McLeod and Balamoutsou 2001). As a researcher with a strong commitment to a grounded theory approach to theory-building (Charmaz 2006; Corbin and Struass 2008), in which concepts emerge from immersion in the data, rather than being derived from theoretical speculation and then imposed on data, I was eager to remain as open as possible to what the case might disclose to me. At the same time, I appreciated that I needed to find some way of handling the massive amount of information that was present in a therapy transcript. What evolved was a set of strategies for segmenting the text into manageable chunks, and then using word processing functions (e.g., cut and paste) to configure the remaining material in ways that made it more interpretable (McLeod and Balamoutsou 2001). Segmenting the text was guided by some tentative theoretical ideas (e.g., the story the client tells at the start of therapy must be important, so look closely at the first 5 minutes of the first session). There were two techniques that we devised for reconfiguring the text. The first of these was to transform key parts of the text from standard transcript sentences and paragraphs, to a poetic 'stanza' format, that presented the text in a way that captured the rhythm of the spoken word. This technique had originally been used by Gee (1991). We found that the meaning and structure of 'event' stories (when the client was talking about something specific that had happened) were much easier to see if the text was arranged in stanza form. The second strategy was to separate out client statements and therapist statements, into separate files. This is a fairly brutal way to approach the analysis of conversation, because it destroys the moment-by-moment co-constructed nature of talk (as many critics have pointed out to us). However, it is also hugely illuminating in terms of (a) being able to follow the unfolding story told by the client; and (b) being able to identify the therapist 'metanarrative' that is fed into the conversation in the form of brief responses to what the client has said. There is not space within this chapter to provide details of how these techniques can be used. The point is that there exist ways of dismantling and displaying qualitative texts so that it becomes possible to carry out theory-oriented micro-analysis on relevant, but manageable segments. Miles and Huberman (1994) offer many further suggestions around how this can be accomplished. A reviews of techniques for analysing therapy transcript data can be found in Riding and Lepper (2005).

Box 9.2

Access to case transcripts for research purposes

The case of Amalia X has become one of the most widely known psychoanalytic cases in recent years. Amalia X was a patient in psychoanalysis who allowed her therapy to be audio recorded, transcribed, and placed in the *Ulm Textbank*, a resource centre for psychotherapy researchers that is based at the University of Ulm in Germany (Mergenthaler 1991). This case has been analysed in different ways by many psychotherapy researchers (Kachele et al. 2006, 2008), and has become the modern-day equivalent of Freud's Dora and Wolfman cases. It may not entirely be a coincidence that Amalia was the name of Freud's mother. There are extensive English-language collections of psychoanalytic and psychodynamic cases at the Penn Institute in the USA (Luborsky et al. 2001) and elsewhere (Mergenthaler 1993). Cases from the York University, Toronto, research into client-centred and experiential therapies have also been made available to researchers from other centres (Angus et al. 2008). A commercially – developed archive of case transcripts has been assembled by the Alexander Street Press (www. alexanderstreet.com). Access to cases that have already been transcribed can be invaluable for theory-building case study researchers. There is also considerable value in analysing a case from different perspectives, as a means of demonstrating convergence and divergence between alternative theoretical approaches.

Theory-building research using therapist notes

The strong recommendation throughout this book is that case studies that rely solely on data from therapist notes are subject to many sources of potential bias, and that if at all possible, it is best to try to assemble a rich case record that includes different kinds of information that are available to independent external scrutiny. However, there are many theoretically interesting case studies that have been published on the basis of evidence from therapist notes. For example, several of the studies published in *Pragmatic Case Studies in Psychotherapy*, such as Karon (2008a), have been based on notes. The use of therapist notes is particularly widely used within the psychoanalytic community. Tuckett (2000: 1067) has written that, in his view:

> careful records of the treatment process or of critical moments in the treatment, kept by psychoanalysts in whatever form best suits their style, are a major source of new ideas and techniques in psychoanalysis.

A good example of disciplined and systematic use of therapist notes in theory-building case study research can be found in the work of the Finnish psychoanalyst Matti Keinanen, who has published a series of case studies in the role of therapy in facilitating the development of a capacity for reflective symbolization of bodily experience in young clients suffering from borderline personality disorder (Keinanen 2006). These cases are convincing because the theory is explained in sufficient detail to allow the reader to evaluate the links between data and theory, the case record includes carefully described examples of specific process events in the therapy and a series of full case studies is used to provide multiple points of contact between observation and theory. Further discussion of the use of therapist notes in systematic case study research can be found in Edelson (1985) and Wallerstein (2009).

Mixed-method theory-building case research

Using a single source of information on a case, such as a set of session transcripts, has the advantage of simplifying the kind of analysis that can be carried out – a transcript can either be coded or interpreted. However, a single source inevitably has limitations. For example, it is very hard, on the basis of a transcript, to know what a client's intentions might have been when he or she said something, or to know whether he or she thought that a particular therapy event was helpful or hindering. As a result, some theory-oriented therapy case study researchers have followed the lead of Elliott (2001, 2002; see Chapter 8) of seeking to assemble a rich case record. In this section of the present chapter, two examples of this approach are discussed.

The role of immediacy in therapy process and outcome (Hill et al. 2008; Kasper, et al. 2008)

The work of Clara Hill and her colleagues at the University of Maryland represents a sustained and highly influential body of research into the process of counselling and psychotherapy, with a primary focus on developing models and principles that can be used to inform training and practice. This programme of research has included a number of notable case study investigations (e.g., Hill 1989; Hill et al. 1983), most recently involving an exploration of the role of immediacy in therapy.

Papers by Kasper et al. (2008) and Hill et al. (2008) present two linked single case studies that aim to develop an understanding of immediacy, defined as 'disclosures within the therapy session of how the therapist is feeling about the client, him- or herself in relation to the client, or about the therapy relationship' (Kasper et al. 2008: 281). Although the first of these papers (Kasper et al. 2008) discussed various ways of understanding this process, drawn from interpersonal theory, psychoanalysis and models of the therapeutic alliance, the investigation did not propose an explicit 'starting-point' theoretical formulation. Instead, the aim was to provide an exploratory mapping of the construct ('we know very little about how much immediacy is used, what types of immediacy are used, and the effects of immediacy; p. 283). In both studies, clients were recruited to take part in a research study, and therapists were chosen who were known to use immediacy interventions, albeit in different ways. A package of outcome and process measures was employed in each study, in order to track change and also to be able to compare client data to wider normative samples. The outcome measures were: *Outcome Questionnaire* (OQ; 45-item symptomatology measure); *Inventory of Interpersonal Problems* (IIP; 32-item measure of relationship problems); *Self-Understanding of Interpersonal Patterns-Revised* (SUIP-R; 28-item measure of client's awareness of relationship patterns). Outcome measures were completed before the start of therapy, at termination and at follow-up. The standardised process measures used in the project were: *Depth Scale of the Session Evaluation Questionnaire* (SEQ-D; 5-item, bipolar, adjective–anchored, self-report measure of client and therapist perceptions of the quality of therapy); *Working Alliance Inventory – Short Form* (WAI-S; 12-item measure of client and therapist perceptions of the therapeutic relationship). In addition, two further process measures were developed for use in the study: *Client Recall Questionnaire* (CRQ; client rating of how much the immediate relationship was discussed during the session, and how useful this was); *Therapist Process Note* (TPN; therapist perceptions of immediacy and reactions of the client). Process scales were completed immediately following each therapy session. All sessions were audio recorded and transcribed, and judges rated the transcript data for categories of therapist immediacy (the *Speaking Turns Immediacy Measure*) and *Client Involvement*. End of therapy interviews were held with clients and therapists. Clients gave ethical consent for their data to be used in publications.

The client in the Kasper et al. (2008) was Lily, a 24-year-old postgraduate student who entered therapy to work on her troubled relationships with men. Her therapist was Dr N, a 51-year-old male interpersonal therapist with 20 years of clinical experience. Therapy consisted of 12 weekly sessions. A team of five researchers was involved in analysing the data. The pattern that emerged in this case, in relation to quantitative process measures, was that Dr N used immediacy in about 30% of the statements he made (a very high proportion). This mainly took the form of inquiring about the relationship between Lily and himself. When Dr N used immediacy, Lily tended to respond with some kind of statement of her own immediate thoughts and feelings. However, she rarely initiated statements about 'here and now' immediate processes. Dr N's use of immediacy tended to have the effect of reducing Lily's involvement in the therapy (comparison of levels of involvement before and after immediacy statements).

Qualitative analysis of the transcripts was used to identify and categorize 33 distinct 'immediacy events'. The most common types of immediacy event were *drawing parallels between external and therapy relationships*, and *encouraging expression of immediate feelings*. The Kasper et al. (2008) article includes detailed descriptions of these events, including analysis of Lily's responses to them. Overall, it appeared that:

> Lily had mixed reactions to Dr N's immediacy. On the one hand, immediacy helped her open up, express feelings that she did not usually allow herself, feel closer to Dr N, feel cared for, and satisfied with the session. On the other hand, immediacy sometimes made her feel pressured to respond, awkward, vulnerable, challenged, and hurt. (p. 291)

The outcome data showed that Lily got worse over the course of therapy in terms of symptoms and interpersonal functioning, but became more aware of her patterns of relating to others. These quantitative findings are consistent with Lily's own appraisal of the therapy. In the final therapy session, Dr N asked Lily what she had gained from therapy. She replied:

> I think the biggest thing is just the self-awareness aspect. That, to me, is the hugest thing 'cause that's something, like I said, I never used to engage in. I just acted upon whim and you know on emotion. Whereas now like I try to, while I still feel the emotion, I try to stop myself and think about that emotion and analyse that emotion, and figure out why am I feeling this? ... Probably that it's okay to be more open with people. I mean just the times that I did kind of open up to you and the way you reacted I think definitely encouraged me to look at myself in a very different perspective and see that you know like maybe other people don't see me the way I always think they do and that maybe I have a lot more to offer than I realize. (p. 293)

Kasper et al. (2008) concluded that immediacy had mixed effects in the case of Lily and Dr N. On the one hand, it helped the client to develop self-awareness around how she related to others. On the other hand, it did not appear to have been possible for the client to translate this awareness into action in terms of on-going difficulties in actual relationships. At the end of the paper, Kasper et al. (2008) identified what they had learned from this case, in respect of formulating a framework for the use of immediacy in therapy:

- more than 12 sessions may be necessary when immediacy is used with a highly defended client;
- it may be helpful to educate clients about the role of immediacy;
- it may be helpful for therapists to assist clients to process the meaning of intense here-and-now events;
- gender and cultural differences are likely to effect the way that therapist immediacy is interpreted by a client;
- therapists who use immediacy should be aware of their countertransference reactions to clients and ensure that they are using immediacy in response to client needs rather than for their own needs … [and] … engage in regular supervision to help manage the complex dynamics of countertransference that result from such intense immediacy focused work. (p. 296)

The paper concludes by suggesting that it is important to test these conclusions in further case studies.

The case of Jo, a 29-year-old black lesbian woman, and Dr W, a 55-year-old white interpersonal therapist, was the arena in which this emerging model of immediacy was then explored in more depth (Hill et al. 2008). For reasons of space, it is not possible to report on the case of Jo in any detail. However, this therapy (17 sessions over 8 months) was clearly a good-outcome case, in terms of outcome measures and follow-up interviews with the client. The methods used in the Hill et al. (2008) study were a modification of the approach taken in the previous study by Kasper et al. (2008). Although the same quantitative measures were employed, there was a much greater emphasis on intensive qualitative analysis of specific immediacy events. A quite different pattern of immediacy was found in this case. Dr W used immediacy only 12% of the time. Also, whereas Dr N had frequently used immediacy to draw parallels between external relationships and the here-and-now therapy relationship, Dr W used this form of immediacy with only relatively few of his responses to Jo. The role of immediacy, in therapy with Dr W, was about inviting collaboration, and offering affirmation and caring. Some of the key findings from this study were:

- immediacy can allow the therapist and client to negotiate their relationship and establish the rules for their interactions;
- expression of real caring for a client can enable the client to express immediate genuine positive feelings about the therapist (but not negative feelings);
- therapist immediacy can encourage a client to open up and explore shame-based personal topics;
- therapist immediacy can provide a client with a 'corrective relational experience (defined as coming to understand or experience relationships in a different and unexpected way);
- immediacy can be helpful in resolving ruptures or breakdowns in the therapeutic relationship;
- immediacy can be useful at the end of therapy, to help the client to look back, look forward, and say goodbye.

Overall, this case study specified a highly positive, empowering role for immediacy in therapy.

By mapping out a range of different types of therapist immediacy, and examining their effects on clients, these two case studies from Clara Hill's research group provide the foundations for a theory of immediacy. These studies demonstrate the way in which qualitative and quantitative data can be combined in the analysis of complex events in therapy. They also show how a team of researchers can collaborate around the tasks of data collection and analysis, and theory-building. Finally, these case studies emphasize the importance of careful case selection. Because the therapists in these two cases were committed to the use of immediacy, the cases yielded plenty of rich data to be analysed. Because they used immediacy in different ways, the theoretical yield from each study was substantial.

Developing a theory of how clients test their therapists (Silberschatz and Curtis 1993)

Another example of a mixed-method approach to theory-building case study research can be found in Silberschatz and Curtis (1993). For reasons of space, it is not possible to examine this study in detail. However, the study is methodologically important, in terms of illustrating the use of a case study approach to explore a theoretical issue that would be extremely difficult to investigate using any other kind of method. The study was carried out as part of a programme of research at the Mount Zion Psychotherapy Research Group in San Francisco. The aim of this pro-gramme has been to develop a deeper understanding of a psychoanalytic idea known as *control-mastery theory*. This theory suggests that people enter therapy because they are troubled by traumatic experiences in childhood that have resulted in 'pathogenic beliefs', and that they use therapy to test out the continued validity of these beliefs in the context of their relationship with their therapist. If the therapist passes the test (i.e., does not behave in a way that reinforces the belief), the client will gradually come to relinquish the belief, and move forward into a more mature way of relating to others, based on current realities rather than buried memories. The methodologically challenging aspect of this theory is that each client possesses their own unique belief/test pattern. It is therefore only possible to investigate this phenomenon by taking the time and trouble to asses each client individually, in terms of categories of interaction pattern that they might be expected to exhibit in their relationship with their therapist.

The study by Silberschatz and Curtis (1993) consists of two case analyses. Pre-therapy assessment interviews were used to derive case formulations for each client, which specified their pathogenic beliefs, the likely ways that the client would test the therapist and the types of therapist response that would be most helpful in enabling the client to disconfirm their beliefs. All therapy sessions were transcribed. A team of five expert therapists independently read through the transcripts, and identified all possible instances where the client might be testing the therapist. Each of these events was then analysed in more depth, in terms of the quality of the therapist's response to the client's test, and the impact of the therapist's reaction on the client's subsequent levels of openness to experience, and willingness to explore difficult issues (assessed by rating scales). The results of the study showed that, in both cases, clients showed immediate improvement when the therapist passed their test.

Unlike the Hill et al. (2008) immediacy studies, which represented the beginning of a process of theory-building, the Silberschatz and Curtis (1993) study was carried out in the context of a theoretical model that was already well established. The theoretical contribution of the Silberschatz and Curtis (1993) study was therefore largely confirmatory, although theoretically interesting comparisons between their two cases were discussed. It is in relation to the literature on theory-building case methodology, however, that the Silberschatz and Curtis (1993) study is of particular interest, in showing how analysis of pre-therapy interview data can be used to develop an individual client-focused framework for analysing therapy transcript data.

Using ethnographic methods in theory-building single case research

An example of the use of ethnographic methods as a means of conducting theory-building research can be found in the work of the Danish psychologist Ole Dreier (1998, 2000, 2008). This research is theoretically innovative in the position that it adopts in relation to therapy process and outcome. Dreier (2008) argues that therapy consists of only a small portion of the life of a client, and that to understand how people actively make use of therapy, it is necessary to examine their everyday lives. He suggests that almost all research in counselling and psychotherapy takes the therapy session as its focus, and assumes that what happens in the session can be generalized to everyday life. Dreier (2008) proposes a 180 degree revolution, in which the standpoint for research is the everyday life of the person looking in to therapy, rather than the other way round.

The theoretical background to this approach lies in critical psychology and specifically in the theory of *social practice* developed by Klaus Holzkamp (Tolman 2009). This theory states that human beings are endlessly engaged in reproducing and changing their social world. A key aspect of the social landscape are the many social contexts or places that function as sites for reproducing this social world; social practice is *situated*. Individuals adopt particular stances in relation to what is happening in different places, and engage in movement across contexts. The implication of this theoretical perspective is 'to gain a richer, more lively, and concrete conception of the person, we must, paradoxically, not look directly into the person, but into the world and grasp the person as a participant in that world' (Dreier 2008: 40).

The case study presented in Dreier (2008) reports on the experiences of a family (two parents; two children) receiving 26 sessions of family therapy over an 18-month period at an outpatient child psychiatry clinic in Copenhagen. The aim of the study was to produce a 'decentered understanding of how therapy works' (Dreier 2008: 48). Participants were given the following information about the study:

> The [therapy] sessions are only a small part of your lives. So we are interested in knowing more about how your everyday lives outside sessions unfold and which changes might be taking place there. This concerns changes with no links to the sessions as well as which links there might be between the sessions and your everyday lives. We would like to know

more about whether the sessions were useful or not or whether they should be different or you have other needs than the ones the sessions cover or may not cover. In that way we want to learn to improve our work. (pp. 48–9)

All therapy sessions attended by the family were recorded and transcribed. The researcher interviewed the family in their home, every three or four weeks throughout therapy, and for six months following therapy. The researcher listened to the therapy recordings in preparation for the interviews. Interviews were conducted with the whole family together, and with individual members. In the interviews, participants were asked about the events and changes in their everyday lives since the previous interview. Only then were they asked about their views on the possible impact of therapy on their lives. The therapists working with the family had access to transcripts of the research interviews. A team of two researchers was involved – Lisbeth Moltzen, who carried out the interviews, and Ole Dreier, who was one of the family therapists.

The analysis of this case comprises seven chapters of a book. A detailed descriptive account is provided of the everyday life of this family, as a group, and then of each of the four family members. Theoretical ideas are woven into the account. For example, there is description of places or contexts, stances taken within these contexts, and trajectories of movement across context, and changes in social practice. Nowhere in the case report is there a summary of the main themes or findings of the study – the intention is to present a contextualized rather than abstract understanding of the case. Dreier (2008: 294) describes the way that theory-building was part of the process of analysing the case material:

analysing my material with my theoretical framework led to many surprises and struggles, which proved analytically very fruitful. They forced me to pay close attention anew to particular episodes and to the clients' statements and the concepts they used in particular situations and contexts ... [for example] the clients' confusion when asked about changes and their not noticing changes forced me to re-consider my preconception of change.

In this kind of study, therefore, theoretical 'discoveries' are not highlighted in the report as specific results, but instead are embedded in the analysis.

The family therapy case published by Dreier (2008) is typical of ethnographic research in that a large amount of qualitative material was collected. Also, the researchers were part of the social world of the people who were being studied – Dreier was one of the therapists for the family, and Moltzen visited the family at home, as well as having meetings with the therapists. On the other hand, the study is not typical of some other ethnographic work, in that the researchers did not collect observational data. The Dreier (2008) study illustrates the potential of an ethnographic approach, in relation to theory-building case study research in counselling and psychotherapy. Anyone reading this case will quickly realize that the methodology that was adopted, particularly the home interviews and asking about everyday life, opened up a dramatically different perspective on the process and outcome of therapy, and indeed on the very meaning of therapy.

A diary method for exploring the everyday lives of clients

The ethnographic approach adopted by Dreier (2008) in his theoretically oriented case study of family therapy represents a highly demanding and time-consuming method of inquiry. Recent research by Mackrill (2007, 2008a,b) used structured client diaries to collect information about the everyday lives of clients. In his research, the therapist also keeps a diary, and therapy sessions are recorded. Taken together, these sources of data represent a rich case record that is attuned to gathering observations around the relationship between therapy and everyday life, and the development of a theoretical framework for making sense of this dimension of therapy (Mackrill 2009).

Box 9.4

Building theory by comparing good- and poor-outcome cases

Theories of counselling and psychotherapy tend to be mainly concerned with attempting to understand and explain what happens in therapy to bring about beneficial change in clients. One of the best ways of finding out about 'what works' in therapy is look at what is going on when therapy is *not* effective. There have been several studies that have compared good outcome and poor outcome cases, with the aim of building a theoretical understanding of the effectiveness of therapy, derived from analysis of what is missing in cases where the client does not improve.

One of the most important studies in the history of psychotherapy research has been the *Vanderbilt I* experiment, carried out by a team of researchers at Vanderbilt University in the USA, directed by Hans Strupp (Strupp 1993; Strupp and Hadley 1979). In this research, male university students suffering from social isolation and anxiety were randomly allocated to either highly experienced professional psychodynamic psychotherapists, or to university lecturers who were known to be sensitive to student problems and interested in student welfare, but who had no experience or training in therapy. Therapy sessions were recorded, and an extensive battery of outcome and process measures was administered to clients before, during and after therapy, and at follow-up. The findings of this study were that there was no difference in outcome between the experienced therapists and college professors. This finding was, of course, unexpected, and Strupp carried out a series of intensive single-case analyses to look more closely at what had happened (Strupp 1980 a,b,c,d). In these case studies, information on all aspects of the case was analysed, with the goal of making sense of the factors in the therapy that contributed to success or failure. The data analysis strategy that was adopted was to take pairs of cases from the same therapist (the most and least effective cases) and display the data in a series of boxes, in which information from each case could be examined side by side. An interpretation was provided of the possible significance of the differences that were apparent between the cases. This approach has the merit of ensuring that all relevant data are examined in a systematic manner. Three of the comparisons looked at cases from professional therapists (Strupp 1980a,b,d). The fourth case analysed data from two clients seen by a lay counsellor (college professor) (Strupp 1980c).

In each of these case study comparisons, there was strong evidence that the therapist had behaved in the same way with each of his cases. Because clients were carefully screened before entering therapy, it seemed unlikely that differential outcomes would be associated with level of client severity. It seemed clear, therefore, that differences in outcome needed to be attributed to relational factors. What Strupp (1980a,b,d) found in the cases that had been handled by professional therapists, was that in the good-outcome cases there was a good match between what the therapist was offering and the client's assumptions and expectations about what might be helpful. By contrast, in the poor-outcome cases, the client appeared to be looking for a different kind of help, and gradually became frustrated with what the therapist had to offer. During this process, the therapist did not appear willing to modify his style, and in some of the cases the client became hostile, which only made things worse, by causing the therapist to retreat. Strupp (1980a,b,d) suggested that, although these clients all had similar problem severity scores at the outset of therapy, they in fact differed in terms of their ability to form relationships: it was only the clients who had some previous capacity to form relationships who seemed to be able to benefit from the relationally oriented psychodynamic therapy that was on offer. In the other case comparison, where the therapist was a college lecturer, the unsuccessful client appeared to have been too disturbed for the lay counsellor, who struggled to know how to help. A further finding that emerged from this case series was that the in-session behaviour of the professional therapists was quite different to that of the lay counsellor, even though their success rate with clients was similar. In his overview of these studies, Strupp (1980a) suggests that all of the poor outcome cases might well have been helped if they had been matched up with a therapist using an approach that was appropriate for that client. He also suggests that a key factor in therapist competence is the ability to respond constructively and flexibly when a client becomes frustrated and hostile. Much of his later research was devoted to exploring this important issue (Strupp 1993), thereby illustrating the effectiveness of his series of case analysis in allowing him to build a theoretical understanding that would have significant implications in terms of both research and practice.

Another example of the use of good/poor outcome case comparison to generate theoretical development can be found in Watson, Goldman and Greenberg (2007). These authors have been (with Robert Elliott and others) in the vanguard of developing *emotional-focused therapy* (also known as *process-experiential psychotherapy*), an approach to therapy that comprises an integration of ideas from client-centred therapy, Gestalt Therapy, constructivist philosophy and research into the psychology of emotion. During the development of this approach to therapy, several randomized controlled studies of EFT were conducted (see Elliott et al. 2004 for a review of these studies). These large-scale studies found that EFT was equivalent in effectiveness to established approaches such as client-centred/person-centred therapy and CBT. Nevertheless, it was clear that some clients in these trials had not benefitted from EFT. The research team therefore decided to carry out a systematic case comparison of good-and poor-outcome cases of EFT for depression (Watson et al. 2007).

The book-length report of this project includes six comprehensive case analyses (three good-outcome, three poor-outcome cases, selected to highlight different aspects of the process of EFT therapy). These case analyses are based on outcome and process data, case transcripts and interviews with clients and therapists. Watson, Goldman and Greenberg (2007) describe each case in turn, then data across all six cases are discussed in relation to a series of key themes (e.g., early environment, social support, affect regulation, readiness to change, etc.). This analysis is used to generate further development of aspects of the theory and practice of EFT. Examples of modifications in the theory include recommending that therapists need to be more aware of the client's level of affect regulation, and placing a greater emphasis on helping clients tell their story in detail as a means of enabling them to understand what has happened in their lives.

The case-comparison strategy used by Strupp (1980a,b,c,d) and Watson, Goldman and Greenberg (2007) has a number of advantages in relation to theory-building research in counselling and psychotherapy. It is extremely interesting to read about cases in which highly trained and skilful therapists are largely ineffective. There are very few explicitly poor-outcome cases published in the literature, for understandable reasons (who wants to tell colleagues that they have failed?). The case comparison research design creates a format that eases the pain of writing about poor-outcome clients. This approach also has the advantage of making it relatively easy to identify (by looking for cross-case differences) factors in therapy that may be of potential theoretical interest. It is important to note, however, that these studies have made use of *extreme* good- and poor-outcome cases. What they found (that client preferences and readiness largely determine what happens) may explain cases where clients experience transformative change, or just get nowhere with the therapy. It seems reasonable to imagine that outcome differences in the middle range might have more to do with therapist skill.

Conclusions

This chapter has discussed a variety of approaches to using case study methods to contribute to the development of theory. It can be seen that a similar inquiry cycle can be identified, even when different kinds of case data are employed. Systematic theory-building case study research begins with careful and detailed specification of theory, which includes identifying how evidence of theoretical concepts might be observed in the case material. The next steps involve comparison between theory and what is observed, leading to the development of new concepts, or more differentiated versions of existing concepts, within the overall structure of the original theory. In the studies outlined in this chapter, this process is carried out in a transparent manner, so that readers are able to make sense of how and why the new theoretical concepts are necessary.

Topics for reflection and discussion

1　In each of the theory-building case studies discussed in this chapter, what is the root metaphor, or underlying philosophical concept, around which the theory is constructed? How explicit are the authors of these case studies, about their underlying assumptions?

2 What therapy theory or model would you like to explore? This might be a new concept, or an aspect of an existing theory that lacks clarity. How might you design a theory-building case study that would enable you to generate a fuller understanding of these ideas? What kind of data would you need, in order to create points of contact with the theory?

3 Identify a theoretical model that is of interest to you. Think about what has been written about this theory. What is the specific evidence that has been put forward to support this theory in the literature that you have read? Does this literature include case study evidence? If it does, how credible are the case analyses? If it does not – what are the implications for the theory of *not* being supported by evidence from individual cases?

4 Case study evidence can be used to *disconfirm* theory as well as to build it. Reflect on the theory-building case studies discussed in this chapter, or on other theory-building case studies with which you are familiar. To what extent have these case analyses sought to refute, or question, certain theoretical propositions? Is it possible to build a theory without implicitly undermining or weakening the plausibility of other, competing, theories? Or is it preferable to adopt a pluralistic perspective, in which all theories are potentially of equal value?

Recommended further reading

The work of Bill Stiles and his research group has been particularly significant in relation to theory-building research, in being explicit about theory-building as a goal, and the stages involved in using case material to develop theory. These ideas are discussed in:

Stiles, W.B. (2003) When is a case study scientific research? *Psychotherapy Bulletin*, 38, 6–11.

Stiles, W.B. (2007) Theory-building case studies of counselling and psychotherapy. *Counselling and Psychotherapy Research*, 7, 122–7.

A series of articles in a special theme issue of the *Pragmatic Case Studies in Psychotherapy* journal provide a range of critical perspectives on this approach to case study inquiry:

Fishman, D.B. (2009) Using case studies to develop theory: roadmap to a dialogue. *Pragmatic Case Studies in Psychotherapy*, 5(3), 1–8. http://pcsp.libraries.rutgers.edu

Further discussion of the role of theory in counselling and psychotherapy research and practice can be found in:

McLeod, J. (2009) *An Introduction to Counselling*, 4th edn. Maidenhead: Open University Press. See Chapter 3.

Exploring the meaning of the therapy experience: narrative case research

Although the genres of therapy case study research that have been discussed in earlier chapters – pragmatic, n=1, HSCED and theory-building – are different from each other in many ways, they nevertheless have one important characteristic in common. Each of these forms of therapy case study research is motivated by professional goals and interests, for example the development of theory, evaluating outcome and documenting professional knowledge. By contrast, the genre of therapy case study research that constitutes the focus of the present chapter has a quite different purpose. The aim of a *narrative* case study is to 'tell the story' of the experience of therapy, to convey what it was like to be a participant in therapy. This kind of case study is successful if it expresses the *meaning* of therapy. In seeking to elucidate meaning, and tell a story, this tradition of case study research is much wider in scope than other case study genres. This is because the meaning of a therapy experience reaches beyond the concepts and categories of counselling and psychotherapy theory. It is also wider in scope because stories of therapy are written by clients and patients as well as by therapists and researchers, they are written for a variety of reasons and they are disseminated through a variety of outlets.

The intention of this chapter is to provide an overview of approaches to conducting narrative case study research. Since this kind of case study does not represent a single approach, it is not possible to identify a set of methodological principles that can be followed. Instead, some brief comments are made concerning possible strategies for assembling a rich narrative case record. A series of exemplar studies is presented, to illustrate different approaches to narrative case study research in the field of counselling and psychotherapy. The chapter concludes with a discussion of the issues and challenges associated with this form of case study inquiry.

Strategies for constructing a narrative case study

As with other approaches to case study research, in carrying out a narrative case study it is necessary to create a rich case record, which incorporates information that is relevant to the aim of the case analysis. A narrative case study is an attempt to tell the story of therapy from the point of view of a participant (usually the client). There are various sources of information that may be useful for the author, in relation to carrying out this task.

Writing an autobiographical retrospective account

The most obvious and straightforward approach to compiling a narrative case study is to sit down and write about what happened and what it felt like. One of the issues in relation to this strategy is whether it is more effective just to start with a blank page, or whether it is helpful to devise (or be given) guidelines or headings that will provide a structure for what is written. Guidelines for writing autobiographical accounts can be found in McAdams (1985) and Adler and McAdams (2007 a,b).

Diary or journal entries

A convincing story includes detailed descriptions of events and experiences as they happened. For most people, it is hard to remember the details of what happened, following the lapse of time. It is also likely that, over time, the meaning of some events is revised in the light of their eventual outcomes, or that some aspects of events are distorted or omitted in an effort to achieve a more coherent account. Diaries can be structured or unstructured, and can take many different forms: written, audio, video. Further information on the use of diaries for research purposes can be found in Alaszewski (2006) and Mackrill (2008b).

Recordings

Audio or video recordings of therapy sessions can provide invaluable narrative material, for example in allowing the author of a narrative case study to use the exact words that he or she uttered during a therapy session.

Artifacts created during therapy, or associated with the therapy

In some forms of therapy, the client may write letters or poems, make pictures or sculptures, or bring in significant objects. Sometimes clients complete questionnaires or worksheets, and keep copies. There may be other physical objects that have meaning in relation to the experience of therapy: a gift from the therapist, a railway ticket for the journey to and from therapy sessions, a photograph of the members of a therapy group. These artifacts can be used both to elicit memories of therapy, and as part of the story that is told.

Interviews

Sometimes it can be easier for a person to tell the story of their therapy in response to questions being asked by another person, or in dialogue with others. The author of a narrative case study may also wish to interview people who were involved in their life at the time of therapy, about their perceptions of how the person may have changed.

It is possible to see that narrative case studies based only on retrospective autobiographical accounts are probably less credible than those that are backed up by other sources of information. A process of actively researching what occurred during a life episode, such as being in therapy, inevitably produces a 'thicker' narrative account.

A further set of issues associated with the construction of narrative case studies concerns how to select, edit and present the narrative information that has been collected. There are examples of narrative case studies of therapy experience, such as those published by Dryden and Yankura (1992) and Yalom and Elkin (1974) that consist of minimally edited diary entries. This type of reporting can be difficult to follow, and leaves the reader to interpret what the text might mean, in the absence of sufficient contextual information. It seems clear, from the pioneering efforts of Irvin Yalom and Windy Dryden to carry out narrative case research, that something more than raw diary entries is required. At the present time, there does not exist an agreed format for the publication of this type of therapy case report. However, there are many examples, in the broader narrative social science literature, of ways in which narrative material can be organized and presented. For example, McLeod (1997) and Richardson (2003) have reviewed how poetic/stanza structures can be used to highlight the meaning of stories. A very useful book by Goodley et al. (2004) explores four alternative styles of writing life history narratives. Davis (2003) discusses the issues and skills involved in writing 'portraits' of individuals. An overview of broader issues in relation to narrative research can be found in Josselson et al. (2003). Some of the possible strategies for writing and presenting narrative case studies of counselling and psychotherapy are exemplified in the case studies that are introduced in the following sections of this chapter.

A multi-method narrative case study

The most completely realized narrative case study of therapy experience that is currently available was published by Kim Etherington, a counsellor and Professor of Narrative and Life Story Research at the University of Bristol. This book-length case report consists of the stories of two male clients, who were brothers, and two therapists involved in working with them. Etherington (2000) describes how she had published a book on the experiences of male survivors of sexual abuse, which was discovered by Stephen, a man who was trying to come to terms with memories of long-term sexual abuse by his grandfather. On the basis of what he had read in her book, Stephen contacted Kim Etherington, and entered therapy with her. Soon afterwards, his brother Mike, who had also been sexually abused by their grandfather, also entered therapy with Etherington. At a later stage in the therapy, both men also received body psychotherapy from another practitioner, Sarasi Rogers. Several years after the therapy was completed, Etherington contacted Stephen and Mike, and asked them if they would be interested in collaborating with her to write something about their experience that would 'offer a lifeline' to other men who had undergone similar experiences. They responded positively.

The book that emerged from these events consists of four sets of stories: the stories of each of the clients, the counsellor's story and the story of the research process that led to the production of the published account of the case. The actual book (Etherington 2000) begins with the stories of Stephen and Mike, written in their own words. However, to understand the methodological approach that informed the construction of this narrative case study, it is necessary to begin by examining the process of ethical negotiation and consent that was implemented at the point where Mike and Stephen were invited to take part in this project. These discussions, between Kim Etherington and her former clients, were audio recorded and are reproduced in the book. What they reflect is a careful attempt to establish an egalitarian, collaborative basis on which to embark on the study. In reading the dialogue that took place, it is important to keep in mind that both Stephen and Mike were experienced health professionals, and as a result understood many of the issues associated with ethical consent. Also, they had both previously read research by Kim Etherington based on in-depth interviews with men who had been abused, so they had some idea of what the eventual book might look like. Finally, the therapy had been successful, had been completed some years previously and some contact had been maintained over the ensuing period. These were all factors that made it more likely that genuine collaboration might take place. Nevertheless, the preparatory discussions reported in Etherington (2000: 268–82) covered a substantial territory, including such issues as the possible impact of revisiting emotional trauma, the effect of reading each other's stories, consequences for family members, the contract with the publisher and much else. This process not only addressed key ethical issues, but enabled a new set of post-therapy collaborative relationships to be established. It is important to emphasize this aspect of the Etherington (2000) study because the case report that was eventually published was enormously revealing, at a personal level, and thus highly ethically sensitive. Additional discussion of the ethical issues arising from this study, and how they were resolved, can be found in Etherington (2007).

The narrative case studies of Stephen and Mike were based on the following sources of information:

- diaries kept by the clients and therapists through the course of therapy;
- letters and poems written by Stephen and Mike during therapy;
- transcripts of individual interviews conducted by Kim Etherington with Stephen and Mike at the point when they agreed to work together on a case study;
- transcripts of conversations between the three participants;
- comments made in response to drafts of the case report prepared by Kim Etherington.

The method of analysis used by Etherington (2000) involved collecting these various narrative sources into a 'multi-layered text', and then spending time reading and reflecting, in a process of immersion:

> as I immersed myself in the multi-layered texts I had gathered, I waited until a shape formed in my mind ... I just began to write and trusted myself to allow whatever was really meaningful to unfold ... It was my background as a woman who was aware of the impact of the socio-political culture on myself, first, and then upon the men in my previous study, that helped me to hear the studies in my own particular way. (p. 297)

The kind of analysis of a 'rich case record' is intentionally different from the approaches described in earlier chapters of this book. What Etherington (2000) is describing is a method that is grounded in personal rather than theoretical sensitivity, and an assumption that meaning will emerge from a process of personal engagement with text ('I waited … I trusted myself') rather than through any technique of rational dissection of that text.

Within the Etherington (2000) book, the narrative case study of the therapy experiences of Stephen and Mike are set alongside passages where the main author explains both her counselling approach and her approach to research. These explanatory sections serve two functions. First, they offer the reader a context through which the experiences of Stephen and Mike might be understood, for example in relation to different stages in the therapy process. Second, they are probably also intended to inform counselling and psychotherapy students and practitioners, and researchers about how to do therapy and/or research. In terms of the different genres of case study discussed in the present book, there are elements of a pragmatic case study approach included in the Etherington (2000) book, in addition to its predominantly narrative focus. It is also worth noting that all this is contained with a 331-page book.

One of the most striking aspects of this study is the way in which the purely client-generated narrative data has relatively little to say about what actually happened in therapy. In their diaries, Stephen and Mike (understandably) write about their attempts to make sense of what has happened in their lives, and what is happening in the present moment, rather than reflect on how helpful their most recent therapy session may or may not have been for them. The diaries are presented in the form in which they were written. The following excerpts (from Stephen, then Mike) have been chosen on the basis that they reflect some of the least harrowing segments that were available (pages 37, 92):

7th September 1995

This started out as a neat chronological list of events BUT again I can't stop writing. I hope this is a positive sign?

20.45 hrs. Dad rang on their way back from holidays. Sounded bright, cheerful.

Normal chit chat.

NOW I FEEL PANIC, ANXIETY, HELP.

21.30 hrs: a very old memory has just come into my head. I remember

HIM taking me to Blackpool, must have been only 8 or 9.

Long coach journey, illuminations, funfair, circus, boarding/guest house:

Him sucking me in a small bedroom.

7.10.95 (...)

Mum rings me (!!) after a couple of days – supposedly at Dad's suggestion – an olive branch? But the same old circular conversation – they just seem oblivious to our feelings.

I am beginning to feel overwhelmed by what has happened – sad and helpless.

Then Helen and Jim are back from holiday. Mum rings briefly to tell me they've had a conference and yes, two of Dad's siblings have admitted to being abused – names no names but thought I ought to know!

These diary entries powerfully convey the lived experience of the process that these men went through during their time in therapy: revisiting memories that had been previously locked away, fluctuating emotional states, shifts in relationships with family members.

By contrast, in conversation with Kim Etherington, as part of research interviews carried out for the purposes of the book, both Stephen and Mike were able to use a more reflective voice, to communicate their experience in terms of themes suggested by the researcher. For example, the excerpts below were in response to questioning about how they perceived the therapeutic relationship:

> *Stephen*: As time went on ... [*long pause*] I got very attached to you but I knew that it would have to end ... and you were quite mysterious in some ways but that was good – you had to be – you had to be quite anonymous for me to be able to tell you all those things ... I didn't know anything about you, but that was OK because it needed to be that way. It was a good counsellor/client relationship – we were very close but there was also a boundary as well – just about in the right order, in the right quantities, looking back on it.
>
> *Kim*: So you were aware of getting attached?
>
> *Stephen*: Yes, I was aware that it would have been easy to get too attached.
>
> *Kim*: Too attached?
>
> *Stephen*: Yes, too dependent upon you – it would have been nice to have seen you every week for ever and just come along, have a chat, and tell you all my problems [*laughs gently*].
>
> *Kim*: Yes [*laughs gently*].

Stephen: It would be good to have you there all the time – 'cos you're so nice and you cared – but I knew it wasn't reality – I couldn't do that forever – I think that went OK – the parting, yes. (p. 127)

*****

Mike: It felt very suddenly that I'd gone into being a little boy and that you were the parent who was going to look after me.

Kim: So once you felt that this person knew what she was doing and was not frail in the sense of being able to deal with this, you could actually let go.

Mike: And I dare say that didn't show, but it feels as if it was very sudden – as if I was sitting on the edge thinking about it, then sliding down.

Kim: Mmm and that felt quite early on for you?

Mike: Yes, although I remember still feeling all shut in as a helpless little boy – but all shut in as the little boy, not as the suspicious, aloof doctor …

Kim: So once you'd established enough trust you were able to be your need child?

Mike: Yes, that did happen almost immediately. (p. 128)

The decision to include the interviewer statements in these excerpts is significant, in relation to the methodological stance adopted by Etherington (2000). Many of the client statements in these passages could easily have been offered as exemplification of researcher-generated categories (e.g., 'I'd gone into being a little boy and that you were the parent who was going to look after me' as an example of transference). By retaining the interviewer questions, Etherington (2000) reminds the reader of the dialogical, co-constructed nature of the narrative that has been created.

The case studies of Stephen and Mike, published in Etherington (2000), provide a sense of the possibilities of the narrative case study genre. This has been an influential and widely read book, which speaks not only to therapy practitioners, but also to people who have experienced childhood sexual abuse. By including a detailed account of the methods that were used to create these narrative case studies, Etherington (2000) provides guidance for other researchers seeking to undertake similar work. There are aspects of this study that would not be applicable to other projects. It is published as a book-length report; other narrative case study researchers would wish to generate outputs that could be accommodated within article-length reports. The Etherington (2000) book includes sections explaining the therapy process (rather like a pragmatic case study), which could be omitted from a straightforward narrative account. The researcher worked alone to carry out data collection and analysis, whereas other researchers might prefer to work in teams or with colleagues. These are all matters of adapting and fine-tuning the methodological template that has been established in this seminal work.

Writing therapy stories

Dan McAdams is one of the leading researchers and theorists in the field of narrative psychology (McAdams 1985, 1993, 1996, 2006). Much of his research has consisted of asking people to create autobiographical life-stories by writing or being interviewed by another person, using a set of guidelines provided in McAdams (1985). The narrative themes that are present in these stories can be analysed, and related to other information about the person, such as their stage of psychological development. In some recent research, he has worked with Jonathan Adler to apply this approach to the study of people's stories of the therapy they have received. This programme of research has generated a number of publications (Adler and McAdams 2007a,b; Adler et al. 2007, 2008). The discussion that follows will focus primarily on Adler and McAdams (2007a,b), which provides the most comprehensive descriptive account of this work that is currently available.

In the study by Adler and McAdams (2007a,b), participants were invited to write about their experience of therapy. The instructions that were given to them, asked them to create five or six 'scenes':

- *The Problem.* A specific scene in which the presenting problem was especially clear or vivid.
- *The Decision.* A scene in which it was decided that the person would go to therapy to address the problem.
- *Most Important Session.* A specific session in therapy that the participant deemed to be the most significant.
- *Another Important Scene.* A specific session, different from the previous one, that the person deems significant.
- *Ending.* A specific scene that describes a time before, at or after termination of therapy in which the impact of the therapy was particularly clear or vivid.
- *Optional sixth scene.* Any other information that the participant thought was not captured in the rest of the narrative.

Participants in the study (76) were recruited from the community, on the basis that they were not currently in therapy and had completed at least eight sessions of therapy within the previous five years. Participants had received a broad range of types of therapy, for a variety of problems: the aim was to focus on the narratives of people who had received 'treatment as usual' in typical outpatient settings. The stories that were created by participants were analysed by a team of five researchers, using a grounded theory approach in which themes emerge from the data rather than being imposed by the researchers on the basis of pre-existing theories. What Adler and McAdams (2007a,b) discovered was that four different types of therapy story could be identified: *personal agency* stories, *healing connection* stories, *self-acceptance* stories and *incoherent* stories.

An example of a *personal agency* therapy narrative was found in the case of Nora (Adler and McAdams 2007b). Nora had developed an eating disorder at the age of 23, and was persuaded by her boyfriend to enter therapy. She was resistant to the idea of therapy, and critical of her therapist. She dropped out of therapy, but experienced a traumatic life crisis (a sexual assault) and re-entered therapy with another counsellor. This time therapy got off to a better start, there were moments of insight or 'revelations', and she 'grew to respect' her therapist. Even so, she felt 'totally betrayed' when he suggested that her parents might attend a therapy session with her. She 'decided I could recover on my own' and left therapy again. Adler and McAdams (2007b) suggest that this kind of story is characteristic of people who view themselves as being in control of their lives. She described herself as a powerful person who was temporarily struggling to cope with specific problems, who used therapy as a means of re-discovering her own sense of agency and purpose. It is not the relationship with the therapist that is viewed as significant in bringing about change, but the capacity of the person to use therapy to bring about personal insights.

A *healing connection* story was told by Willy (Adler and McAdams 2007b). Willy was 44 when he entered therapy. Estranged from his wife and daughter, Willy had struggled for many years with depression and alcoholism, while managing to cope with a successful career as an advertising executive. Eventually, a severe alcoholic binge caused him to lose his job. At this point, a friend persuaded him to enter therapy. For Willy, the success of his therapy was attributable to the caring approach taken by his therapist, and the quality of their relationship. The story of Willy's therapy was typical of others in the *healing connection* group. These stories described longstanding and wide-ranging problems, which the person was powerless to cope with until they met a therapist with a powerful and caring presence.

The third category of therapy narrative uncovered by Adler and McAdams (2007a) placed a strong emphasis on *self-acceptance*. Adler and McAdams (2007a) described these stories as reflecting conventional ideas about therapy. The person resolved his or her problems by admitting that the problems existed, and facing up to them, thus achieving higher levels of self-esteem. The final category of therapy narratives included those that lacked clarity about the sources of problems, and the processes through which these problems were addressed in therapy. They were somewhat vague stories, in which the identity of the central character, the writer, was not clear.

The research carried out by Adler and McAdams (2007a,b) was not primarily focused on constructing individual case studies that were analysed in depth. Instead, they collected stories from a large number of participants, found themes across these stories and were then able to use these themes to identify distinctive story types. However, there are two ways in which their approach has important implications for the field of narrative case study research in counselling and psychotherapy. First, their method of inviting participants to write about their experience of therapy in terms of discrete 'scenes' appears to have produced a great deal of useful data. The idea of 'scenes' is consistent with the construction of everyday narratives – people tend to share stories of their life in terms of specific concrete events or scenes. The 'scene' structure is therefore likely to make sense to participants, and be viewed as more manageable than an open-ended invitation to 'just write' (or talk) about the experience of therapy. Also, the idea of scenes is neutral in terms of what the scenes might include, whereas more specific questions ('what was the therapy relationship like?' 'how helpful were the interventions used by your therapist?') inevitably lead the informant in the direction of therapist-defined categories. In a more intensive case study setting, it would be possible either to increase the number of scenes that the person was being asked to write about, or to use the scene-based narrative as the basis for an interview that encouraged the informant to expand and 'fill-in' further detail.

The other significant implication of the Adler and McAdams (2007a,b) research is that it suggests that there are different types of therapy story, and that it would therefore be reasonable to expect that, for example, a series of narrative case studies of the experience of therapy for sexual abuse would in fact yield a range of different accounts. Research by Kuhnlein (1999) (not case-study-based) showed that clients tell different types of story, even when their therapy has been effective, and they have all received one type of therapy for one type of problem in one clinic. Adler and McAdams (2007a,b) suggest that differences between the therapy narratives they collected can mainly be attributed to the personality of the narrator, and possibly also influenced by cultural factors, rather than by the actual therapy that was undergone. However, Adler and McAdams (2007a,b) did not have access to independent data on the therapy experiences of their research participants. The point here is that it does not seem sensible to expect that narrative case studies will necessarily (or only) illuminate what happened in therapy – they will function as an expression of culturally specific ideas about identity and human agency. McAdams (2006) makes a compelling argument in support of the idea that the stories told by people in mainstream American culture tend to take the form of 'redemption' narratives (e.g., George W. Bush, Bill Clinton …). Narrative case study research that built on the Adler and McAdams (2007a,b) paradigm, but which explored individual cases in more depth, might be able to throw light on the ways in which this prevailing cultural narrative shapes therapy in the USA (and how alternative cultural narratives shape therapy in other societies).

A final comment on the Adler and McAdams (2007a,b) research – one that has no direct bearing on narrative case study methodology but is nevertheless intriguing. The structure of the 'agency' stories told by participants in this study (about 28% of the overall sample) has an uncanny resemblance to the kind of story that clients are encouraged to tell in the narrative therapy developed by White and Epston (1990) – the person is fundamentally capable and agentic, their 'problem' is an external force that they already possess the tools to overcome, and the relationship with the therapist is relatively unimportant. Could it be that narrative therapy is based on a strategy of teaching clients to narrate their lives in the way that 'successful' people do?

Ideal type analysis

A method of analysing client narratives of their experience of therapy, that is similar to the approach taken by Adler and McAdams (2007a,b), but which has emerged from a different research tradition, is the technique of *ideal type* analysis. The concept of an 'ideal type' was used by the German sociologist Max Weber to describe a composite case that embodied the key attributes of a set of similar cases. In recent years, idea type analysis has been employed by a number of European psychodynamically oriented psychotherapy researchers with the goal of producing case analyses that are particularly relevant for clinical practice (Frommer and Langenbach 2001; Stuhr and Wachholz 2001). This approach has been used to analyse narrative accounts of client experiences of therapy (Kuhnlein 1999), client ideas about how therapy works (Philips et al. 2007a; Philips et al. 2007b), subjective theories of illness (Frommer et al. 1996), clients' memories of their therapists (Wachholz and Stuhr 1999), and types of suicidal clients (Lindner 2006; Lindner et al., 2006). In each of these studies, ideal type analysis has been used to generate composite cases that practitioners can compare against the patterns within cases that they encounter within their own practice. A further advantage of ideal type analysis is that it allows complex case material to be presented in a way that does not risk breaching the confidentiality of individual clients.

Box 10.1

Life history approaches to therapy case study research

The narrative case studies that have been discussed in earlier sections of this chapter have largely focused on the client's experience of a course of therapy. Another approach to making sense of the meaning of therapy for a person is to consider the significance of a therapy episode in the context of that person's life as a whole. This strategy can be viewed as a *life history* approach – therapy is viewed from the perspective of broader life patterns. There are few studies that have attempted to carry out this kind of investigation. McKenna and Todd (1997) interviewed people who had experienced multiple episodes of therapy over the course of their life, and used a time-line technique to help informants to identify different therapy episodes and relate these events to other issues that were around for them at that time. Because they interviewed several informants, the case report on each individual was somewhat brief. However, it was clear that the time-line technique was effective in eliciting life-history narrative accounts. An interesting set of life history accounts of psychotherapy experience can be found in *The Psychotherapist's Own Psychotherapy: Patient and Clinician Perspectives*, edited by Geller, Norcross and Orlinsky (2005). This book includes invited narrative accounts of lifetime therapy experiences from five well-known contemporary psychotherapists: Windy Dryden (2005), Jesse Geller (2005), Clara Hill (2005), William Pinsof (2005) and Bryan Wittine (2005). These accounts were written in response to a set of guidelines provided by Geller, Norcross and Orlinsky (2005; 419–20). The book also includes a copy of a previously published account by the psychoanalyst Harry Guntrip (2005) of his experiences as an analysand of Donald Fairbairn and D.W. Winnicott. Although it is clear that these writers, mindful of their professional and collegial audience, have produced somewhat selective accounts of their therapy experiences, what they produced is nevertheless extremely informative. Their stories support the conclusions of the McKenna and Todd (1997) study, that the meaning of therapy is shaped both by the person's stage in the life course, and by the impact of previous therapies that they have tried. A recurring theme in all of these narratives is that of the search for the right therapy or therapist, and how helpful it is for the person when that emotional home is found. In the light of these life-histories, apparently unsuccessful therapy experiences may still be regarded as useful if they leave the person with a clearer understanding of what it is that they still need to do.

It is a pity that more life history research has not been carried out in relation to the role of therapy in a person's life. There is a thriving academic field of life history research, represented in texts such as Bertaux (1981), Goodley et al. (2004) and Runyan (1980, 1981a,b, 1997), and in the *Narrative Study of Lives* series edited by Ruthellen Josselson, Amia Lieblich and Dan McAdams. There also exists important and relevant work in the field of auto-ethnography (the systematic exploration of personal life experiences for research purposes; Speedy 2007). However, for the most part, ideas and methods from these methodological traditions have not filtered through into the psychotherapy and counselling case study research community.

Methods of eliciting narrative data

Box 10.2

At the heart of counselling and psychotherapy research is an abiding interest in the process of change that occurs in therapy. A huge array of outcome measures and process scales have been developed over the years, in order to assess different aspects of change in therapy clients who participate in large-scale research studies. It is important to recognize that these methods have been primarily designed for the purpose of collecting aggregate data across group samples, and have limitations when it comes to single-case research. For example, in a case study of an individual client, the person's idiosyncratic interpretation of the meaning of questionnaire items can become apparent, in a way that would be hidden in a study with a large sample of participants. One of the emerging issues in therapy case study research, therefore, is the task of developing research tools that are specifically oriented toward the needs of case-level inquiry. The structured therapy story technique devised by Adler and McAdams (2007 a,b), is an example of a research instrument that has been designed to generate data that is particularly relevant in terms of understanding change in an individual case. Another useful technique is the Life Space Map (LSM) interview (Rodgers 2006), in which the client is invited to make a drawing of his or her life at various points in therapy, and then to talk about the image they have created. This technique has proved to be highly effective in eliciting life-story material that is relevant to an understanding of how the person has changed (or not) in therapy.

Autobiographical and fictional narrative case studies

There are many counselling and psychotherapy case studies that are written and published by clients in the guise of autobiographical books and chapters, or as fictional pieces. Client accounts of therapy can be found in books such as *Consuming Psychotherapy*, by Anne France (1988; summary available in House 2006), *Folie à Deux: An Experience of One-to-one Therapy* by Rosie Alexander (1995) and *The Analysand's Tale* (Morley 2007a). Rosemary Dinnage (1988) interviewed 20 people about their experiences of psychotherapy. *Shouldn't I Be Feeling Better by Now? Client Views of Therapy*, edited by Yvonne Bates (2006), includes six first-person accounts of therapy experiences, written by people who have been victims of therapy malpractice. These are just some of the autobiographical accounts of counselling and psychotherapy experience that are in circulation. In addition to these factual accounts, fictional narratives of therapy have been published by David Lodge (1995) and other novelists.

The autobiographical and fictional literature outlined above represents an important evidence base, because it consists of a body of therapy narrative that has been produced out of the control or influence of therapists or therapy researchers. It therefore seems likely that it will convey perceptions of therapy that have been overlooked by professional writers, and/or will communicate ideas and insights that will be uncomfortable for members of the therapy professions to hear. At the present time, however, there is little sign that the therapy professions and their research divisions have paid much attention to this literature. This situation sits in contrast to recent developments in the field of mental health, in which user accounts are increasingly being taken seriously (Hatfield 1989; Marsh 2000), and are informing new approaches to policy and practice around the 'recovery' movement (Davidson et al. 2005, 2006). One of the ways in which a professional group can take user narratives seriously is to collect, catalogue and review them, as a means of distilling the wisdom that they contain. It would be a good idea for someone to undertake this task in respect of the counselling and psychotherapy literature.

Box 10.3

Integrating a narrative perspective into other genres of case study research

The main interest of this chapter is case studies that have a predominant narrative focus, where the aim is to convey the client's story of the therapy they have received, and the meaning that this experience has had for them. However, it is also possible to include a narrative perspective into other genres of therapy case study research. Baines and Wills (2002) published a case series of three clients undergoing CBT-oriented counselling for long-term obsessive–compulsive disorder (OCD). Clients completed standard pre- and post-therapy measures, and were also interviewed about their experience of therapy. The information from these qualitative interviews is not reported in any great detail in Baines and Wills (2002), for reasons of space. However, even the limited qualitative material that is used in this article manages to convey a client narrative that diverges from the picture of therapy arising from analysis of quantitative measures, and from certain aspects of theoretical accounts of how and why CBT is effective. For example, all three clients identified significant changes in their life that had not been picked up by the outcome measures used in the study. In addition, what had been most helpful in the therapy was the chance to talk:

> all three clients described an overwhelming need to talk through their problems with someone who understood their, often bizarre, illness. It seems that OCD can be very difficult for non-sufferers to empathise with and this can put an enormous strain on the client's family, leading to feelings of isolation. The opportunity to be listened to and understood within a confidential and non-judgemental relationship was stated to be the most important factor in therapy for all three clients. (p. 274)

The Baines and Wills (2002) study provides an example of how valuable it can be to elicit the client's narrative account of their therapy experience, as an adjunct to other methods. It also shows that, where necessary, this kind of information can be meaningfully condensed in order to highlight central themes, rather than being reported in full.

Narrative case studies as therapeutic resources

One of the threads running through this chapter is an acknowledgement that few narrative case studies of counselling and psychotherapy are being carried out, and that this type of case study research has had a minimal impact on theory and research in counselling and psychotherapy. However, there is considerable evidence that narrative case studies play a significant role in therapy practice, perhaps a greater role than any other form of research and inquiry. Surveys of therapists in the USA carried out by Clifford et al. (1999) and Sommer (2003) found that over 70% of practitioners had recommended autobiographical 'personal journey of psychotherapy' books to their clients, and had received positive feedback from the vast majority (95%) of clients who had read such books, on the contribution that these sources had made to their therapy. In a different light, within the narrative therapy tradition, former clients are routinely used as 'consultants', and invited to share their 'insider knowledge' of how they overcame fear, depression, eating problems, etc., with clients in treatment or with therapists in training (Epston 1992). A further example of the use of service user narratives can be observed in the *Directory of Patient Experience* project (www.dipex. org.uk/), now called *Health Talk Online*. This is a website that carries patient interviews, talking about their experiences of a wide range of medical conditions, as a means of informing and empowering other patients and carers.

Conclusions

The field of narrative case study research in counselling and psycho-therapy is at a different stage of development, when compared to the case study approaches discussed in earlier chapters. In all of the other approaches, guidelines and protocols have been developed for therapy case study researchers. In the domain of n=1 single subject case studies, a range of introductory textbooks are available to inform new research-ers. By contrast, nothing at all like this exists in relation to narrative case study research. This chapter has attempted to pull together some ideas and techniques for carrying out narrative case studies, and has high-lighted some examples of interesting and useful case studies that have been carried out. But much more needs to be done, in terms of method development, to give writers of narrative case studies a framework for organizing autobiographical and descriptive materials. It would probably also be helpful if more clear-cut publication opportunities were availa-ble. Who wants to put the work into writing a narrative case study and then not be able to publish it? Not many people will have the energy and motivation to produce book-length case studies. Academic journals are possibly not the best outlet for first person accounts of therapy, because they tend to limit the availability of what has been written to selective academic audiences. The example of authors such as Rosemary Dinnage and Yvonne Bates, who have assembled edited collections of narrative case studies, disseminated by publishers who will ensure a rea-sonable market, may be a good route to follow.

Case studies of counselling and psychotherapy always tell some kind of story. However, the story can be used in two ways (Polkinghorne 1995). On the one hand, the story of a therapy can be analysed in terms of general categories and themes. This strategy, which has been described as *analysis of narrative,* was used by Adler and McAdams (2007a,b) when they collected therapy stories from former clients, but then used this material to build a general model of story themes. In contrast, it is possible for a story to convey meaning in itself (*narrative analysis*), because a story functions as a basic human means of organizing and communicating information about life experience. The study by Etherington (2000) mainly uses this approach, in allowing the story of therapy to be told, with relatively little attempt to categorize or interpret what happened. The therapy stories reported in Dinnage (1988) reflect a pure form of narrative analysis – the accounts of therapy that are collected together in that book include no commentary or analysis at all. The value of narrative case studies, for the field of counselling and psychotherapy as a whole, lies in the fact that they underline the essential knowledge function of narrative knowing. The writings of Jerome Bruner (1986, 1990, 2002) and Donald Polkinghorne (1988, 1995) have emphasized the significance of narrative and storytelling in the development of culture and human action. A therapy profession certainly needs abstract, general theories (what Bruner calls *paradigmatic* knowing). But it also needs stories.

Topics for reflection and discussion

1. Reflect on your personal experience of therapy, as a client. How would you feel, if someone asked you if you would be willing to write an account of what your therapy was like for you? How likely is it that you would agree? What kinds of consideration would make it more, or less likely that you would agree? If you did accept the invitation to write, how useful would you find Jonathan Adler's set of instructions, based on 'scenes' (page 198)? If you did not use these guidelines, how else would you set about the task of writing?

2. The clients who collaborated with Kim Etherington had undergone sustained sexual abuse in childhood, and wished to tell their stories in order to support other people with similar experiences. What categories of therapy client do you believe might be less interested in sharing their experience, or might even be actively opposed to doing so? What are the different sources of motivation that might be associated with willingness to take part in writing a narrative case study?

3. To what extent are the same, or different ethical issues raised by the publication of narrative case studies, written by clients, as opposed to the publication of other types of case study (e.g., pragmatic, n=1, HSCED)?

4. In Chapter 2, traditional clinical case studies were criticized on the basis that case reports based on therapist recall were likely to be biased in the direction of the therapist's pre-existing theoretical assumptions. To what extent will similar processes occur in client reports of therapy? What are the implications of this issue for narrative case study research?

Recommended further reading

The key source of further information about the challenges and possibilities of narrative case study research is:

Etherington, K. (2000) *Narrative Approaches to Working with Adult Male Survivors of Child Sexual Abuse: The Client's, the Counsellor's and the Researcher's Story*. London: Jessica Kingsley.

A fascinating and informative review of different strategies for writing life stories can be found in:

Goodley, D., Lawthom, R., Clough, P. and Moore, M. (2004) *Researching Life Stories: Method, Theory and Analyses in a Biographical Age*. London: RoutledgeFalmer.

Good examples of chapter-length client narrative accounts of therapy are available in:

Dinnage, R. (1988) *One to One: Experiences of Psychotherapy*. London: Penguin.

Hill, C.E. (2005) The role of individual and marital therapy in my development. In J.D. Geller, J.C. Norcross and D.E. Orlinsky (eds), *The Psychotherapist's Own Psychotherapy: Patient and Clinician Perspectives*. New York: Oxford University Press.

Team-based case study research for practitioners and students

Case study research has the potential to make a major contribution to the evidence base for counselling and psychotherapy practice. The preceding chapters of this book have described a set of methodological approaches to systematic and rigorous case study inquiry that demonstrate the ways that case-based research can be used to address a range of questions around the process and outcomes of therapy, and the construction of theory. However, this potential is not being realized. Few good quality case studies are being published. As a result, the enormous reservoir of knowledge that is created on a daily basis by client and therapist reflections on their experiences of therapy, is draining away and leaving little trace. In recent years there have been many pleas from within the academic community, from champions of case study research, exhorting practitioners to be more willing to write up their cases. These pleas appear to have had little effect, in relation to the flow of cases being submitted for publication.

Why are practitioners resistant to doing case study research? One factor must surely be that counsellors and psychotherapists who make a living seeing clients are busy, and do not have time to do research. This is undoubtedly true. On the other hand, the majority of therapists do manage to find the time to read, attend supervision, have person therapy and engage in on-going training. So, busy practitioners do have time for other activities, and generally agree that these activities are crucial to their well-being and professional effectiveness – just seeing clients leads to burnout. I believe that the difference between the learning activities that practitioners tend to be enthusiastic about (e.g., supervision and training), and activities that they avoid (such as research) is that the former is viewed as personally satisfying and relevant to work with clients, whereas the latter are regarded as unsatisfying, not personally meaningful, and a duty to be performed to fulfil someone else's agenda.

Further barriers to practitioner case study research include the perceived ethical difficulties associated with publishing client material, and uncertainty about the publication criteria for case reports. Hopefully these issues have been addressed in earlier chapters of this book.

What is being suggested in this chapter is a radically different way of thinking about the role of case study research in counselling and psychotherapy, a refocusing of the debate. It is proposed that the profession might move toward a position in which case study research and inquiry should be considered primarily as a vehicle for fulfilling the learning and support needs of both students/trainees and experienced practitioners. For counsellors and psychotherapists, personal and professional development involves a broad agenda for reflection on practice. The reflective learning that counsellors need to do incorporates examination of the relationship between theory and practice, the personal meaning of engagement with clients, and the moral and ethical issues arising from the work. Practitioners also need to be mindful of the contribution they make to the on-going sustainability of the profession as a whole, and the particular groupings in the profession with which they identify. In addition, practitioners are mindful of a need to build a career, to develop expertise, experience and reputation in specific areas of knowledge and competence. Case study research brings these areas of professional activity together.

The aim of this chapter is to offer an outline of how case study research can be reconceptualized as a form of professional learning that has two areas of added value: contributing to the evidence base for the profession and career building. Case study projects can serve some of the functions of training and supervision, while allowing participants to be professional 'good citizens' by generating new knowledge.

The chapter addresses these issues in three ways. First, a basic format for group- or team-based practitioner case study research is described, that can be incorporated into initial professional training programmes and continuing professional development provision. Second, a more ambitious format, the *adjudicated clinical trial* is discussed as a means through which members of practitioner research networks can work together to carry out case-based outcome research that will feed into evidence-based practice reviews. The final section of the chapter considers some of the issues involved in implementing a reconceptualization of case study research.

The case study inquiry group: a model of team-based practitioner research

One of the central arguments of this book is that counselling and psychotherapy case studies in which the therapist is the sole researcher (traditional clinical case studies) are fundamentally not a good idea. There are clearly many therapist-generated case studies that have been interesting and stimulating, and have made a valuable contribution to knowledge and understanding. Nevertheless, taken as a whole, this is a research tradition that is grounded in a flawed methodology. It would be better for the profession, and the research community, if single-authored case studies became the exception rather than the norm. There will always be some situations where therapists will rightly believe that there is value in writing up their work with a client, and for whatever reason are not able to work with colleagues in analysing their data. However, it will be to everyone's advantage if it becomes accepted that good quality case study research is based in a rigorous and critical use of *externality* – the involvement of people who are fresh to the situation and do not have a stake in interpreting case data in a way that will promote the merits of any particular therapeutic ideology.

Team-based practitioner case study research involves a group of people (trainees or qualified practitioners) working together to plan a case study project, obtain ethical consent, collect and analyse data, submit their conclusions to external adjudication and prepare a case report for publication as an article, chapter or book, or dissemination through alternative media such as the Internet. A case study inquiry group of this type is structured in such a way that it contributes to the personal and professional development of its members, as well as yielding a publishable product.

At the present time, few people have had the experience of taking part in a case study group, and as a consequence, any such group would need to spend time at the start, defining and clarifying its mode of operation. However, as more members of the profession gain experience of this type of learning, for example through having been introduced to it in training, it will become easier to implement. The following structure is based on a model of a group of four to six members, that might get together for a 3 hour meeting, once each month, with email communication between meetings. Time can be organized in different ways. For example, a group of colleagues who live in close proximity to each other might hold an evening meeting every fortnight, while a case study group that involved long-distance travelling might meet for a whole weekend every 4 months. There are many ways that case study inquiry groups might be formed or convened, for example through identification of shared interests, through meeting colleagues at conferences and seminars, or placing notices in local or national professional journals and websites.

The sequence of meetings described below, and time-scale, is based on a scenario in which no one in the group has already collected case data, and the group is in the business of designing a case study project from the ground up. In a situation in which a member of the group has already assembled a rich case record, and is recruiting others to assist him or her to analyse it, fewer meetings would be required. However, the same basic sequence would need to be followed.

Stage 1: Convening the group (2 or 3 meetings)

The group gets together; members introduce themselves and share information about personal and professional background and experience. Discussion of hopes and fears for the group, personal goals, ground rules, length of commitment to the group, and future meeting schedule. Discussion of case study ideas and possibilities. Agreement over aims and scope of first case study project. Allocation of tasks.

Stage 2: Detailed planning (2 or 3 meetings)

Developing a research protocol (the aims of the case study, what data will be collected, how it will be analysed, etc.), negotiating ethical approval. It is usually more interesting for a practitioner case study group to design a project that encompasses both an outcome dimension ('is this a good outcome case' – examined using an n=1 or HSCED approach) *and* a theory-building dimension ('how can this case material be used to develop a richer understanding of the concept or theory of X …?'). It is necessary to plan to collect data on more than one case, to allow for the possibility that clients may decline permission, at the end of therapy or at follow-up, for the case to be analysed or published.

Stage 3: Collecting data

The length of this phase of a group will depend on the length of therapy. It is ethically problematic to analyse case material while a case is on-going, for two reasons. First, if the therapist is part of the inquiry group (which would usually happen) then concurrent analysis of the case might interfere with the therapy process. Second, the client should always be able to withdraw consent at any point – if a group has invested a lot of time in transcribing session recordings and analysing data during the course of therapy, a situation is created in which team members may exert unconscious pressure on the client to agree to allow the material to be written up. Nevertheless, there are data-collection activities that may allow group members to remain involved at this stage, such as interviewing the client, interviewing the therapist, collating information, and entering quantitative data into a database to be ready for later analysis. If a group has obtained ethical permission to study a few cases, the likelihood is that at least one of the therapies will be finished within three months. If all the cases become long-term, the group will need to be patient, or to decide to reconvene when the first client comes to an end. The group may also wish to use the data collection stage to refine its 'starting point' theoretical model, complete a review of relevant literature and write a draft of the method section of an eventual article.

Stage 4: Analysing the case (4–6 meetings)

The group works together to analyse the case material. Further suggestions on how this might be accomplished are discussed below. However, the analysis process would always begin with each member of the group independently reading the rich case record, and sharing their initial analysis with colleagues, at a meeting of the group. The end-point of the analysis involves assembling the rich case record and analysis, and sending it to external adjudicators.

Stage 5: Writing up the case (2–4 meetings)

Members of the team take on different roles in relation to writing the final report, submitting it for publication and responding to reviewer feedback. At some point in this stage the group reviews its experience in terms of either an ending of the team, or learning to be taken forward to another project.

This schedule provides an outline of a project in which a group goes through a whole cycle of convening and completing one case study, over a period of about 18 months. If a group already has a rich case record to start with, the process can be condensed into about 6 months. If, on the other hand, the group decides to work on multiple cases, it could remain in existence for several years, and might have an evolving membership.

Box 11.1

What needs to be done: a task analysis of the functioning of a case study inquiry group

Within a case study inquiry group, there are multiple opportunities for participants to carry out tasks that either make use of their existing skills and knowledge, or allow the development of new areas of competence. These tasks include:

- selecting data collection tools such as outcome and process measures;
- developing an ethics protocol (information sheet and consent form);
- dealing with ethics committees/approval processes;
- recruiting clients and negotiating ethical consent;
- carrying out research interviews with clients and therapists;
- facilitating the process of the inquiry group;
- making arrangements for group meetings;
- collating and organizing information;
- reviewing, reading and summarizing relevant theoretical and research literature;
- analysing different kinds of data (qualitative and quantitative);
- supporting fellow group members to articulate their ideas; challenging the ideas of fellow members;
- acting with courage in voicing and facing up to moral, existential and personal dilemmas faced by the group and its members;
- recruiting and liaising with external adjudicators;
- writing;
- dealing with journal editors, reviewers or publishers.

Reflecting on this list of research group tasks makes it easier to understand why individual practitioners have found it hard to carry out case research – there is a lot to do, on top of existing work commitments. However, divided out between the members of a research group, and with the support of other members of the group, these tasks seem a lot more manageable. Also, the task list suggests ways in which members can learn from each other. Not everyone in the group needs to know about research methodology (e.g., selection of outcome measures), have read everything that is available on a particular theoretical approach, or be skilled in bringing the best out of members of a group. All it needs is one person in the group who is competent in any of these areas (or willing to learn), and who is willing to share their knowledge with others.

Making case study research relevant to personal and professional development

The model of stages in the life of a case study group, outlined above, is mainly focused on the sequence of research tasks that need to be completed in order to carry through a case study project to completion. In parallel to these research tasks are a corresponding set of personal and professional development topics. For example, exploring the personal meaning of the research creates opportunities for reflection on issues that may have both personal and professional implications. The experience of being a member of a group that meets over an extended period of time, and whose participants are called upon to collaborate around a complex, open-ended set of goals, generates further opportunities for learning. The process of analysing case material leads inquiry group participants in the direction of questioning their pre-existing assumptions about the nature of therapy. For example, formulating a therapy model or concept in a way that is specific enough to guide the analysis of case material requires thinking with more clarity than is demanded in everyday practice. A final aspect of the personal and professional development potential of case study groups lies in the fact that immersion in a case will inevitably include thinking about what the therapist has done in the case, and what the effects of these actions appear to have been. Always, when reading a detailed account of a case, a practitioner will have the thought: 'I would have done something different here'. The practitioner-inquirer is therefore faced with resolving a tension between what he or she might have done, and what the actual therapist might have done. It is through the process of resolving this tension, or at least reflecting on it, that a practitioner opens up a broader sense of possibilities for practice. This tension is more acute when the practitioner-inquirer was also the therapist in the case.

These four areas of personal and professional development – the personal meaning of the research, being a member of a group, refining professional knowledge and enhancing practice – represent some of the areas of learning that can be stimulated by participation in a case study group. It remains a matter for future research, to determine the extent and persistence of these forms of learning, and how they compare with personal and professional development outcomes achieved through other activities such as supervision, private study, personal therapy and training workshops.

Working as a team to analyse a rich case record

How can members of a case study inquiry group work effectively together, to produce a case study report? Given that time is likely to be at a premium, how can a group organize itself to get maximum benefit from members' investment? How can a group operate to ensure that their case study 'products' are of a high quality, rather than reflecting a collusive avoidance of the challenges of this type of research? On the basis of the methodological issues discussed in earlier chapters of this book, there would appear to be a set of core principles that need to be taken into account when deciding how the group will function:

- A step-by-step approach: carrying out a case study involves a complex set of tasks; to avoid confusion and wasted effort, everyone needs to be clear about what they are doing, and why.
- Enabling everyone to make a contribution: the point of assembling an inquiry team is to be able to move beyond the limitations of a single 'reading' of the data – for this to work, there needs to be a format in which everyone's voice can be heard. It is not useful if there is one dominant member (the learned professor or wise therapist) and everyone else just turns up to agree with them.
- Achievement of consensus: the aim is to construct an agreed document that can be published or disseminated. While some degree of alternative interpretation can be interesting and valuable, a group that never manages to come together will end up either not producing anything, or will produce a report that is too fragmented to be readable.
- Creative use of dissensus and challenge: the logic of a quasi-judicial or adversarial approach seems well-suited to case study inquiry. Case reports are generally regarded as more plausible if readers can see that alternative interpretations of the data have been taken into consideration.
- Use of externality: the credibility or validity of the group's decisions is evaluated by a person or persons external to the group process.

There are a number of models available in the literature of how case study inquiry groups might function:

- *The co-operative inquiry model.* A model of co-operative inquiry (also known as collaborative inquiry, or participatory inquiry) has been developed by Peter Reason, Judi Marshall, John Heron and their colleagues at the University of Bath, and elsewhere. This approach is based on an action research conception of inquiry, in which a group proceeds through a series of research cycles as it collectively reflects on experience, collects and analyses data, and initiates further action arising from what has been learned. There is an emphasis on authentic participation by group members, with attention to emotional, spiritual and social justice dimensions of what might be happening in the group. Members are encouraged, at any stage, to take on the role of 'devil's advocate', and challenge anything that might be happening or being said. There are no specific analytic procedures associated with the co-operative inquiry approach; rather, the group selects or improvises methods to suit its particular aims. Further information on this approach can be found in Reason (1988, 1994, 1998) and Heron and Reason (2001).

- *Consensual qualitative research* is a team-based (usually 4–6 members) method for carrying out qualitative research, developed by Clara Hill (Hill et al. 1997, 2004). Research data (e.g., a rich case record) is analysed first in terms of broad domains, selected in advance. Within each domain, a version of an open-ended grounded theory approach is then used to generate categories. Each individual member of the group independently analyses the material, and shares what they have found. The group then discusses emerging categories, and reaches a consensus. There is an auditor, usually an experienced researcher, who is an adjunct member of the group, who regularly checks that the analysis being developed by the group is backed up by the data.
- *The Ward method.* Anthony Ward devised a format in which a team of architects could work together to produce the best possible response to a commission. Each member of the team produces a draft plan, and presents it to the group. In the ensuing discussion, the rule is that no one expresses a positive or negative critique of anyone else's ideas – the aim is to create a conversation in which the focus is on understanding ideas and the reasoning behind them. A record is kept of the discussion at each session. After each meeting, each member returns to independent work, building on the efforts of others that they have heard in the group, and produces another draft, which is then shared at the next meeting of the group. This procedure continues until there is sufficient convergence between the different plans to enable acceptance of a final agreed version. The Ward method has been applied in team-based therapy research by Bill Stiles and his group (Schielke et al. 2009).
- *Quasi-judicial structures.* There have been several approaches to organizing research teams along quasi-judicial lines, as a means of structuring the process of data analysis. Within the field of personality research, DeWaele and Harré (1976) and Murray and Morgan (1945) created two parallel groups of researchers, who worked independently on the same analysis and met periodically to compare results. Elliott et al. (2000) used a version of this strategy in the HSCED study described in Chapter 9, but with each team given a different brief (affirmative or sceptic positions in relation to the question: 'is this a good outcome case?'), leading to a final presentation of each case for adjudication by a panel of independent judges. Miller (2008) has described an adjudication process that operated as a live 'court-case' over the course of one day, with presentations of affirmative and sceptic positions, and cross examination, in the presence of expert judges who based their decision on what they had heard on the day.

Each of these models represents a means of harnessing the wisdom, insight and experience of members, while attenuating individual prejudice and any tendency to rush to premature judgement. The goal is to democratize the research process, by creating contexts in which authority judgements can be challenged.

At this stage in the development of case study inquiry group methodology, it is premature to recommend any one of these models, over the others. There are valuable aspects to all of them. Also, it is likely that increasing use of a team-based approach will bring further innovation. It would seem sensible, therefore, to select aspects of different models in accordance with the goals of the case study investigation being undertaken and the organizational context. For example, the guidelines and materials that Elliott has developed around sceptic and affirmative briefs are invaluable for any group that is analysing a case in terms of outcome. However, Elliott et al. (2009) found that team members could be uncomfortable when forced into one of these roles. As a result, some inquiry groups may prefer to have all members undertake affirmative/sceptic appraisals, rather than splitting the group. The use of an auditor on the Consensual Qualitative Research approach may be particularly effective when team members are students being supervised by a tutor. Compared to the other models, the co-operative inquiry method places a stronger emphasis on personal learning of group members and action outcomes.

The way that external adjudication is used will depend on the type of case study that is being carried out. When students or trainees are working together in a case study inquiry group, external adjudication may be provided by other groups of students, or by tutors.

By contrast, a case study inquiry group that is working toward publication will usually want to arrange external adjudication from experts in the field. These people may be experts in the therapy orientation that has been studied, or experts from rival orientations. For example, a published single case outcome study of psychodynamic therapy will gain in credibility if judged by a leading CBT researcher, or biological psychiatrist to be an example of good outcome. In some circumstances, service users (experts-by-experience) and even lay people (as in a normal jury) may be appropriate judges.

In this section, the case study inquiry group has been suggested as a means of integrating practice-oriented research, and personal and professional development. Some ideas have been offered regarding the way that such groups might operate. There is no doubt that further ideas will emerge as case study inquiry groups become more widely implemented. It is to be hoped that organizations that employ counsellors and psychotherapists, and practitioners working privately, will see advantages in allocating some of the time currently devoted to supervision and training to involvement in team-based case study research.

The case study inquiry group is a method that can be used in relation to any genre of case study research: pragmatic case studies, outcome-oriented case studies, theory-building case studies and narrative studies. Many practitioner inquiry groups will find, when they get together, that their interests cut across several of these genres. For example, there may be valuable theoretical insights to be gained from a primarily outcome-oriented case analysis. However, groups need to keep sight of the risk of trying to do too much in the time available, and the fact that it is easier to publish papers that focus on specific research goals. A case study inquiry group that decides to adopt a comprehensive approach to a case may need to budget for enough time to prepare more than one article for publication.

Using practitioner case studies to influence evidence-based practice policies: the adjudicated clinical trial

The case study inquiry group format is designed to allow practitioners to generate publishable research, and make a contribution to the knowledge base for counselling and psychotherapy. Some practitioner-based case studies may be able to be entered into systematic reviews, and some may serve as the groundwork for eventual large-scale randomized trials. However, on its own, a small-scale practitioner study can only have a limited impact on policy decision-making, such as the NICE guidelines process. To have influence at that level, practitioners need to work together in *practitioner research networks*, and carry out studies that are based on multiple cases. It is possible for practitioner research networks to carry out randomized controlled trials, or non-randomized outcome studies, in which large numbers of clients or patients complete outcome measures before therapy, at the end, and at follow-up. However, it is also possible for practitioner research networks to set up projects that involve multiple intensive case studies. There are several examples in the literature of case series of n=1 single subject case studies of therapy with specific client groups (see Chapter 7). This type of evidence has been accepted by policy-making groups in the USA as supporting the probable efficacy of such therapies (Chambless and Hollon, 1998; Chambless et al. 1998). The approach described below goes further than the n=1 studies, in outlining a case-based methodology that incorporates additional validity checks: the *adjudicated clinical trial*.

An adjudicated clinical trial (ACT) consists of a series of outcome-oriented case studies carried out by case study inquiry groups, using a combination of techniques from randomized clinical trial methodology, and both n=1 and HSCED case study methods. An adjudicated clinical trial represents a model of research that would be co-ordinated by a practitioner research network. The network would develop a standard research protocol that would be implemented by local inquiry groups, and would monitor the compliance of these groups to the research procedures. Just as in a randomised controlled trial the aim of an ACT study is to evaluate the efficacy of a therapy intervention under controlled conditions.

The key features of an adjudicated clinical trial are:

1 A research protocol that specifies the delivery of a specific form of therapy to clients with a specific set of problems. The protocol would encompass inclusion and exclusion criteria for clients, a manualized therapy, procedures for assessing adherence to the therapy, outcome measures to be used, and timing of administration of measures.
2 A case study inquiry group protocol that specifies how data are to be analysed. This would specify the collection of rich case data that would include a combination of n=1 time-series analysis, the preparation of sceptic/affirmative briefs, and narrative research.
3 Local case study inquiry groups are established, and trained in the procedures for the study.
4 A set of counsellors and psychotherapists working in everyday practice agree to submit clients who fulfil the criteria for the study and who are willing to take part, into the trial.
5 Research data are collected by the therapists (e.g., weekly outcome scales) and members of the inquiry groups (e.g., end of therapy Change Interview).
6 Each case is analysed by a case study inquiry group. The case analysis is passed on to external adjudicators. The client is invited to comment on a summary of the case analysis.
7 External adjudicators are selected to reflect a mix of different stakeholders (e.g., experienced therapists who work within the approach being studied; therapists from other approaches; other mental health professionals; service users/experts-by-experience).
8 The whole process is monitored by representatives of the practitioner research network, for example to ensure that poor-outcome cases do not get 'lost', etc.

This type of efficacy study has a number of strengths and weaknesses in comparison with other types of efficacy research in counselling and psychotherapy. Its weakness in contrast to RCTs is that it does not include random allocation to different treatments. On the other hand, random allocation of therapy clients raises ethical issues and compliance difficulties. The advantage over an RCT is that an ACT incorporates two levels of user involvement (the client and adjudicators) and allows for causal links between intervention and outcome to be examined at the case level. In contrast to n=1 studies, ACTs are more complex and take more time. The advantage over n=1 series is that the ACT model includes all cases (including poor outcome) rather than focusing solely on examples of where the therapy has clearly been effective, and encompasses a wider data set on each case. An ACT can be seen as a 'scaled-up', multi-site version of an HSCED study, but with an explicit incorporation of n=1 techniques (e.g., baseline data, time-series analysis, specifying the intervention) and client/user adjudication.

The adjudicated clinical trial method addresses some of the funda-mental political difficulties associated with outcome research in counsel-ling and psychotherapy. At the moment, RCTs are very expensive to implement, and require a high level of technical skill around statistical analysis, randomization techniques, etc. As a result, RCTs can only really be attempted by researchers in departments of psychology and psychia-try, and are therefore carried out on the therapies with which they are familiar (e.g., CBT, psychodynamic). Also, there is evidence that there is a strong 'experimenter effect' in RCT studies – where two therapies are compared in an RCT, the one that comes out as more effective is usually the one to which the lead researcher has a professional allegiance (Luborsky et al. 1999). Finally, service users and clients have no effective voice in the policy-making process. The ACT design goes some way to addressing each of these issues, and producing evidence of efficacy that is more transparent – findings can be drilled down to individual cases, and the client's view as to the extent to which the case summary sensi-tively captures their experience of therapy.

Integrating case study research into training: two examples

In many counselling and psychotherapy training programmes, students may attend a research module or research workshops, and receive an introduction to case study methods. There are two recently published examples of pro-grammes that attempt to go beyond this kind of introductory approach, and integrate the practice of case study research into the training experience of the student. In the person-centred/experiential psychotherapy training programme at the University of Leuven, students undertake a case study project throughout most of the course (Stinckens et al. 2009). In the first year of this four-year training programme, students attend lectures on research methods and are introduced to a case study research protocol that includes outcome and process

Box 11.2

(Continued)

measures, and a post-therapy Change Interview. In the second year, they collect data on at least one case. In the third year, they work with a supervisor to analyse the data. In the final year of the programme, they present a paper on their case to the course community, and the case becomes part of an archive that is available for other students to read. The focus of student case studies varied a great deal, with some students focusing on an area of client problem (e.g., eating disorders, depression) while others used their case study to explore process issues such as alliance ruptures or early dropout. Stinckens et al. (2009) evaluated the attitudes of students toward the case study element of their programme. They found that at the beginning of the course, 47% of students reported negative feelings about the case study assignment (not interested, fearful of failure, overwhelmed). By the end of the third year, however, all students reported positive attitudes. Another example of the integration of case study research into a training programme is found in the work of Esten Hougaard and colleagues at the Anxiety Clinic of the University of Aarhus in Denmark (Hougaard 2008; Hougaard et al. 2008). In this project, students and staff worked together to co-facilitate a group-based CBT programme for clients with social anxiety. In addition to the group, the students offered individual therapy to the clients before and after the group experience (this was the first client they had seen). Standard outcome data were collected for all clients. Each of the students wrote up a case study assignment on their client, following the format of the *Pragmatic Case Studies in Psychotherapy* journal. The clinic director then wrote a composite paper on all the client cases in the group, which was published with the students as co-authors (Hougaard et al. 2008). Students rated this whole learning experience as highly satisfactory.

Conclusions: an action plan for the development of practitioner-based case research

There have been relatively few references in this chapter, because it is looking forward rather than reviewing what has been done in the past. Case study inquiry groups and adjudicated clinical trials represent ways that practitioners can take well-established research tools and strategies and apply them in ways that are beneficial for their personal and professional development, as well as contributing to building a case-based research literature. Of course, so far, relatively little of this is in place, and none of it can happen overnight. It will take time to create a new tradition of practitioner case study research. The aim of the final section of this chapter, therefore, is to consider what can be done to support this endeavour. What follows is an action list.

Counsellor and psychotherapist training

It would be useful if training courses could introduce students/trainees to different genres of case study research, the use of data collection techniques such as outcome measures and the Change Interview, and the experience of working in groups to analyse case material. Trainees are usually required to submit at least one case study during their training, so there already exist areas of the training curriculum that could be augmented by the adoption of a more research-informed approach. It would also be valuable if university programmes were to support and encourage students to carry out case-based studies for their Masters and Doctoral dissertations, and to find ways of rewarding students for working in teams, rather than necessarily having to carry out single-researcher studies.

Journal policies

The editorial boards of counselling and psychotherapy journals could support practitioner case study research in a number of ways. Elliott et al. (1999) made a major contribution to the advancement of qualitative research in psychology and psychotherapy by publishing a set of 'publishability guidelines' for qualitative research. It would be helpful if this could be achieved for case study research, either across the field as a whole or in the context of specific journals and their instructions for authors. It will be easier for practitioners (and others) to think about submitting case study articles to journals if they know in advance about the criteria that reviewers and editors will use in evaluating their manuscripts. Journals could also help the case study cause by further developing their practices around on-line publication of supplementary material. It is difficult to do justice to a case study within the normal word length of a journal article, and the knowledge that data can be included in an on-line appendix would be valuable for authors.

Ethics procedures

Many practitioners are wary of getting involved in case study research because of the ethical complexities and sensitivities associated with this form of inquiry. The discussion in Chapter 4 of this book is intended to clarify some of these ethical issues, and suggest ethical procedures that might be followed. It would be better if these suggestions could be given further consideration by the relevant professional bodies, leading to a consensus statement on how the ethics of case study research in counselling and psychotherapy should be handled by practitioner-researchers. The existence of such a consensus statement (which would need to be periodically revised in the light of experience) would be very helpful for practitioners seeking to gain ethical approval for case study projects.

Funding support for case study inquiry groups and practitioner research networks

At the time of writing this book, all the advanced technical-industrial economies were in recession, and facing a decade of public spending cuts in order to pay for the rescue of the banking system. The near future is certain to bring increased demand on state resources to pay for the costs associated with global warming, and an ageing population. As a consequence, there seems to be absolutely no chance of an expansion in finding support for counselling and psychotherapy training and research. In this context, practitioner-based, low-cost 'grass roots' research may come to be increasingly popular with funding agencies, particularly if it incorporates the views of service users. It may be possible to make an argument that focused investment in practitioner research networks can yield big gains in research knowledge (compared to the same amount invested in an RCT). It may be realistic to bid for the appointment of researcher officers to facilitate practitioner research networks, or short-term sabbaticals for practitioner-researchers. It may be possible to encourage larger counselling and psychotherapy agencies to re-direct some of the money they already spend on staff training and supervision into case study inquiry groups and involvement in practitioner research networks.

University researchers as resources for practitioner research networks

It can be hard for practitioners who are interested in research to gain access to the knowledge and skills of researchers based in universities. The organizational structure and priorities of most universities means that researchers are largely restricted to supervising Masters and Doctoral students, and conducting funded research. The needs of practitioner-researchers, who may not wish to do a PhD, and certainly cannot pay for consultation time, get lost in all this. Greater publicity needs to be given to those university groups that have been able to act as resources for practitioner research groups, so that their success experiences can be replicated more widely.

Establishing a list of volunteer adjudicators

Case study research that involves the use of external adjudicators would be greatly facilitated if there was a directory of people who might be willing to fulfil this role, and had received some training in what might be involved. Professional bodies such as the British Association for Counselling and Psychotherapy might be in a good position to co-ordinate this activity.

Criteria for inclusion in systematic reviews

In the UK, the National Institute for Health and Clinical Excellence (NICE) is a government organization that has responsibility for deciding on treatments that will be made available within the National Health Service (NHS). There are similar bodies in other countries (and in the UK). At the present time, it is not clear that NICE will take case study evidence on counselling and psychotherapy into consideration, or the kind of weighting it might give to different types of case study. This absence may be because little or no relevant case study evidence has hitherto been submitted to it. It would be useful if NICE and other bodies could clarify their position in respect of case-based outcome evidence. Recently, NICE indicated the conditions under which qualitative evidence would be appraised, by publishing on its website a checklist for evaluating the methodological rigour of qualitative studies. It would be helpful if a similar exercise could be undertaken for case study and case-series evidence.

This action list is intended as a means of enabling interested stakeholders to think about what might be done to promote practitioner-based case study research in counselling and psychotherapy. It is a list of what to do, what to ask for, and what might be given. However, it would be a big mistake to think that all (or indeed any) of this needs to be in place before practitioner case study inquiry groups and research networks can flourish. My own belief is that the main priority is actually to get on and do this kind of research, but in a way that strikes a balance between research outputs and personal/professional development outputs. More published examples of case study research that speaks to practitioners, and speaks to policy issues, will be the single most powerful way of inducing leverage in terms of increased support from government agencies, professional bodies and universities. Meaningful personal learning experiences in students and practitioners engaged in case study inquiry groups is the way to make this happen.

Topics for reflection and discussion

1   How might your own personal and professional development as a counsellor or psychotherapist be facilitated by participation in a case study inquiry group? Reflect on the list of group tasks outlined in Box 11.1 and the discussion of developmental themes on pages 214–15. Which of these opportunities for learning are most relevant for you at this point in your career? What would be the advantages and disadvantages of pursuing these learning possibilities through case study research, as opposed to other activities such as supervision, personal therapy and training workshops?

2   If you were part of a case study inquiry group, who would you ideally want the other members to be? What does your answer imply, in terms of criteria for establishing the size and composition of effective research teams?

Recommended further reading

In terms of developing an appreciation of how a case study inquiry group might function, it is necessary to explore the literature on research teams:

Heron, J. and Reason, P. (2001) The practice of co-operative inquiry: research 'with' rather than 'on' people. In P. Reason and H. Bradbury (eds), *Handbook of Action Research.* London: Sage.

Hill, C.E., Thompson, B.J. and Nutt-Williams, E. (1997) A guide to conducting consensual qualitative research. *Counseling Psychologist*, 25, 517–72.

Hill, C.E., Knox, S., Thompson, B.J., Williams, E.N., Hess, S.A. and Ladany, N. (2004) Consensual qualitative research: an update. *Journal of Counseling Psychology*, 52, 196–205.

Schielke, H.J., Fishman, J.L., Osatuke, K. and Stiles, W.B. (2009) Creative consensus on interpretations of qualitative data: the Ward method. *Psychotherapy Research*, 19, 558–65.

References

Ablon, J.S. and Jones, E.E. (1998) How expert clinicians' prototypes of an ideal treatment correlate with outcome in psychodynamic and cognitive-behavioral therapy. *Psychotherapy Research*, 8, 71–83.

Adler, J.M. and McAdams, D.P. (2007a) The narrative reconstruction of psychotherapy. *Narrative Inquiry*, 17, 179–202.

Adler, J.M. and McAdams, D.P. (2007b) Telling stories about therapy: ego development, well-being, and the therapeutic relationship. In R. Josselson, A. Lieblich and D.P. McAdams (eds), *The Meaning of Others: Narrative Studies of Relationships*. Washington, DC: American Psychological Association.

Adler, J.M., Skalina, L.M. and McAdams, D.P. (2008) The narrative reconstruction of psychotherapy and psychological health. *Psychotherapy Research*, 18, 719–34.

Adler, J.M., Wagner, J.W. and McAdams, D.P. (2007) Personality and the coherence of psychotherapy narratives. *Journal of Research in Personality*, 41, 1179–98.

Alaszewski, A. (2006) *Using Diaries for Social Research*. London: Sage.

Alexander, R. (1995) *Folie à Deux: An Experience of One-to-one Therapy*. London: Free Association.

Angus, L. (1996) An intensive analysis of metaphor themes in psychotherapy. In J.S. Mio and A. Katz (eds), *Metaphor: Pragmatics and Applications*. New York: Erlbaum.

Angus, L., Goldman, R. and Mergenthaler, E. (2008) Introduction. One case, multiple measures: an intensive case-analytic approach to understanding client change processes in evidence-based, emotion-focused therapy of depression. *Psychotherapy Research*, 18(6), 629–33.

APA Presidential Task Force on Evidence-Based Practice (2006) Evidence-based practice in psychology. *American Psychologist*, 61, 271–85.

Argyris, C. and Schön, D. (1974) *Theory in Practice: Increasing Professional Effectiveness*. San Francisco, CA: Jossey–Bass.

Aveline, M. (2005) Clinical case studies: their place in evidence-based practice. *Psychodynamic Practice*, 11, 133–52.

Axline, V. (1971) *Dibs: In Search of Self*. Harmondsworth: Penguin.

BACP (2007) *Ethical Framework for Good Practice in Counselling and Psychotherapy*, rev. edn. Rugby, UK: British Association for Counselling and Psychotherapy.

Baines, K. and Wills, F. (2002) Beyond beliefs: challenging obsessive thoughts and compulsive behaviours within a collaborative counselling relationship. *Counselling and Psychotherapy Research*, 2, 269–76.

Barker, C., Pistrang, N. and Elliott, R. (2002) *Research Methods in Clinical and Counselling Psychology*, 2nd edn. Chichester: Wiley.

Barkham, M., Mellor-Clark, J., Connell, J. and Cahill, J. (2006) A core approach to practice-based evidence: a brief history of the origins and applications of the CORE-OM and CORE System. *Counselling and Psychotherapy Research*, 6(1), 3–15.

Barlow, D.H. and Hersen, M. (1986) *Single Case Experimental Designs: Strategies for Studying Behavior Change*, 2nd edn. New York: Pergamon.

Barlow, D.H., Hayes, S.C. and Nelson, R.O. (1984) *The Scientist Practitioner: Research and Accountability in Clinical and Educational Settings*. New York: Pergamon.

Barrett-Lennard, G.T. (1978) *The Relationship Inventory: Later Development and Adaptations. JSAS Catalog of Selected Documents in Psychology*, 8, 68.

Barrett-Lennard, G.T. (1986) The Relationship Inventory now: issues and advances in theory, method and use. In L.S. Greenberg and W.M. Pinsof (eds), *The Psychotherapeutic Process: A Research Handbook*. New York: Guilford.

Bates, C.M. and Brodsky, A.M. (1989) *Sex in the Therapy Hour: A Case of Professional Incest*. London: Guilford Press.

Bates, Y. (ed.) (2006) *Shouldn't I Be Feeling Better by Now? Client Views of Therapy*. London: Palgrave.

Beauchamp, T.L. and Childress, J.F. (1979) *Principles of Biomedical Ethics*. Oxford: Oxford University Press.

Beitman, B.D. (1991) Medications during psychotherapy: case studies of the reciprocal relationship between psychotherapy process and medication use. In B.D. Beitman and G.L. Klerman (eds), *Integrating Pharmacotherapy and Psychotherapy*. Washington, DC: American Psychiatric Association.

Bernheimer, C. and Kahane, C. (eds) (1986) *In Dora's Case*. London: Virago.

Bertaux, D. (ed.) (1981) *Biography and Society*. London: Sage.

Bichi, E.L. (2008) A case history: from traumatic repetition towards psychic representability. *International Journal of Psychoanalysis*, 89, 541–60.

Billig, M. (1997) Freud and Dora: repressing an oppressed identity. *Theory, Culture and Society*, 14, 29–55.

Bjelland, I., Dahl, A.A., Haug, T.T. et al. (2002) The validity of the Hospital Anxiety and Depression Scale: an updated literature review. *Journal of Psychosomatic Research*, 52, 69–77.

Blampied, N.M. (1999) A legacy neglected: restating the case for single-case research in cognitive-behaviour therapy. *Behaviour Change*, 16, 89–104.

Blampied, N.M. (2000) Single-case research designs: a neglected alternative. *American Psychologist*, 55, 960.

Blampied, N.M. (2001) The third way: single-case research training and practice in clinical psychology. *Australian Psychologist*, 36, 157–63.

Blanton, H. and Jaccard, J. (2006) Arbitrary metrics in psychology. *American Psychologist*, 61, 27–41.

Blotzer, M.A. and Ruth, R. (eds) (1995) *Sometimes You Just Want to Feel Like a Human Being: Case Studies of Empowering Psychotherapy with People with Disabilities*. Baltimore, MD: Paul H. Brookes Publishing.

Bohart, A.C. (2000) The client is the most important common factor: clients' self-healing capacities and psychotherapy. *Journal of Psychotherapy Integration*, 10, 127–48.

Bohart, A.C. and Boyd, G. (1997) A qualitative analysis and study of outcome in psychotherapy. Paper distributed at the 1997 North American Society for Psychotherapy Research Conference, Tucson, AZ.

Bohart, A.C. and Humphreys, C. (2000) A qualitative 'adjudicational' model for assessing psychotherapy outcome. Paper presented at the meeting of the International Society for Psychotherapy Research, Chicago, Illinois.

Bohart, A.C. and Tallman, K. (1996) The active client: therapy as self-help. *Journal of Humanistic Psychology*, 3, 7–30.

Bohart, A.C. and Tallman, K. (1998) The person as an active agent in experiential therapy. In L.S. Greenberg, J.C. Watson and G. Lietaer (eds), *Handbook of Experiential Psychotherapy*. New York: Guilford Press.

Bohart, A.C. and Tallman, K. (1999) *How Clients Make Therapy Work: The Process of Active Self-healing*. Washington, DC: American Psychological Association.

Bolgar, H. (1965) The case study method. In B. Wolman (ed.), *Handbook of Clinical Psychology*. New York: McGraw–Hill.

Borckardt, J.J., Nash, M.R., Murphy, M.D., Moore, M., Shaw, D. and O'Neil, P. (2008) Clinical practice as natural laboratory for psychotherapy research. A guide to case-based time-series analysis. *American Psychologist*, 63, 77–95.

Borkovec, T.D., Echemendia, R.J., Ragusea, S.A. and Ruiz, M. (2001) The Pennsylvania Practice Research Network and future possibilities for clinically meaningful and scientifically rigorous psychotherapy effectiveness research. *Clinical Psychology: Science and Practice*, 8, 155–67.

Borrill, J. and Foreman, E.I. (1996) Understanding cognitive change: a qualitative study of the impact of cognitive-behavioural therapy on fear of flying. *Clinical Psychology and Psychotherapy*, 3(1), 62–74.

Bowling, A. (2001) *Measuring Disease*, 2nd edn. Maidenhead: Open University Press.

Bowling, A. (2004) *Measuring Health*, 3rd edn. Maidenhead: Open University Press.

Braud, W. and Anderson, R. (eds) (1998) *Transpersonal Research Methods for the Social Sciences: Honoring Human Experience*. Thousand Oaks, CA: Sage.

Brinegar, M.G., Salvi, L.M., Stiles, W.B. and Greenberg, L.S. (2006) Building a meaning bridge: therapeutic progress from problem formulation to understanding. *Journal of Counseling Psychology*, 53, 165–80.

Bromley, D. (1981) *Personality Description in Ordinary Language*. Chichester: Wiley.

Bromley, D. (1986) *The Case-Study Method in Psychology and Related Disciplines*. Chichester: Wiley.

Bruner, J. (1986) *Actual Minds, Possible Worlds*. Cambridge, MA: Harvard University Press.

Bruner, J. (1990) *Acts of Meaning*. Cambridge, MA: Harvard University Press.

Bruner, J. (2002) *Making Stories. Law, Literature, Life*. New York: Farrar, Straus and Giroux.

Byrne, D. and Ragin, C.C. (eds) (2009) *The Sage Handbook of Case-Based Methods*. Thousand Oaks, CA: Sage.

Campbell, D.T. and Stanley, J.C. (1963) *Experimental and Quasi-Experimental Designs for Research*. Chicago, IL: Rand McNally.

Carvalho, M.J., Faustino, I., Nascimento, A. and Sales, C.M.D. (2008) Understanding Pamina's recovery: an application of the hermeneutic single-case efficacy design. *Counselling and Psychotherapy Research*, 8, 166–73.

Casement, P. (1985) *On Learning from the Patient*. London: Tavistock.

Casement, P. (1990) *Further Learning from the Patient: The Analytic Space and Process*. London: Tavistock/Routledge.

Caspar, F. (2007) Plan analysis. In T.D. Eells (ed.), *Handbook of Psychotherapy Case Formulation*, 2nd edn. New York: Guilford Press.

Caspar, F. (2009) Plan analysis in action. *Pragmatic Case Studies in Psychotherapy*, 5(2), 25–27. http://hdl.rutgers.edu/1782.1/pcsp_journal

Chambless, D.L. and Hollon, S.D. (1998) Defining empirically supported therapies. *Journal of Consulting and Clinical Psychology*, 66, 7–18.

Chambless, D.L., Baker, M.J. Baucom, D.H. et al. (1998) Update on empirically validated therapies II. *The Clinical Psychologist*, 51, 1–16.

Charmaz, K. (2006) *Constructing Grounded Theory: A Practical Guide through Qualitative Analysis*. Thousand Oaks, CA: Sage.

Clifford, J.S., Norcross, J.C. and Sommer, R. (1999) Autobiographies of mental health clients: psychologists' uses and recommendations. *Professional Psychology: Research and Practice*, 30, 56–9.

Cohen, S., Kamarck, T. and Mermelstein, R. (1983) A global measure of perceived stress. *Journal of Health and Social Behavior*, 24, 386–96.

Cone, J.D. (2001) *Evaluating Outcomes: Empirical Tools for Effective Practice*. Washington, DC: American Psychological Association.

Connolly, M.B., Crits-Christoph, P., Kurtz, J., (1999) The reliability and validity of a measure of self-understanding of interpersonal patterns. *Journal of Counseling Psychology*, 46, 472–82.

Cooper, M. (2008) *Essential Research Findings in Counselling and Psychotherapy: The Facts Are Friendly*. London: Sage.

Corbin, J. and Strauss, A. (2008) *Basics of Qualitative Research: Techniques and Procedures for Developing Grounded Theory*, 3rd edn. Thousand Oaks, CA: Sage.

Cronbach, L.J. (1975) Beyond the two disciplines of scientific psychology. *American Psychologist*, 30, 116–27.

Crosby, F. (1979) Evaluating psychohistorical explanations. *Psychohistory Review*, 7(4), 6–16.

Cushman, P. (1995) *Constructing the Self, Constructing America: A Cultural History of Psychotherapy*. Reading, MA: Addison-Wesley.

Davidson, L. (2008) From 'incurable' schizophrenic to person in recovery: a not so uncommon story. *Pragmatic Case Studies in Psychotherapy*, 4(1), 25–34. http://hdl.rutgers.edu/1782.1/pcsp_journal

Davidson, L., Harding, C. and Spaniol, L. (eds) (2005) *Recovery from Severe Mental Illnesses: Research Evidence and Implications for Practice, Volume 1*. Boston: Boston University Center for Psychiatric Rehabilitation.

Davidson, L., Harding, C. and Spaniol, L. (eds) (2006) *Recovery from Severe Mental Illnesses: Research Evidence and Implications for Practice, Volume 2*. Boston, MA: Boston University Center for Psychiatric Rehabilitation.

Davis, J.H. (2003) Balancing the whole: portraiture as methodology. In P.M. Camic, J.E. Rhodes and L. Yardley (eds), *Qualitative Research in Psychology: Expanding Perspectives in Methodology and Design*. Washington, DC: American Psychological Association.

Deane, F.P., Spicer, J. and Todd, D.M. (1997) Validity of a simplified target complaints measure. *Psychological Assessment*, 4, 119–30.

DeWaele, J. and Harré, R. (1976) The personality of individuals. In R. Harré (ed.), *Personality*. Oxford: Blackwell.

Dinnage, R. (1988) *One to One: Experiences of Psychotherapy*. London: Penguin.

Dixon, M.R., Jackson, J.W. and Small, S.L. (2009) Creating single-subject design graphs in Microsoft Excel™ 2007. *Journal of Applied Behavior Analysis*, 42(2), 277–93.

Donmoyer, R. (1990) Generalizability and the single case study. In E.W. Eisner and A. Peshkin (eds), *Qualitative Inquiry in Education: The Continuing Debate*. New York: Teachers College Press.

Dreier, O. (1998) Client perspectives and uses of psychotherapy. *European Journal of Psychotherapy, Counselling and Health*, 1, 295–310.

Dreier, O. (2000) Psychotherapy in clients' trajectories across contexts. In C. Mattingly and L. Garro (eds), *Narratives and the Cultural Construction of Illness and Healing*. Berkeley, CA: University of California Press.

Dreier, O. (2008) *Psychotherapy in Everyday Life*. Cambridge: Cambridge University Press.

Dryden, W. (2005) The personal therapy experience of a Rational Emotive Therapist. In J.D. Geller, J.C. Norcross and D.E. Orlinsky (eds), *The Psychotherapist's Own Psychotherapy: Patient and Clinician Perspectives*. New York: Oxford University Press.

Dryden, W. and Yankura, J. (1992) *Daring to be Myself: A Case Study in Rational-Emotive Therapy*. Maidenhead: Open University Press.

Dukes, W.F. (1965) N=1. *Psychological Bulletin*, 53, 74–9.

Edelson, M. (1985) The hermeneutic turn and the single case study in psychoanalysis. *Psychoanalysis and Contemporary Thought*, 8, 567–614.

Edelson, M. (1986) Causal explanation in science and in psychoanalysis: implications for writing a case study. *Psychoanalytic Study of the Child*, 41, 89–127.

Edwards, D.J.A. (1998) Types of case study work: a conceptual framework for case-based research. *Journal of Humanistic Psychology*, 38(3), 36–70.

Edwards, D.J.A. (2007) Collaborative versus adversarial stances in scientific discourse: implications for the role of systematic case studies. *Pragmatic Case Studies in Psychotherapy*, 3(1), 6–34. http://pcsp.libraries.rutgers.edu

Edwards, D.J.A., Dattilio, F. and Bromley, D.B. (2004) Developing evidence-based practice: the role of case-based research. *Professional Psychology: Research and Practice*, 35, 589–97.

Eells, T. (ed.) (2007a) *Handbook of Psychotherapy Case Formulation*, 2nd edn. New York: Guilford Press.

Eells, T.D. (2007b) Generating and generalizing knowledge about psychotherapy from pragmatic case studies. *Pragmatic Case Studies in Psychotherapy*, 3(1), 35–54. http://pcsp.libraries.rutgers.edu

Eells, T.D. and Lombart, K.G. (2003) Case formulation and treatment concepts among novice, experienced and expert cognitive-behavioural and psychodynamic therapists. *Psychotherapy Research*, 13, 187–204.

Eells, T.D, Lombart, K.G., Kendjelic, E.M., Turner, L.C. and Lucas, C.P. (2005) The quality of psychotherapy case formulations: a comparison of expert, experienced, and novice cognitive-behavioral and psychodynamic therapists. *Journal of Consulting and Clinical Psychology*, 73, 579–89.

Elliott, R. (1983) 'That in your hands ...': a comprehensive process analysis of a significant event in psychotherapy. *Psychiatry*, 46, 113–29.

Elliott, R. (1984) A discovery-oriented approach to significant change events in psychotherapy: Interpersonal Process Recall and Comprehensive Process

Analysis. In L.N. Rice and L.S. Greenberg (eds), *Patterns of Change: Intensive Analysis of Psychotherapy Process*. New York: Guilford Press.

Elliott, R. (1993) *Comprehensive Process Analysis: Mapping the Change Process in Psychotherapy*. Unpublished manual. Available from Department of Psychology, University of Toledo, Toledo, Ohio, USA.

Elliott, R. (1998) A guide to the empirically supported treatments controversy. *Psychotherapy Research*, 8, 115–25.

Elliott, R. (2001) Hermeneutic single-case efficacy design: an overview. In K.J. Schneider, J. Bugental and J.F. Pierson (eds), *The Handbook of Humanistic Psychology: Leading Edges in Theory, Research and Practice*. Thousand Oaks, CA: Sage.

Elliott, R. (2002) Hermeneutic Single Case Efficacy Design. *Psychotherapy Research*, 12, 1–20.

Elliott, R. and Shapiro, D.A. (1992) Client and therapist as analysts of significant events. In S.G. Toukmanian and D.L. Rennie (eds), *Psychotherapy Process Research: Paradigmatic and Narrative Approaches*. London: Sage.

Elliott, R., Fischer, C.T. and Rennie, D.L. (1999) Evolving guidelines for the publication of qualitative research studies in psychology and related fields. *British Journal of Clinical Psychology*, 38, 215–29.

Elliott, R., Greenberg, L.S. and Lietaer, G. (2004) Research on experiential psychotherapies. In M.J. Lambert (ed.), *Bergin and Garfield's Handbook of Psychotherapy and Behavior Change*, 5th edn. New York: Wiley.

Elliott, R., Partyka, R., Wagner, J., Alperin, R., Dobrenski, R., Messer, S.B., Watson, J.C. and Castonguay, L.G. (2009) An adjudicated Hermeneutic Single Case Efficacy Design study of experiential therapy for panic/phobia. *Psychotherapy Research*, 19, 543–57.

Elliott, R., Shapiro, D.A. and Mack, C. (1999) *Simplified Personal Questionnaire*. Toledo, OH: Department of Psychology, University of Toledo.

Elliott, R., Shapiro, D.A., Firth-Cozens, J., Stiles, W.B., Hardy, G.E., Llewelyn, S.P. and Margison, F.R. (1994) Comprehensive Process Analysis of insight events in cognitive-behavioral and psychodynamic-interpersonal psychotherapies. *Journal of Counseling Psychology*, 41, 449–63.

Elliott, R. and Zucconi, A. (2006) Doing research on the effectiveness of psychotherapy and psychotherapy training: a person-centered/experiential perspective. *Person-Centered and Experiential Psychotherapies*, 5, 81–100.

Ellis, C. (2007) Telling secrets, revealing lives: relational ethics in research with intimate others. *Qualitative Inquiry*, 13, 3–29.

Ellis, C. and Bochner, A.P. (eds) (1996) *Composing Ethnography: Alternative Forms of Qualitative Writing*. Walnut Creek, CA: AltaMira Press.

Epston, D. (1992) Consulting your consultants: the documentation of alternative knowledges. In D. Epston and M. White (eds), *Experience, Contradiction, Narrative and Imagination*. Adelaide, Australia: Dulwich Centre Publications.

Eriksen, E, (1986) Reality and actuality: an address. In C. Bernheimer and C. Kahane (eds), *In Dora's Case*. London: Virago.

Etherington, K. (2000) *Narrative Approaches to Working with Adult Male Survivors of Child Sexual Abuse: The Client's, the Counsellor's and the Researcher's Story*. London: Jessica Kingsley.

Etherington, K. (2004) *Becoming a Reflexive Researcher – Using Our Selves in Research*. London: Jessica Kingsley.

Etherington, K. (2007) Ethical research in reflexive relationships. *Qualitative Inquiry*, 13, 599–616.

Evans, D. (2003) Hierarchy of evidence: a framework for ranking evidence evaluating healthcare interventions. *Journal of Clinical Nursing*, 12, 77–84.

Faith, M.S., Allison, D.B. and Gorman, B.S. (1996) Meta-analysis of single-case research. In R.D. Franklin, D.B. Allison and B.S. Gorman (eds), *Design and Analysis of Single-Case Research*. Mahwah, NJ: Lawrence Erlbaum.

Farber, B.A., Brink, D.C. and Raskin, P.M. (eds) (1996) *The Psychotherapy of Carl Rogers: Cases and Commentary*. New York: Guilford Press.

Finlay, L. and Gough. B. (eds.) (2003) *Reflexivity: A Practical Guide for Researchers in Health and Social Science*. Oxford, Blackwell.

Firth-Cozens, J. (1992) Why me? A case study of the process of perceived occupational stress. *Human Relations*, 45, 131–42.

Fisher, P.L. and Wells, A. (2008) Metacognitive therapy for obsessive–compulsive disorder: a case series. *Journal of Behavior Therapy*, 29, 117–32.

Fishman, D.B. (1999) *The Case for a Pragmatic Psychology*. New York: New York University Press.

Fishman, D.B. (2000) Transcending the efficacy versus effectiveness research debate: proposal for a new, electronic 'Journal of Pragmatic Case Studies.' *Prevention and Treatment*, 3, Article 8.

Fishman, D.B. (2005) Editor's introduction to PCSP – From single case to database: a new method for enhancing psychotherapy practice. *Pragmatic Case Studies in Psychotherapy*, 1(1), 1–50. http://pcsp.libraries.rutgers.edu

Fishman, D.B. (2006) Finding legitimacy for case study knowledge. *Pragmatic Case Studies in Psychotherapy*, 2(4), 1–6. http://pcsp.libraries.rutgers.edu/

Fishman, D.B. (2009) Using case studies to develop theory: roadmap to a dialogue. *Pragmatic Case Studies in Psychotherapy*, 5(3), 1–8. http://pcsp.libraries.rutgers.edu

Flybjerg, B. (2006) Five misunderstandings about case-study research. *Qualitative Inquiry*, 12(2): 219–45.

Foa, E.B. and Rothbaum, B.O. (1998) *Treating the Trauma of Rape: Cognitive Behavioral Therapy for PTSD*. New York: Guilford Press.

France, A. (1988) *Consuming Psychotherapy*. London: Free Association.

Freud, S. (1901/1979) The case of Dora. *Pelican Freud Library*, vol. 8: *Case Histories I*. Harmondsworth: Penguin.

Freud, S. (1909/1979) Notes upon a case of obsessional neurosis (the 'Rat Man'). *Pelican Freud Library*, vol. 9: *Case Histories II*. Harmondsworth: Penguin.

Freud, S. (1910/1979) Psychoanalytic notes on an autobiographical account of a case of paranoia (Dementia Paranoides) (Schreber). *Pelican Freud Library*, vol. 9: *Case Histories II*. Harmondsworth: Penguin.

Frommer, J. and Langenbach, M. (2001) The psychoanalytic case study as a source of epistemic knowledge. *Psychologische Beitrage*, 43, 50–68.

Frommer, J., Reissner, V., Tress, W. and Langenbach, M. (1996). Subjective theories of illness in patients with personality disorders: qualitative comparison of twelve diagnostic interviews. *Psychotherapy Research*, 6, 56–69.

Furedi, F. (2004) *Therapy Culture: Cultivating Vulnerability in an Uncertain Age*. London: Routledge.

Furlong, A. (2006) Further reflections on the impact of clinical writing on patients. *International Journal of Psychoanalysis*, 87, 747–68.

Furlong, M.J. and Wampold, B. (1982) Intervention effects and relative variation as dimensions in experts' use of visual inference. *Journal of Applied Behavior Analysis*, 15, 415–421.

Gabbard, G.O. (2000) Disguise or consent: problems and recommendations concerning the publication and presentation of clinical case material. *International Journal of Psychoanalysis*, 81, 1071–86.

Gabbard, G.O. and Williams, P. (2001) Preserving confidentiality in the writing of case reports. *International Journal of Psychoanalysis*, 82, 1067–8.

Galassi, J.P. and Gersh, T.L. (1991) Single-case research in counselling. In C.E. Watkins and L.J. Schneider (eds), *Research in Counseling*. Hillsdale, NJ: Lawrence Erlbaum.

Galatzer-Levy, R. (2003) Psychoanalytic research and confidentiality dilemmas. In C. Levin, A. Furlong and M.K. O'Neil (eds), *Confidentiality: Ethical Perspectives and Clinical Dilemmas*. Hillsdale, NJ: Analytic Press.

Gavey, N. and Braun, V. (1997) Ethics and the publication of clinical case material. *Professional Psychology: Research and Practice*, 28, 399–404.

Gee, J.P. (1991) A linguistic approach to narrative. *Journal of Narrative and Life History*, 1, 15–39.

Geller, J.D. (2005) My experiences as a patient in five psychoanalytic psychotherapies. In J.D. Geller, J.C. Norcross and D.E. Orlinsky (eds), *The Psychotherapist's Own Psychotherapy: Patient and Clinician Perspectives*. New York: Oxford University Press.

Geller, J.D., Norcross, J.C. and Orlinsky, D.E. (eds) (2005) *The Psychotherapist's Own Psycotherapy: Patient and Clinician Perspectives*. New York: Oxford University Press.

Gergen, K.J. (1999) *An Invitation to Social Construction*. Thousand Oaks, CA: Sage.

Gerring, J. (2006) *Case Study Research: Principles and Practices*. New York: Cambridge University Press.

Gomm, R., Hammersley, R. and Foster, P. (eds) (2000) *Case Study Method*. London: Sage.

Goodley, D., Lawthom, R., Clough, P. and Moore, M. (2004) *Researching Life Stories: Method, Theory and Analyses in a Biographical Age*. London: RoutledgeFalmer.

Gorman, B.S. and Allison, D.B. (1996) Statistical alternatives for single-case designs. In R.D. Franklin, D.B. Allison and B.S. Gorman (eds), *Design and Analysis of Single-Case Research*. Mahwah, NJ: Lawrence Erlbaum.

Grafanaki, S. (1996) How research can change the researcher: the need for sensitivity, flexibility and ethical boundaries in conducting qualitative research in counselling/psychotherapy. *British Journal of Guidance and Counselling*, 24, 329–38.

Grafanaki, S. (2001) What counselling research has taught us about the concept of congruence: main discoveries and unresolved issues. In G. Wyatt (ed.), *Rogers' Therapeutic Conditions: Evolution, Theory and Practice. Volume 1: Congruence*. Ross-on-Wye: PCCS Books.

Grafanaki, S. and McLeod, J. (1999) Narrative processes in the construction of helpful and hindering events in experiential psychotherapy. *Psychotherapy Research*, 9, 289–303.

Graves, P.L. (1996) Narrating a psychoanalytic case study. In R. Josselson (ed.), *Ethics and Process in the Narrative Study of Lives*. Thousand Oaks, CA: Sage.

Greenberg, L. (2002) *Emotion-Focused Therapy: Coaching Clients to Work Through Feelings*. Washington, DC: American Psychological Association.

Greenberg, L.S. and Pinsof, W.M. (eds) (1986) *The Psychotherapeutic Process: A Research Handbook*. New York: Guilford Press.

Greenberg, L.S., Rice, L.N. and Elliott, R. (1993) *Facilitating Emotional Change: The Moment-by-Moment Process*. New York: Guilford Press.

Gresham, F.M. (1996) Treatment integrity in single-subject research. In R.D. Franklin, D.B. Allison and B.S. Gorman (eds), *Design and Analysis of Single-Case Research*. Mahwah, NJ: Lawrence Erlbaum.

Guillemin, M. and Gillam, L. (2004) Ethics, reflexivity and 'ethically important moments' in research. *Qualitative Inquiry*, 10, 261–80.

Guntrip, H. (2005) My experience of analysis with Fairbairn and Winnicott: how complete a result does psychoanalytic therapy achieve? In J.D. Geller, J.C. Norcross and D.E. Orlinsky (eds), *The Psychotherapist's Own Psychotherapy: Patient and Clinician Perspectives*. New York: Oxford University Press.

Hargaden, H. and Sills, C. (2002) *Transactional Analysis: A Relational Perspective*. London: Brunner Routledge.

Hatcher, R.L. and Gillaspy, J.A. (2006) Development and validation of a revised short form of the Working Alliance Inventory. *Psychotherapy Research*, 16, 12–25.

Hatfield, A.B. (1989) Patients' accounts of stress and coping in schizophrenia. *Hospital and Community Psychiatry*, 40, 1141–5.

Hembree, E.A. and Brinen, A.P. (2009) Prolonged exposure (PE) for treatment of childhood sexual abuse-related PTSD: Do we need to augment it? *Pragmatic Case Studies in Psychotherapy*, 5(2), 35–44. http://hdl.rutgers.edu/1782.1/pcsp_journal

Heron, J. and Reason, P. (2001) The practice of co-operative inquiry: research 'with' rather than 'on' people. In P. Reason and H. Bradbury (eds), *Handbook of Action Research*. London: Sage.

Hill, C.E. (1989) *Therapist Techniques and Client Outcomes: Eight Cases of Brief Psychotherapy*. London: Sage.

Hill, C.E. (2005) The role of individual and marital therapy in my development. In J.D. Geller, J.C. Norcross and D.E. Orlinsky (eds), *The Psychotherapist's Own Psychotherapy: Patient and Clinician Perspectives*. New York: Oxford University Press.

Hill, C.E., Carter, J.A. and O'Farrell, M.K. (1983) A case study of the process and outcome of time-limited counseling. *Journal of Counseling Psychology*, 30, 3–18.

Hill, C.E., Knox, S., Thompson, B.J., Williams, E.N., Hess, S.A. and Ladany, N. (2004) Consensual qualitative research: an update. *Journal of Counseling Psychology*, 52, 196–205.

Hill, C.E., Sim, W.E., Spangler, P., Stahl, J., Sullivan, T. and Teyber, E. (2008) Therapist immediacy in brief psychotherapy: Case Study 2. *Psychotherapy: Theory, Research, Practice and Training*, 45(3), 298–315.

Hill, C.E., Thompson, B.J. and Nutt-Williams, E. (1997) A guide to conducting consensual qualitative research. *Counseling Psychologist*, 25, 517–72.

Hilliard, R.B. (1993) Single-case methodology in psychotherapy process and outcome research. *Journal of Consulting and Clinical Psychology*, 61(3), 373–80.

Honos-Webb, L., Stiles, W.B., Greenberg, L.S. and Goldman, R. (1998) Assimilation analysis of process-experiential psychotherapy: a comparison of two cases. *Psychotherapy Research*, 8, 264–86.

Honos-Webb, L., Stiles, W.B. Greenberg, L.S. and Goldman, R. (2006) An assimilation analysis of psychotherapy: responsibility for 'being there.' In C.T. Fisher (ed.), *Qualitative Research Methods For Psychologists: Introduction Through Empirical Studies*. New York: Academic Press.

Honos-Webb, L., Surko, M., Stiles, W.B. and Greenberg, L.S. (1999) Assimilation of voices in psychotherapy: the case of Jan. *Journal of Counseling Psychology*, 46, 448–60.

Hougaard, E. (2008) Further reflections on the therapy training program in Aarhus, and the role of case studies in psychotherapy research. *Pragmatic Case Studies in Psychotherapy*, 4(4), 76–91. http://pcsp.libraries.rutgers.edu

Hougaard, E., Madsen, S.S., Hansen, L.M., Jensen, M., Katborg, G.S., Morsaa, L., Pedersen, M., Pedersen, S.M. and Piet, J. (2008) A novel group therapeutic format in cognitive behavioral treatment for clients with social phobia in a training setting: a case study of one treatment group with nine clients. *Pragmatic Case Studies in Psychotherapy*, 4(4), 1–52. http://pcsp.libraries. rutgers.edu

House, R. (2006) A digest of Anne France's *Consuming Psychotherapy*. In Y. Bates (ed.), *Shouldn't I Be Feeling Better by Now? Client Views of Therapy*. London: Palgrave.

Humphreys, C., Bohart, A. and Dutile, R. (2000) Adjudication model for psychotherapy research: psychotherapy outcome. Paper presented at the American Psychological Association Convention, Washington, DC.

Ingram, B.I. (2009) The case of Ms Q: A demonstration of integrative psychotherapy guided by 'core clinical hypotheses'. *Pragmatic Case Studies in Psychotheraphy*, 5(1.1), 1–42. http://pcsp.libraries.rutgers.edu

Iwakabe, S. and Gazzola, N. (2009) From single-case studies to practice-based knowledge: aggregating and synthesizing case studies. *Psychotherapy Research*, 19, 601–11.

Jacobson, N.S., Follette, W.C. and Revenstorf, D. (1984) Psychotherapy outcome research: methods for reporting variability and evaluating clinical significance. *Behavior Therapy*, 15, 336–52.

Jacobson, N.S. and Revenstorf, D. (1988) Statistics for assessing the clinical significance of psychotherapy techniques: issues, problems and new developments. *Behavioral Assessment*, 10, 133–45.

Javidi, Z., Battersby, M. and Forbes, A. (2007) A case study of trichotillomania with social phobia: treatment and 4-year follow-up using cognitive-behaviour theraphy. *Behaviour Change*, 24, 231–43.

Jensen, C. (1994) Psychosocial treatment of depression in women: nine single-subject evaluations. *Research on Social Work Practice*, 4, 267–82.

Johnstone, L. and Dallos, R. (eds) (2006) *Formulation in Psychology and Psychotherapy: Making Sense of People's Problems*. London: Routledge.

Jones, E.E. and Pulos, S.M. (1993) Comparing the process in psychodynamic and cognitive-behavioral therapies. *Journal of Consulting and Clinical Psychology*, 61, 306–16.

Josseleson, R., Lieblich, A. and McAdams, D.P. (eds) (2003) *Up Close and Personal: The Teaching and Learning of Narrative Research*. Washington, DC: American Psychological Association.

Josselson, R. (1987) *Finding Herself: Pathways to Identity Development in Women*. Chichester: Wiley.

Josselson, R. (ed.) (1996a) *Ethics and Process in the Narrative Study of Lives*. Thousand Oaks, CA: Sage.

Josselson, R. (1996b) On writing other people's lives: self-analytic reflections of a narrative researcher. In R. Josselson (ed.), *Ethics and Process in the Narrative Study of Lives*. Thousand Oaks, CA: Sage.

Kachele, H., Albani, C., Buchheim, A. et al. (2006) The German specimen case, Amalia X: Empirical studies. *International Journal of Psychoanalysis*, 87, 809–26.

Kachele, H., Schachter, J. and Thomae, H. (2008) *From Psychoanalytic Narrative to Empirical Single Case Research: Implications for Psychoanalytic Practice*. New York: Routledge.

Kantrowitz, J.L. (2006) *Writing about Patients: Responsibilities, Risks and Ramifications*. New York: Other Press.

Karon, B.P. (2008a) An "incurable" schizophrenic: the case of Mr. X. *Pragmatic Case Studies in Psychotherapy*, 4(1), 1–24. http://hdl.rutgers.edu/1782.1/pcsp_journal

Karon, B.P. (2008b) Psychotherapy of schizophrenia works. *Pragmatic Case Studies in Psychotherapy*, 4(1), 55–61. http://hdl.rutgers.edu/1782.1/pcsp_journal

Kasper, L.B., Hill, C.E. and Kivlighan, D.E. (2008) Therapist immediacy in brief psychotherapy: Case Study 1. *Psychotherapy: Theory, Research, Practice and Training*, 45(3), 281–97.

Kazdin, A.E. (1981) Drawing valid inferences from case studies. *Journal Of Consulting and Clinical Psychology*, 49, 183–92.

Kazdin, A.E. (1982) Single-Case Research Design: Methods for Clinical and Applied Settings. New York: Oxford University Press.

Kazdin, A.E. (2006) Arbitrary metrics in psychology: implications for identifying evidence-based treatments. *American Psychologist*, 61, 42–9.

Keinanen, M. (2006) *Psychosemiosis as a Key to Body–Mind Continuum: The Reinforcement of Symbolization-Reflectiveness in Psychotherapy*. New York: Nova Science.

Kendall, P.C., Holmbeck, G. and Verduin, T. (2004) Methodology, design, and valuation in psychotherapy research. In M.J. Lambert (ed.), *Bergin and Garfield's Handbook of Psychotherapy and Behavior Change*, 5th edn. Chichester: Wiley.

Kitchener, K.S. (1984) Intuition, critical evaluation and ethical principles: the foundation for ethical decisions in counseling psychology. *Counseling Psychologist*, 12, 43–55.

Klein, M.H., Mathieu-Coughlan, P. and Kiesler, D.J. (1986) The Experiencing Scales. In L.S. Greenberg and W.M. Pinsof (eds), *The Psychotherapeutic Process: A Research Handbook*. New York: Guilford Press.

Knight, B.G. (1992) *Older Adults in Psychotherapy: Case Histories*. Thousand Oaks, CA: Sage.

Kottler, J.A. and Carlson, J. (2002) *Bad Therapy: Master Therapists Share Their Worst Failures*. New York: Brunner/Routledge.

Kottler, J.A. and Carlson, J. (2003) *The Mummy At the Dining Room Table: Eminent Therapists Reveal Their Most Unusual Cases and What They Teach Us About Human Behavior*. San Francisco, CA: Jossey-Bass.

Kottler, J.A. and Carlson, J. (2006) *The Client Who Changed Me: Stories of Therapist Personal Transformation*. New York: Brunner/Routledge.

Kottler, J.A. and Carlson, J. (2008) *Their Finest Hour: Master Therapists Share Their Greatest Success Stories*, 2nd edn. Bethel, CT: Crown Publishing.

Kottler, J.A. and Carlson, J. (2009) *Creative Breakthroughs in Therapy: Tales of Transformation and Astonishment*. New York: Wiley.

Kramer, U. (2009a) Individualizing exposure therapy for PTSD: the case of Caroline. *Pragmatic Case Studies in Psychotherapy*, 5(2), 1–24. http://hdl.rutgers.edu/1782.1/pcsp_journal

Kramer, U. (2009b) Between manualized treatments and principle-guided psychotherapy: illustration in the case of Caroline. *Pragmatic Case Studies in Psychotherapy*, 5(2), 45–51. http://hdl.rutgers.edu/1782.1/pcsp_journal

Kroenke, K., Spitzer, R.L. and Williams, J.B. (2001) The PHQ-9: validity of a brief depression severity measure. *Journal of General Internal Medicine*, 16(9), 606–13.

Kromrey, J.D. and Foster-Johnson, L. (1996) Determining the efficacy of intervention: the use of effect sizes for data analysis in single-subject research. *Journal of Experimental Education*, 65, 73–93.

Kuhnlein, I. (1999) Psychotherapy as a process of transformation: the analysis of posttherapeutic autobiographical narrations. *Psychotherapy Research*, 9, 274–88.

Kutash, I.L. and Wolf, A. (eds) (1986) *The Psychotherapist's Casebook*. San Francisco' CA: Jossey–Bass.

Kvale, S. (2001) The psychoanalytic interview as qualitative research. In J. Frommer and D. Rennie (eds), *Qualitative Psychotherapy Research: Methods and Methodology*. Lengerich, Germany: Pabst Science.

Lakoff, G. and Johnson, M. (1980) *Metaphors We Live By*. Chicago, IL: University of Chicago Press.

Lakoff, G. and Johnson, M. (1999) *Philosophy in the Flesh: The Embodied Mind and Its Challenge to Western Thought*. New York: Basic Books.

Lambert, M. (ed.) (2004) *Bergin and Garfield's Handbook of Psychotherapy and Behavior Change*, 5th edn. Chichester: Wiley.

Lambert, M.J. (2007) What we have learned from a decade of research aimed at improving psychotherapy outcome in routine care. *Psychotherapy Research*, 17(1), 1–14.

Lazarus, A.A. and Zur, O. (eds) (2002) *Dual Relationships in Psychotherapy*. New York: Springer.

Leitenberg, H. (1973) The use of single-case methodology in psychotherapy research. *Journal of Abnormal Psychology*, 82, 87–101.

Lepper, G. and Riding, N. (2006) *Researching the Psychotherapy Process: A Practical Guide to Transcript-based Methods*. Basingstoke: Palgrave Macmillan.

Levine, M. (1974) Scientific method and the adversary model: some preliminary thoughts. *American Psychologist*, 29, 661–77.

Lieblich, A. and Josselson, R. (eds) (1997) *Narrative Studies of Lives*, Vol. 5. Thousand Oaks, CA: Sage.

Lincoln, Y.S. and Guba, E.G. (1989) Judging the quality of case study reports. *Qualitative Studies in Education*, 3, 53–9.

Lincoln, Y.S. and Guba, E.G. (2000) The only generalization is: there is no generalization. In R. Gomm, R. Hammersley and P. Foster (eds), *Case Study Method*. London: Sage.

Lindner, R. (2006) Suicidality in men in psychoanalytic psychotherapy. *Psychoanalytic Psychotherapy*, 20, 197–217.

Lindner, R., Fiedler, G., Altenhofer, A., Gotze, P. and Happach, C. (2006) Psychodynamic ideal types of elderly suicidal persons based on counter transference. *Journal of Social Work Practice*, 20, 347–65.

Lipton, E.L. (1991) The analyst's use of clinical data, and other issues of confidentiality. *Journal of the American Psychoanalytic Association*, 39, 967–86.

Llewelyn, S. (1988) Psychological therapy as viewed by clients and therapists. *British Journal of Clinical Psychology*, 27, 223–38.

Lo, Y. and Konrad, M. (2007) A field-tested task analysis for creating single-subject graphs using Microsoft Office Excel. *Journal of Behavioral Education*, 16, 166–8.

Lodge, D. (1995) *Therapy*. London: Secker and Warburg.

Luborsky, L., Barber, J.P., Siqueland, L., Johnson, S., Najavits, L.M., Frank, A. and Daley, D. (1996) The Revised Helping Alliance Questionnaire (HAq-11): pychometric properties. *Journal of Psychotherapy Practice*, 5, 260–71.

Luborsky, L., Diguer, L., Seligman, D.A. et al. (1999) The researcher's own therapy allegiances: a 'wild card' in comparisons of treatment efficacy. *Clinical Psychology: Science and Practice*, 6, 95–106.

Luborsky, L., Stuart, J., Friedman, S. et al. (2001) The Penn psychoanalytic treatment collection: a set of complete and recorded psychoanalyses as a research resource. *Journal of the American Psychoanalytic Association*, 49, 217–34.

Lysaker, P.H. and Lysaker, J.T. (2002) Narrative structure in psychosis: schizophrenia and disruptions in the dialogical self. *Theory and Psychology*, 12, 207–20.

Lysaker, P.H., Buck, K.D. and Ringer, J. (2007a) The recovery of metacognitive capacity in schizophrenia across 32 months of individual psychotheraphy: a case study. *Psychotherapy Research*, 17(6), 713–20.

Lysaker, P.H., Davis, L.W., Eckert, G.J., Strasburger, A.M., Hunter, N.L. and Buck, K.D. (2005) Changes in narrative structure and content in schizophrenia in long term individual psychotherapy: a single case study. *Clinical Psychology and Psychotherapy*, 12, 406–16.

Lysaker, P.H., Davis, L.W., Jones, A.M., Strasburger, A.M. and Beattie, N.L. (2007b) Relationship and technique in the long-term integrative psychotherapy of schizophrenia: a single case study. *Counselling and Psychotherapy Research*, 7, 79–85.

Lysaker, P.H., Lysaker, J.T. and Lysaker, J.T. (2001) Schizophrenia and the collapse of the dialogical self: recovery, narrative and psychotherapy. *Psychotherapy*, 38, 252–61.

Mackrill, T. (2007) Using a cross-contextual qualitative diary design to explore client experiences of psychotherapy. *Counselling and Psychotherapy Research*, 7, 233–9.

Mackrill, T. (2008a) Exploring psychotherapy clients' independent strategies for change while in therapy. *British Journal of Guidance and Counselling*, 36, 441–53.

Mackrill, T. (2008b) Solicited diary studies of psychotherapeutic practice – pros and cons. *European Journal of Psychotherapy and Counselling*, 10, 5–18.

Mackrill, T. (2009) A cross-contextual construction of clients' therapeutic practice. *Journal of Constructivist Psychology*, 22, 283–305.

Mahony, P.J. (1996) *Freud's Dora. A Psychoanalytic, Historical, and Textual Study*. New Haven, CT: Yale University Press.

Malan, D.H. (1979) *Individual Psychotherapy and the Science of Psychodynamics*. London: Butterworths.

Marsh, D.T. (2000) Personal accounts of consumers/survivors: insights and implications. *Journal of Clinical Psychology*, 56, 1447–57.

Marshall, R.D., Spitzer, R.L., Vaughan, S. et al. (2001) Assessing the subjective experience of being a participant in psychiatric research. *American Journal of Psychiatry*, 158, 3019–21.

Masters, W.H. and Johnson, V.E. (1970) *Human Sexual Inadequacy*. New York: Bantam Books.

McAdams, D.P. (1985) *Power, Intimacy, and the Life Story: Personological Inquiries into Identity*. New York: Guilford Press.

McAdams, D.P. (1993) *The Stories We Live By: Personal Myths and the Making of the Self*. New York: William Murrow.

McAdams, D.P. (1996) Personality, modernity, and the storied self: a contemporary framework for studying persons. *Psychological Inquiry*, 7, 295–321.

McAdams, D.P. (2006) *The Redemptive Self: Stories Americans Live By*. New York: Oxford University Press.

McAdams, D.P., Josselson, R. and Lieblich, A. (eds) (2001) *Turns in the Road: Narrative Studies of Lives in Transition*. Washington, DC: American Psychological Association.

McCann, D.L. (1992) Post-traumatic stress disorder due to devastating burns overcome by a single session of eye movement desensitization. *Journal of Behaviour Therapy and Experimental Psychiatry*, 23(4), 319–23.

McKenna, P.A. and Todd, D.M. (1997) Longtitudinal utilization of mental health services: a time-line method, nine retrospective accounts, and a preliminary conceptualization. *Psychotherapy Research*, 7, 383–96.

McLeod, J. (1992) The story of Henry Murray's diagnostic council: a case study in the demise of a scientific method. *Clinical Psychology Forum*, No. 44 (June), 6–12.

McLeod, J. (1997) *Narrative and Psychotherapy*. London: Sage.

McLeod, J. (1999) Counselling as a social process. *Counselling*, 10, 217–26.

McLeod, J. (2002) Lists, stories and dreams: strategic invitation to relationship in psychotherapy narrative. In W. Patterson (ed.), *Strategic Narrative: New Perspectives on the Power of Personal and Cultural Stories*. Lanham, MA: Lexington.

McLeod, J. (2003) *Doing Counselling Research*, 2nd edn. London: Sage.

McLeod, J. (2004a) Social construction, narrative and psychotherapy. In L. Angus and J. McLeod (eds), *Handbook of Narrative and Psychotherapy*. Thousand Oaks, CA: Sage.

McLeod, J. (2004b) The significance of narrative and storytelling in postpsychological counselling and psychotherapy. In A. Lieblich, D. McAdams and R. Josselson (eds), *Healing Plots: The Narrative Basis of Psychotherapy*. Washington, DC: American Psychological Association.

McLeod, J. (2005) Counselling and psychotherapy as cultural work. In L.T. Hoshm and (ed.), *Culture, Psychotherapy and Counseling: Critical and Integrative Perspectives*. Thousand Oaks, CA: Sage.

McLeod, J. (2009) *An Introduction to Counselling*, 4th edn. Maidenhead: Open University Press.

McLeod, J. and Balamoutsou, S. (1996) Representative narrative process in therapy: qualitative analysis of a single case. *Counselling Psychology Quarterly*, 9, 61–76.

McLeod, J. and Balamoutsou, S. (2000) Narrative process in the assimilation of a problematic experience: qualitative analysis of a single case. *Zeitshrift fur qualitative Bildungs- Beratungs- und Sozialforschung*, 2, 283–302.

McLeod, J. and Balamoutsou, S. (2001) A method for qualitative narrative analysis of psychotherapy transcripts. In J. Frommer and D. Rennie (eds), *Qualitative Psychotherapy Research: Methods and Methodology*. Lengerich, Germany: Pabst Science.

McLeod, J. and Lynch, G. (2000) 'This is our life': Strong evaluation in psychotherapy narrative. *European Journal of Psychotherapy, Counselling, and Health*, 3, 389–406.

McNeilly, C.L. and Howard, K.I. (1991) The Therapeutic Procedures Inventory: psychometric properties and relationship to phase of treatment. *Journal of Psychotherapy Integration*, 1, 223–34.

Mellor-Clark, J. and Barkham, M. (2006) The CORE system: quality evaluation to develop practice-based evidence base, enhanced service delivery and best practice management. In C. Feltham and I. Horton (eds), *Handbook of Counselling and Psychotherapy*. London: Sage.

Mergenthaler, H. (1991) University of Ulm: The Ulm Textbank Research Program. In L. Beutler and M. Crago (eds), *International Psychotherapy Research Programs*. New York: Pergamon,

Mergenthaler, H. (1993) Locating text archives for psychotherapy research. In N.E. Miller, L. Luborsky, J.P. Barber and J. Docherty (eds), *Psychodynamic Treatment Research: A Handbook for Clinical Practice*. New York: Basic Books.

Messer, S.B. (2007) Psychoanalytic case studies and the pragmatic case study method. *Pragmatic Case Studies in Psychotherapy*, 3(1), 55–8. http://pcsp.libraries.rutgers.edu.

Miles, M. and Huberman, A. (1994) *Qualitative Data Analysis: A Sourcebook of New Methods*, 2nd edn. London: Sage.

Miller, R.B. (2004) *Facing Human Suffering: Psychology and Psychotherapy as Moral Engagement*. Washington, DC: American Psychological Association.

Miller, R.B. (2008) Rules of evidence for narrative data. Paper presented at the Societ for Pychotherapy Research Annual Conference, Barcelona, June 2008.

Miller, S.D., Duncan, B.L. and Hubble, M.A. (2005) Outcome-informed clinical work. In J.C. Norcross and M.R. Goldfried (eds), *Handbook of Psychotherapy Integration*. New York: Oxford University Press.

Molloy, G.N., Murphy, G.C. and King, N.J. (2007) The decline of *n*=1 research in *Behaviour Change:* the rise of the evidence-based practice movement as one explanation for the trend. *Behaviour Change*, 24, 114–21.

Moras, K., Telfer, L.A. and Barlow, D.H. (1993) Efficacy and specific effects data on new treatments: a case study strategy with mixed anxiety-depression. *Journal of Consulting and Clinical Psychology*, 61, 412–20.

Morgan, D.L. and Morgan, R.K. (2003) Single-participant research design: bringing science to managed care. In A.E. Kazdin (ed.), *Methodological Issues and Strategies in Clinical Research*, 3rd edn. Washington, DC: American Psychological Association.

Morgan, D.L. and Morgan, R.K. (2009) *Single-case Research Methods for the Behavioural and Health Sciences*. Thousand Oaks, CA: Sage.

Morley, R. (2007a) *The Analysand's Tale*. London: Karnac.

Morley, S. (2007b) Single case methodology in psychological therapy. In S.J.E. Lindsay and G.E. Powell (eds), *A Handbook of Clinical Adult Psychology*, 3rd edn. London: Brunner Routledge.

Morrow, S.L. (2005) Quality and trustworthiness in qualitative research in counseling psychology. *Journal of Counseling Psychology*, 52, 250–60.

Moustakas, C. (1990) *Heuristic Research: Design, Methodology and Applications*. Thousand Oaks, CA: Sage.

MRC (2008) *Developing and Evaluating Complex Interventions: New Guidance*. London: Medical Research Council. Available at: www.mrc.ac.uk/complexinterventions-guidance

Muller, K. (2009) Manualized psychotherapies in the 'real world.' *Pragmatic Case Studies in Psychotherapy*, 5(2), 28–34. http://hdl.rutgers.edu/1782.1/pcsp_journal

Murray, H.A. (1938) *Explorations in Personality: A Clinical and Experimental Study of Fifty Men of College Age*. New York: Oxford University Press.

Murray, H.A. and Morgan, C.D. (1945) A clinical study of sentiments. *Genetic Psychology Monographs*, 32, 3–311.

Ogles, B., Lambert, M. and Fields, S. (2002) *Essentials of Outcome Assessment*. New York: Wiley.

Ogles, B., Lunnen, K. and Bonesteel, K. (2001) Clinical significance: history, application, and current practice. *Clinical Psychology Review*, 21, 421–46.

Parry, G., Shapiro, D.A. and Firth, J. (1986) The case of the anxious executive: a study from the research clinic. *British Journal of Medical Psychology*, 59, 221–33.

Peirce, C.S. (1965) *Collected Papers of Charles Sanders Peirce*. Cambridge, MA: Belknap Press.

Pepper, S. (1970) *Root Metaphors and World Hypotheses*. Berkeley, CA: University of California Press.

Peterson, D.R. (1991) Connection and disconnection of research and practice in the education of professional psychologists. *American Psychologist*, 46, 422–9.

Philips, B., Wennberg, P. and Werbart, A. (2007a) Ideas of cure as a predictor of premature termination, early alliance and outcome in psychoanalytic psychotherapy. *Psychology and Psychotherapy: Theory, Research and Practice*, 80, 229–45.

Philips, B., Werbart, A., Wennberg, P. and Schubert, J. (2007b) Young adults' ideas of cure prior to psychoanalytic psychotherapy. *Journal of Clinical Psychology*, 63, 213–32.

Pinsof, W.M. (2005) A Shamanic tapestry: my experiences with individual, marital and family therapy. In J.D. Geller, J.C. Norcross and D.E. Orlinsky (eds), *The Psychotherapist's Own Psychotherapy: Patient and Clinician Perspectives*. New York: Oxford University Press.

Polkinghorne, D.E. (1988) *Narrative Knowing and the Human Sciences*. Albany, NY: State University of New York Press.

Polkinghorne, D.E. (1992) Postmodern epistemology of practice. In S. Kvale (ed.), *Psychology and Postmodernism*. London: Sage.

Polkinghorne, D.E. (1995) Narrative configuration in qualitative analysis. In J.A. Hatch and R. Wisniewski (eds), *Life History and Narrative*. London: Falmer Press.

Prochaska, J.O. and DiClemente, C.C. (1982) Transtheoretical therapy: toward a more integrative model of change. *Psychotherapy*, 19, 276–88.

Ragin, C. and Becker, H.S. (eds) (1992) *What Is a Case? Exploring the Foundations of Social Inquiry*. Cambridge: Cambridge University Press.

Randall, E.J. and Thyer, B.A. (1998) Combining guided dialog with cognitive therapy for depressed women: six single-case studies. *Journal of Cognitive Psychotherapy: An International Quarterly*, 12, 331–42.

Rapaport, D. and Gill, M. (1959) The points of view and assumptions of metapsychology. *International Journal of Psycho-Analysis*, 40, 153–62.

Reason, P. (1998) Co-operative inquiry as a discipline of professional practice. *Journal of Interprofessional Care*, 12, 419–36.

Reason, P. (ed.) (1988) *Human Inquiry in Action: Developments in New Paradigm Research*. London: Sage.

Reason, P. (ed.) (1994) *Participation in Human Inquiry*. London: Sage.

Rennie, D.L. (2000) Grounded theory methodology as methodical hermeneutics: reconciling realism and relativism. *Theory and Psychology*, 10, 481–502.

Rennie, D.L. (2001) Grounded theory methodology as methodological hermeneutics: reconciling realism and relativism. In J. Frommer and D.L. Rennie (eds), *Qualitative Psychotherapy Research: Methods and Methodology*. Lengerich, Germany: Pabst Science.

Richards, P.S. and Bergin, A.E. (1997) Case reports of spiritual issues and interventions in psychotherapy. In P.S. Richards and A.E. Bergin (eds), *A Spiritual Strategy for Counseling and Psychotherapy*. Washington, DC: American Psychological Association.

Richardson, L. (2003) Poetic representation of interviews. In J.F. Gubrium and J.A. Holstein (eds), *Postmodern Interviewing*. Thousand Oaks, CA: Sage.

Riding, N. and Lepper, G. (2005) *Researching the Psychotherapy Process: A Practical Guide to Transcript-Based Methods*. London: Palgrave/Macmillan.

Rodgers, B. (2006) Life space mapping: preliminary results from the development of a new method for evaluating counselling outcomes. *Counselling and Psychotherapy Research,* 6(4), 227–32.

Rowland, N. (2007) BACP and NICE. *Therapy Today*, 18(5), 27–30.

Rowland, N. and Goss, S. (eds) (2000) *Evidence-based Counselling and Psychological Therapies: Research and Applications*. London: Routledge.

Runyan, W.M. (1980) Alternative accounts of lives: an argument for epistemological relativism. *Biography*, 3, 209–24.

Runyan, W.M. (1981a) Why did Van Gogh cut off his ear? The problem of alternative explanations in psychobiography. *Journal of Personality and Social Psychology*, 40(6), 1070–7.

Runyan, W.M. (1981b) *Life Histories and Psychobiography: Explorations in Theory and Method*. New York: Oxford University Press.

Runyan, W.M. (1997) Studying lives: psychobiography and the conceptual structure of personality psychology. In R. Hogan and J. Johnson (eds), *Handbook of Personality Psychology*. New York: Academic Press.

Russell, R.L. (ed.) (1994) *Reassessing Psychotherapy Research*. New York: Guilford Press.

Ryle, A. and Kerr, I.B. (2002) *Introducing Cognitive Analytic Therapy: Principles and Practice*. Chichester: Wiley.

Sato, T., Yasuda, Y., Arakawa, A., Mizoguchi, H. and Valsiner, J. (2007) Sampling reconsidered: idiographic science and the analysis of personal life trajectories. In J. Valsiner and A. Rosa (eds), *The Cambridge Handbook of Sociocultural Psychology*. New York: Cambridge University Press.

Schielke, H.J., Fishman, J.L., Osatuke, K. and Stiles, W.B. (2009) Creative consensus on interpretations of qualitative data: the Ward method. *Psychotherapy Research*, 19, 558–65.

Schneider, K.J. (1999) Multiple-case depth research. *Journal of Clinical Psychology*, 55, 1531–40.

Schofield, J.W. (1990) Increasing the generalizability of qualitative research. In E.W. Eisner and A. Peshkin (eds), *Qualitative Inquiry in Education: The Continuing Debate*. New York: Teachers College Press.

Schön, D.A. (1983) *The Reflective Practitioner: How Professionals Think in Action*. New York: Basic Books.

Scruggs, T.E. and Mastropieri, M. (1998) Summarizing single-subject research: issues and applications. *Behavior Modification*, 22(3), 221–42.

Sechrest, L., Stewart, M., Stickle, T.R. and Sidani, S. (1996) *Effective and Persuasive Case Studies*. Cambridge, MA: Human Services Research Institute.

Seikkula, J. and Arnkil, T.E. (2006) *Dialogical Meetings in Social Networks*. London: Karnac.

Shapiro, D.A. and Firth, J. (1987) Prescriptive vs. exploratory psychotherapy. Outcomes of the Sheffield psychotherapy project. *British Journal of Psychiatry*, 151: 790–9.

Shapiro, D.A. and Firth-Cozens, J.A. (1990) Two-year follow-up of the Sheffield psychotherapy project. *British Journal of Psychiatry*, 157, 389–91.

Shapiro, F. (1989) Eye movement desensitization: a new treatment for post-traumatic stress disorder. *Journal of Behavior Therapy and Experimental Psychiatry*, 20, 211–17.

Shapiro, M.B. (1961) The single case in fundamental clinical psychological research. *British Journal of Medical Psychology*, 34, 255–62.

Sharpley, C.F. (2003) N=1 research methodology in counselling: focusing on the individual client. *Australian Journal of Guidance and Counselling*, 13, 133–44.

Sharpley, C.F. (2005) On the decline of *n*=1 Research in Behaviour Change: a comment and some questions. *Behaviour Change*, 22, 249–56.

Sharpley, C.F. (2007) So why aren't counselors reporting *n*=1 research designs? *Journal of Counseling and Development*, 84, 359–86.

Shneidman, E.S. (ed.) (1981) *Endeavors in Psychology: Selections from the Writings of Henry A. Murray*. New York: Harper and Row.

Sidman, M. (1960) *Tactics of Scientific Research*. New York: Basic Books.

Silberschatz, G. and Curtis, J.G. (1993) Measuring the therapist's impact on the patient's therapeutic progress. *Journal of Consulting and Clinical Psychology*, 61, 403–11.

Silver, A.-L. (2008) Karon's case of 'Mr. X' and the 'International Society for the Psychological Treatments of Schizophrenia and Other Psychoses' (ISPS). *Pragmatic Case Studies in Psychotherapy*, 4(1), 44–54. http://hdl.rutgers. edu/1782.1/pcsp_journal

Simons, H. (2009) *Case Study Research in Practice*. London: Sage.

Skovholt, T.M. and Jennings, L. (2004) *Master Therapists: Exploring Expertise in Therapy and Counseling*. New York: Allyn and Bacon.

Sloman, S. (1978) What is conceptual analysis? Chapter 4 of *The Computer Revolution in Philosophy* . Available on-line at: www.cs.bham.ac.uk/research/ cogaff/crp/chap4.html

Smith, J.A., Flowers, P. and Larkin, M. (2009) *Interpretive Phenomenological Analysis: Theory, Method and Research*. London: Sage.

Sommer, R. (2003) The use of autobiography in psychotherapy. *Journal of Clinical Psychology*, 59, 197–205.

Speedy, J. (2007) *Narrative Inquiry and Psychotherapy*. London: Palgrave Macmillan.

Spence, D.P. (1982) *Narrative Truth and Historical Truth: Meaning and Interpretation in Psychoanalysis*. New York: Norton.

Spence, D.P. (1986) Narrative smoothing and clinical wisdom. In T.R. Sarbin (ed.), *Narrative Psychology: The Storied Nature of Human Conduct*. New York: Praeger.

Spence, D.P. (1989) Rhetoric vs. evidence as a source of persuasion: a critique of the case study genre. In M.J. Packer and R.B. Addison (eds), *Entering the Circle: Hermeneutic Investigation in Psychology*. Albany, NY: State University of New York Press.

Spence, D.P. (2001) Dangers of anecdotal reports. *Journal of Clinical Psychology*, 57, 37–41.

Spitzer, R.L., Kroenke, K., Williams, J.B., et al. (2006) A brief measure for assessing generalized anxiety disorder: the GAD-7. *Archives of Internal Medicine*, 166(10), 1092–7.

Stake, R.E. (1978) The case study method in social inquiry. *Educational Researcher*, 7, 5–8.

Stake, R.E. (2005) Qualitative case studies. In N.K. Denzin and Y.S. Lincoln (eds), *Handbook of Qualitative Research*, 3rd edn. Thousand Oaks, CA: Sage.

Stiles, W.B. (1980) Measurement of the impact of psychotherapy sessions. *Journal of Consulting and Clinical Psychology*, 48, 176–85.

Stiles, W.B. (1993) Quality control in qualitative research. *Clinical Psychology Review*, 13, 593–618.

Stiles, W.B. (2002) Assimilation of problematic experiences. In J.C. Norcross (ed.), *Psychotherapy Relationships that Work*. New York: Oxford University Press.

Stiles, W.B. (2003) When is a case study scientific research? *Psychotherapy Bulletin*, 38(1), 6–11.

Stiles, W.B. (2005) Case studies. In J.C. Norcross, L.E. Beutler and R.F. Levant (eds), *Evidence-based Practices in Mental Health: Debate and Dialogue on the Fundamental Questions*. Washington, DC: American Psychological Association.

Stiles, W.B. (2007) Theory-building case studies of counselling and psychotherapy. *Counselling and Psychotherapy Research*, 7, 122–7.

Stiles, W.B. and Shapiro, D.A. (1989) Abuse of the drug metaphor in psychotherapy process-outcome research. *Clinical Psychology Review*, 9, 521–43.

Stiles, W.B., Gordon, L.E. and Lani, J.A. (2002) Session evaluation and the Session Evaluation Questionnaire. In G.S. Tryon (ed.), *Counseling Based on Process Research: Applying What We Know*. Boston, MA: Allyn and Bacon.

Stiles, W.B., Honos-Webb, L. and Surko, M. (1998) Responsiveness in psychotherapy. *Clinical Psychology: Science and Practice*, 5, 439–58.

Stiles, W.B. and Snow, J. (1984) Dimensions of psychotherapy session impact across sessions and across clients. *British Journal of Clinical Psychology*, 23, 59–63.

Stiles, W.B., Meshot, C.N., Anderson, T.M. and Sloan, W.W. (1992) Assimilation of problematic experiences: the case of John Jones. *Psychotherapy Research*, 2(2), 81–101.

Stiles, W.B., Morrison, L.A., Haw, S.F., Harper, H., Shapiro, D.A. and Firth-Cozens, J. (1991) Longitudinal study of assimilation in exploratory psychotherapy. *Psychotherapy*, 28, 195–206.

Stinckens, N., Elliott, R. and Leijssen, M. (2009) Bridging the gap between therapy research and practice in a person-centered/experiential therapy training program: the Leuven Systematic Case Study Protocol. *Person-Centered and Experiential Psychotherapies*, 8, 143–62.

Stricker, G. and Gold, J. (eds) (2006) *A Casebook of Psychotherapy Integration*. Washington, DC: American Psychological Association.

Strupp, H.H. (1980a) Success and failure in time-limited psychotherapy. A systematic comparison of two cases: comparison 1. *Archives of General Psychiatry*, 37, 595–603.

Strupp, H.H. (1980b) Success and failure in time-limited psychotherapy: a systematic comparison of two cases: comparison 2. *Archives of General Psychiatry*, 37, 708–16.

Strupp, H.H. (1980c) Success and failure in time-limited psychotherapy: with special reference to the performance of the lay counselor. *Archives of General Psychiatry*, 37, 831–41.

Strupp, H.H. (1980d) Success and failure in time-limited psychotherapy. Further evidence: comparison 4. *Archives of General Psychiatry*, 37, 947–54.

Strupp, H.H. (1993) The Vanderbilt psychotherapy studies: synopsis. *Journal of Consulting and Clinical Psychology*, 61, 431–3.

Strupp, H.H. and Hadley, S.W. (1979) Specific vs nonspecific factors in psychotherapy: a controlled study of outcome. *Archives of General Psychiatry*, 36, 1125–36.

Stuhr, U. and Wachholz, S. (2001) In search for a psychoanalytic research strategy: the concept of ideal types. In J. Frommer and D. Rennie (eds), *Qualitative Psychotherapy Research: Methods and Methodology*. Lengerich, Germany: Pabst Science.

Teasdale, J. D. and Barnard, P.J. (1993) *Affect, Cognition and Change: Re-modelling Depressive Thought*. Hove: Lawrence Erlbaum.

Tennant, R., Hiller, L., Fishwick, R. et al. (2007) The Warwick–Edinburgh Mental Well-being Scale (WEMWBS): development and UK validation. *Health and Quality of Life Outcomes*, 5, 63.

Timulak, L. (2008) *Research in Counselling and Psychotherapy*. London: Sage.

Tolman, C.W. (2009) Holzkamp's Critical Psychology as a science from the standpoint of the human subject. *Theory and Psychology*, 19, 149–60.

Toukmanian, S. and Rennie, D. (eds) (1992) *Psychotherapy Process Research: Paradigmatic and Narrative Approaches*. London: Sage.

Toulmin, S. (1958) *The Uses of Argument*. Cambridge: Cambridge University Press.

Townend, M. and Smith, M.E. (2007) A case study of cognitive-behavioral psychotherapy with a perpetrator of domestic abuse. *Clinical Case Studies*, 6, 443–53.

Trijsburg, R.W., Lietaer, G., Colijn, S., Abrahamse, R.M., Joosten, S. and Duivenvoorden, H.J. (2004) Construct validity of the Comprehensive Therapeutic Interventions rating scale. *Psychotherapy Research*, 14, 346–66.

Tryon, G.S. (ed.) (2002) *Counseling Based on Process Research: Applying What We Know*. Boston, MA: Allyn and Bacon.

Tuckett, D. (2000) Editorial. Reporting clinical events in the journal: towards the construction of a special case. *International Journal of Psychoanalysis*, 81, 1065–69.

Turpin, G. (2001) Single case methodology and psychotherapy evaluation: from research to practice. In C. Mace, S. Moorey and B. Roberts (eds), *Evidence in the Psychological Therapies: A Critical Guide for Practitioners*. London: Brunner–Routledge.

Van den Noortgate, W. and Onghena, P. (2003) Combining single-case experimental data using hierarchical linear models. *School Psychology Quarterly*, 18, 325–46.

VandenBos, G.R. (2008) Psychotherapy can be helpful for schizophrenics. *Pragmatic Case Studies in Psychotherapy*, 4(1), 35–43. http://hdl.rutgers.edu/1782.1/pcsp_journal

Wachholz, S. and Stuhr, U. (1999) The concept of ideal types in psychoanalytic follow-up research. *Psychotherapy Research*, 9, 327–41.

Wagner, J. and Elliott, R. (2001) *The Simplified Personal Questionnaire*. Unpublished manuscript, Department of Psychology, University of Toledo.

Wallerstein, R.S. (1986) *Forty-two Lives in Treatment: A Study of Psychoanalysis and Psychotherapy*. New York: Guilford Press.

Wallerstein, R.S. (1989) The Psychotherapy Research Project of the Menninger Foundation: an overview. *Journal of Consulting and Clinical Psychology*, 57, 195–205.

Wallerstein, R.S. (2009) What kind of research in psychoanalytic science? *International Journal of Psychoanalysis*, 90, 109–33.

Waters, A.M., Donaldson, J. and Zimmer-Gembeck, M.J. (2008) Cognitive behavioural therapy combined with an interpersonal skills component in the treatment of generalized anxiety disorder in adolescent females: A case series. *Behaviour Change*, 25, 35–43.

Watkins Jr, C.E. and Campbell, V.L. (eds) (2000) *Testing and Assessment in Counseling Practice*, 2nd edn. Hillsdale, NJ: Lawrence Erlbaum.

Watson, J.C., Goldman, R.N. and Greenberg, L.S. (2007) *Case Studies in Emotion-focused Treatment of Depression: A Comparison of Good and Poor Outcomes*. Washington, DC: American Psychological Association.

Wedding, D. and Corsini, R. (eds) (1979) *Great Cases in Psychotherapy*. Itasca, IL: F.E. Peacock.

Westen, D., Novotny, C.M. and Thompson-Brenner, H. (2004) The empirical status of empirically-supported psychotherapies: assumptions, findings, and reporting in controlled clinical trials. *Psychological Bulletin*, 130, 631–63.

White, M. and Epston, D. (1990) *Narrative Means to Therapeutic Ends*. New York: Norton.

Winship, G. (2007) The ethics of reflective research in single case study inquiry. *Perspectives in Psychiatric Care*, 43, 174–82.

Wise, E.A. (2004) Methods for analysing psychotherapy outcomes: a review of clinical significance, reliable change and recommendations for future directions. *Journal of Personality Assesssment*, 82, 50–9.

Wittine, B. (2005) The I and the Self: reminiscences of existential-humanistic therapy. In J.D. Geller, J.C. Norcross and D.E. Orlinsky (eds), *The Psychotherapist's Own Psychotherapy: Patient and Clinician Perspectives*. New York: Oxford University Press.

Wolpe, J. (1958) *Psychotherapy by Reciprocal Inhibition*. Palo Alto, CA: Stanford University Press.

Yalom, I.D. (1989) *Love's Executioner and Other Tales of Psychotherapy*. Harmondsworth: Penguin.

Yalom, I.D. and Elkin, G. (1974) *Every Day Gets a Little Closer: A Twice-Told Therapy*. New York: Basic Books.

Yin, R.K. (2004) *The Case Study Anthology*. Thousand Oaks, CA: Sage.

Yin, R.K. (2009) *Case Study Research: Design and Methods*, 4th edn. Thousand Oaks, CA: Sage.

Zigmond, A.S. and Snaith, R.P. (1983) The hospital anxiety and depression scale. *Acta Psychiatrica Scandinavica*, 67, 361–70.

Index